# FLEETING ATTRACTION

# FLEETING ATTRACTION

## A SOCIAL HISTORY OF AMERICAN SERVICEMEN IN WESTERN AUSTRALIA DURING THE SECOND WORLD WAR

ANTHONY J BARKER       LISA JACKSON

UNIVERSITY OF WESTERN AUSTRALIA PRESS

First published in 1996 by
University of Western Australia Press
Nedlands, Western Australia 6907

National Library of Australia
Cataloguing-in-Publication entry:

Barker, Anthony J.
    Fleeting attraction: a social history of American
    servicemen in Western Australia during the Second World War.

    ISBN 1 875560 74 2.

    1. Americans—Western Australia—History—20th century.
    2. Americans—Western Australia—Public opinion. 3. World
    War, 1939–1945—Social aspects—Western Australia.
    4. Public opinion—Western Australia. 5. United States—
    Armed Forces—Western Australia. I. Jackson, Lisa, 1970–    . II. Title.

940.53941

Front cover photograph: West Australian Newspapers
Photographs on back cover and page 250: Pat Tully's private collection

Edited by Allan Watson, Perth Editorial Service, Perth
Designed by Rosalie Okely, Perth
Typeset in 11 point Berkeley Book by Lasertype, Perth
Printed by Frank Daniels Pty Ltd, Perth

# CONTENTS

# CONVERSION TABLES

IMPERIAL TO METRIC

| | |
|---|---|
| one inch | = 2.54 centimetres |
| one foot: 12 inches | = 30.5 centimetres |
| one yard: 3 feet | = 0.91 metre |
| one mile: 1760 yards | = 61 kilometres |
| one pint | = 568 millitres |
| one gallon: 8 pints | = 4.55 litres |
| one ton | = 1.02 tonnes |

MONETARY

| *Pre-1966* | *Post-1966* |
|---|---|
| one penny (plural pence) | = 0.83 cents |
| one shilling ('bob'): twelve pence | = 10 cents |
| one pound (£): twenty shillings | = $2 |

# ACKNOWLEDGMENTS

This book could not have been written without the help of many people. The most important are all those listed in the 'Oral History' section of the bibliography. Probably most of these prefaced their interviews by expressing doubts about the value of what they could offer, but we can say without distortion or flattery that every interview enhanced our understanding of the period. We greatly appreciate the willingness of so many to share their experiences with us. They not only provided us with indispensable information but also redoubled our enthusiasm for the whole project, as we saw so clearly how people's lives had been uniquely touched by the wartime experience. Obviously some had more to tell than others and some made a greater contribution by leading us on to further interviewees. But there is a real danger of oversights and mistakes in trying to differentiate between so many people, Australian and American, who helped us in our research, so we prefer to say a heartfelt thankyou to all who agreed to be interviewed.

We must also warmly acknowledge the help of the custodians of the various libraries and archives we have used: these include the Australian Archives in Perth, Melbourne, Sydney and Canberra; the Australian National Library in Canberra; and the Reid Library of The University of Western Australia. We obtained not only documentary but also pictorial material from the Australian War Memorial in Canberra, the Battye Library in Perth, the Fremantle City Library, the National Archives in Washington, DC, and The University of Western Australia Archives. We thank those institutions and also West Australian Newspapers and Currie Hall for permission to reproduce many of the illustrations we have used. We give special thanks to Pat Tully of Karrinyup, who lent us photographs for a much longer period than either we or she expected, and Mathew Kelley of Mask Productions for lending illustrations obtained in connection with the documentary 'Secret Fleets', shown on ABC television in November 1995.

All of the aforementioned people and institutions have been helpful to both authors. So, ultimately, have others whom we would nevertheless like to acknowledge separately for the particular attention they gave to one or other of us. Two people gave Lisa Jackson invaluable help at the stage when this project was an honours dissertation rather than the book it has become: Jacquie Bunney, who undertook some of the earliest of the oral history interviews, and Lindsay Peet of Dalkeith, who provided great amounts of background information.

Tony Barker is indebted especially to William Itoh, former US Consul-General in Perth, for his interest in the project over a long period, for his hospitality during the research visit to Washington, DC, for copies of documents he had acquired himself during his time in Perth and for his introduction to James Purcell, wartime director of the American Red Cross in Perth. On a visit to eastern Australia Alan Magnusson provided welcome hospitality in Sydney, while Carolyn Holbrook greatly facilitated research in Canberra through the loan of her car. She also volunteered to pursue various research tasks in later months, both at the War Memorial and in the National Library.

A number of friends read and commented on late versions of the manuscript before it was submitted for publication: Joy Anderson, Jacquie Bunney, Chris Brockman, Georgina Cope and Sue Penberthy. Chris Dixon of the University of Newcastle provided detailed comments with impressive speed, while Carolyn Holbrook devoted many hours to the most thorough of all the critical readings. We are grateful indeed to all these people for the way their criticisms enhanced our work. And we also thank Allan Watson most sincerely for the tact and professionalism he displayed as editor of the final version.

Finally, Lisa is indebted to Luke for his patience and good humour and Tony would like to thank Rosie for her constant moral and practical support, especially during what was for her a rather lonely period in Washington.

# INTRODUCTION

IN MARCH 1942 the respected American journalist Joseph C. Harsch wrote a series of articles for his compatriots about the arrival of United States forces in Australia a short time previously. In addition to offering some propagandist platitudes about the warmth of the welcome the troops had received, he attempted to predict the longer term impact on this hitherto 'sheltered child of the British Empire'. General MacArthur's inspiring arrival had brought 'a sense of momentous impending changes which will be a by-product of this struggle to preserve Western civilisation in Australia':

> Today one hears such things as 'MacArthur has an opportunity to do all
> the things which should have been done years ago but were never done'.
> They indicate a feeling that the time has come to sweep away encrusted
> encumbrances of the colonial past and open Australia's visions and horizon
> to a new future.[1]

The prediction was less than amazing. It followed just three months after Prime Minister John Curtin's announcement that Australia was now looking to America 'free of any pangs as to our traditional links or kinship with the United Kingdom',[2] and a mere six weeks after the fall of Britain's 'impregnable' fortress of Singapore. On the formal level of international relations it was to be a prediction fulfilled in the years immediately ahead, as the Japanese were repulsed and eventually defeated, and also in the much longer term, as Britain withdrew from 'East of Suez' and as Australia became America's faithful ally in Korea, Vietnam and the Gulf War.

Yet it is one thing for an emerging nation to make pragmatic choices about new directions in foreign policy, quite another to discard abruptly all the emotional and cultural baggage of a long colonial history. Whatever eager Australians may have told the journalist Harsch in the heat of a very difficult moment, it was at least possible that American impatience with colonial 'encumbrances' would lead to Australian irritation with Americans.

Certainly the two substantial studies that have been made of the impact of American servicemen on Australia in this period have found plenty of evidence of friction, and have struggled to identify lasting effects as far-reaching as those predicted by Harsch.[3] Neither, however, does justice to the interaction between Americans and the people of Western Australia. To make good that omission is to do more than fill in an empty corner of a coherent picture, for Western Australia in the post-war world presents a unique case study of confused identity and divided loyalties.

The uniqueness of Western Australia has always been self-evident to its inhabitants, even though their fervent conviction may be a matter of indifference or amusement to the rest of the country. In the late twentieth century the feeling is sufficiently entrenched for some to revive the notion of secession, without fear of general ridicule, even though economic and demographic circumstances are very different from the situation in the 1930s, when a majority voted for such a separation from Australia.

Underlying this intense parochialism is, at first glance, a strange ambiguity, which makes Harsch's prediction 'that the arrival of the American troops will prove a dividing point in Australian history' seem crudely simplistic. A state arguably more pro-American than any other in the Commonwealth is also demonstrably more British. With higher levels of United Kingdom immigration than other states in the post-war era, it is perhaps not risky for less rabid conservatives than the secessionists to talk seriously about retaining the monarchy, should fellow-Australians opt for a republic. But how can this loyalty to a colonial past be reconciled with a popular enthusiasm for America arguably greater than in other states?

The evidence for such enthusiasm does not lie in the American names of the sporting teams with which the West confronts eastern Australia. The 'Eagles', the 'Wildcats', the 'Warriors' and the 'Heat' are products of an Americanisation and commercialisation of sport which affects the whole country and much of the world. Similarly, stealing the 'State of Excitement' car number plate slogan from Oregon in the 1970s was typical of an Australia-wide tendency to the derivative.

Replacing it after 1983 with the presumptuous 'Home of the America's Cup' was a proprietorial claim to an achievement celebrated with giddy abandon by the whole nation.

Rather, enthusiasm for America by this most British state has been seen consistently in the welcome lavished on the visiting United States Navy. American sources confirm that it is not another example of parochialism that insists Perth is the Navy's most favoured rest and recreation centre.[4] In the 1980s a handful of American ships visiting eastern ports were met by vociferous protests on the wharves, and by flotillas of obstruction on the water. In the same period much larger numbers of ships were greeted ecstatically in Western Australia.

There are of course obvious economic advantages in welcoming warmly tens of thousands of well-paid sailors on leave. Although the numbers of personnel slumped from a high of 37,749 in 1983 to a mere tenth of that figure in the year of the Gulf War, 1991, they had returned to just short of thirty thousand in 1993.[5] Yet money alone cannot explain why small voices of protest in Fremantle are over-whelmed by the sounds of welcome, and the occasional cold shoulder is invisible among the open arms of hospitality.

The reasons for a unique and apparently unrelenting enthusiasm do not necessarily lie in some folk memory of a special relationship forged in the Second World War. They may have just as much to do with distance from the Vietnam War and from the growing disillusion-ment felt by Sydney, in particular, at the presence on rest and recreation leave in the later 1960s of a very different generation of American servicemen, befuddled by drugs and hardened by cynicism.

In either case, and in any other that may be conjured up, it is impossible to ignore the isolation of Western Australia and the special feelings that go with it—a need more urgent even than that felt by other Australians to seek the reassurance of outside attention, the validation conferred by outside approval and, in some cases, even the means of escape into that outside world. If such feelings had long been acknowledged by some Western Australians and had nagged the subconscious of others, the Second World War brought them to the surface as never before.

Given the strength of these feelings, the already published studies of American forces in Australia during that war might have been deliberately designed to antagonise Western Australians. If there is one thing that annoys Sandgropers almost as much as being ignored entirely, it is being taken for granted as simply another part of Australia.

In the first book published on the theme, *Over-Sexed, Over-Paid and Over Here: Americans in Australia 1941–1945*, John Hammond Moore argues that the Americans were initially warmly welcomed as heroes and saviours but that most Australians were not sad to see them leave, the relationship having been soured by a series of murders committed by Private Edward Leonski in Melbourne and the constant brawling between Allied soldiers in the streets and bars of many other Australian cities. Primarily concerned with the logistical aspects of the American presence, Moore uses oral history anecdotes and contemporary journalism to chart the experience of the American servicemen in areas where large numbers of troops were concentrated, mainly northern Queensland and Melbourne.

*Yanks Down Under 1941–45: The American Impact on Australia*, by E. Daniel Potts and Annette Potts, takes a more sociological approach to the examination of the American presence, basing the study on a comprehensive oral history programme supplemented by the letters, diaries and journals of those experiencing the realities of wartime Australia. The book covers many aspects of the official relations between the United States and Australia. The authors claim that, because of the Second World War experience, the United States and Australia reached a 'lasting alliance' long before formal military and diplomatic bonds were created, offering examples of diplomatic ties and long-term friendships as evidence.[6]

The authors of both *Over-Sexed, Over-Paid and Over Here* and *Yanks Down Under* observe Australians trying to adjust to American cultural influences, which many saw as threatening to basically British traditions. In Rosemary Campbell's view the threat was to a national identity based on the rugged masculine world of the bush. In *Heroes and Lovers: A Question of National Identity* Campbell points out that American servicemen were concentrated in cities, where historically the majority of Australians had always lived and worked, but which had never featured in a rural-centred cultural ideology that downgraded women to domestic roles or saw them as sex objects. The presence of the Americans threatened an image of toughened, beer-swilling bushmen, diggers and shearers which excluded sensitive or romantic attitudes toward women. The smooth-talking, considerate, polite and present-laden 'Yank' may have been sneered at in comics, in the press and in the pub, but his 'success' and popularity with Australian women was astounding.[7]

There can be little doubt that challenges were there to both British and Australia-centred traditions, but there must be a great deal of uncertainty about the extent to which attitudes were changed. And it is here, in this general assumption that all of Australia was, and is, the same, that all these works fail to consider, let alone do justice to, the Western Australian experience. It was a unique experience because circumstances and sensitivities in the West were indeed different, and also unique because the Americans were themselves different from their counterparts in the east.

Both John Hammond Moore and the Pottses struggle to find convincing evidence that the American presence in the war period had a long-term impact. Moore is both more confident and less convincing that he has done so. In the absence of physical evidence such as monuments, he turns to the less tangible aspects of the Australian–American relationship, citing song lyrics, immigration figures and attitudinal changes to conclude that the presence of the American forces set Australia on a 'new path', free from the geographical and social isolation it had experienced previously.[8] Ironically, he pays virtually no attention to the state obsessed with its isolation, not only from the world but from the rest of Australia.

Moore briefly acknowledges that Fremantle was home to the more important of the two United States submarine bases in Australia. In terms of the numbers of servicemen involved he is certainly right to assert that 'in contrast to the GI, the American sailor did not loom large in Australia'. It is his privilege to choose the focus of his book and to decide that naval units are to 'play a small part' in the story he has to tell of a predominantly US Army presence in other parts of Australia. But his assertion that 'by the very nature of their work they usually had much less contact with Australia and its citizens'[9] must be regarded as extraordinary by anybody who has witnessed the welcome given to brief visits by the US Navy in the 1980s and 1990s. It seems provocative to discount the possibility of extremely close contact, considering that the Americans were not brief visitors but occupants of major naval bases in the heart of the Perth metropolitan area from 1942 to 1945.

Perhaps more attention should not be given to a book without footnote documentation of its assertions and with an index that refers to 'Freemantle' and carries no entry for 'Catalinas'. It will be necessary later, however, to give brief attention to its references to wartime violence in Perth, based on undocumented private correspondence thirty years after the event.

Read from a Western Australian perspective, the Pottses' book, *Yanks Down Under,* also has one disconcerting flaw in its methodology. Its only reference to American consular staff mentions Mason Turner as if he were the Consul in Brisbane.[10] Turner may well have made the comments attributed to him about the notorious 'Battle of Brisbane', but if so he did it from Perth, where he was Consul throughout the war years. This lapse is puzzling, and leads on to the rather worrying realisation that the authors have not used consular records at all.[11]

Despite that concern, *Yanks Down Under* is a much more impressive work than *Over-Sexed, Over-Paid and Over Here.* It has footnote references to arguments drawn from a large array of archival, printed and oral sources. It is convincing in its treatment of many significant themes, including the incidence and nature of violence, the ambiguities of racism, the role of wartime censorship and relations between the sexes. It would not be sensible to challenge as mere fence-sitting its well-argued conclusion that 'the effect of the American presence on Australia—the exposure to hundreds of thousands of men and women from a different society—is much more difficult to establish than their contribution to victory in the Pacific'.[12]

The Pottses' book also includes far more references to Western Australia, yet in doing so it takes the state for granted as just another part of Australia. Events and situations in the west are incorporated in discussions of Australia-wide trends, with no sense of different circumstances and sensitivities.

The attitudes underlying this approach are brought most sharply into focus at the very end of the book. 'Ultimately', say the authors, 'the question of "who saved Australia?" resolves itself into the question of "who won the war in the Pacific?"' There can be no quibbling with the conclusions that follow: these emphasise the pre-eminent American contribution without belittling the extent of Australian self-help.[13] But to quote generally the gratitude of Australians, both famous and little known, is to ignore the especial sense of threat experienced in the west in late 1941 and early 1942, when advancing Japanese forces were far closer than those of Australia huddled behind the hated 'Brisbane Line'.

One looks in vain in the index of this well-researched book, purporting to be about the whole of Australia, for references to any of the Western Australian places bombed by the Japanese—Broome, Exmouth, Onslow, Port Hedland or Wyndham. Missing also are any references to the sinking of HMAS *Sydney* off the Western Australian coast, with the loss of more than six hundred lives. Proximity may have made Australia's greatest ever naval disaster particularly shocking to Western Australians, but the occurrence of Pearl Harbour just three weeks afterwards gave this isolated population a semblance of hope that the outside world might provide the protection that the rest of Australia could not.

It was a handful of people on the wharf at Geraldton who eventually saw the only debris from the *Sydney*—a life raft scarred with jagged holes—brought ashore months after the disaster. It might have been mere chance that it was a small American vessel that brought it in.[14] But, as far as the locals were concerned, it was more than lucky that an American Catalina flying-boat base had been established there by this time. Again, neither this town, five hundred kilometres north of Perth, nor the fears that had led many people to evacuate further south—nor indeed the base itself—play any part in the Pottses' book.

Published historical work specifically about the American presence in Western Australia during the Second World War has been concerned with formal military relations rather than with any social impact the visiting troops may have had.[15] David Creed's *Operation of the Fremantle Submarine Base 1942–1945* is a detailed account of the naval activities taking place in the port during the war. Lynne Cairns's *Submarines in the Harbour: The World War Two Allied Submarine Base at Fremantle* has much valuable detail about local facilities for Dutch and British as well as American submariners. But it concludes by acknowledging the neglect of significant studies of the 'home front'.[16]

It has been left to the writers of fiction to convey something of the social effects of the American presence. Robin Sheiner's *Smile, the War is Over* and Lois Battle's *War Brides* both describe relationships between local civilians and American servicemen. Randolph Stow's *The Merry-Go-Round in the Sea* is set in wartime Geraldton and especially effective in setting the scene before the arrival of the Americans, with its vignettes of civil defence preparations, the arrival of evacuees from the Dutch East Indies and departure of locals to less threatened latitudes. Its relatively few references to the Americans are probably in proportion to their numerical presence, but scarcely do justice to the reassurance they offered a community in nervous disarray. With the probable exception of Stow's work, these various novels complement, rather than seriously modify, the themes of fictional works set in other Australian cities, notably *Come In Spinner* by Dymphna Cusack and Florence James, *The Fatal Days* by Henrietta Drake-Brockman and *Soldiers' Women* by Xavier Herbert.[17]

Certainly no work, published or unpublished, has so far attempted to record the impressions of some of the individuals most closely affected by the American presence in Western Australia, let alone evaluated its general social impact. Whether the Americans wrought the major changes predicted by Joseph Harsch for the whole of Australia in 1942, or whether they indeed prepared the way for generation after generation of young women to 'Dial-a-Sailor' with such enthusiasm, it is surely appropriate, fifty years after the event, to give substance to experiences still vivid in the memories of many older Western Australians.

# FLEETING ATTRACTION

## Chapter One

## ANXIOUS ISOLATION

FOR AMERICANS, the Japanese attack on Pearl Harbour in early December 1941 meant an end to lingering hopes of isolation from wars that had been raging in Europe for the previous two years and in Asia much longer. For Australians, longstanding suspicions of Asia and more recent concerns about Japanese intentions became urgent fears. But the accelerating momentum of the Japanese advance also offered fulfilment of hopes that the United States might replace Britain as the guarantor of Australian security.

These fears and hopes, held throughout Australia, had a special poignancy in the west. Traditional loyalties had been clear enough a mere eight years before, when Western Australians voted to secede from the Australian Commonwealth but not from the British Empire. It was logical that such sentiments should lead to general support for Prime Minister Robert Menzies' announcement that Australia was automatically joining Britain's war in 1939. But, however distant the European theatre might at first have seemed, from mid-1941 the potential of attack and invasion by Japan made Australians increasingly aware that the war might come to them long before their fighting men could return from Europe and the Middle East.

9

More acutely than most other Australians, those in the west were confronted with the dangers and proximity of the war in late November 1941, as news gradually emerged that HMAS *Sydney* had been sunk off the undefended western coast by a German raider. It probably helped local morale that the Prime Minister was now John Curtin, federal Member for Fremantle. But it was more important that practical assistance for this uniquely isolated population should come from somewhere. For some time a few local voices had been calling loudly and persistently for strengthened ties with the still neutral United States. Now their advocacy rang true with a population conditioned by Hollywood myth-making to believe that America was wealthy, powerful and magnanimous.

Western Australia greeted the Second World War with traditional attitudes enhanced by recent hardship. In 1933 almost 25 per cent of men living in the city had been unemployed, with another 25 per cent on shortened time.[1] Hundreds of civil servants were either dismissed or had their working hours reduced. Unemployed men were put to work on relief projects in the Darling Range, on the Causeway or in Kings Park to earn their 'sustenance' of twenty-five shillings per week. Many large-scale unemployment demonstrations took place in Perth in the early 1930s, organised by trade unions and often addressed by people with Communist Party sympathies.

The Great Depression may have been no more severe than in other states but it had reinforced the sense of vulnerable isolation that was every Sandgroper's birthright. Despite the internal social tensions, resentment against unemployment and social hardship was expressed most clearly in the secession movement. 'An honourable and friendly withdrawal' from federal control would rescue Western Australia from adversity.[2] The outcome of the 1933 referendum is often seen as essentially a protest against the failure of governments, both state and federal, to solve the problems of the Depression. Even though the result was an overwhelming approval of secession, the electorate simultaneously voted into power the Labor Party, which had opposed it.

Despite this ambiguity, and despite the fact that secessionist sentiment faded as the economy improved, the 1930s had done nothing to soothe longstanding Western Australian sensitivities. There was traditional parochialism in the secessionists' contention that 'the various needs and requirements of Western Australia can never really be properly understood by legislators residing and remaining in a centre which is over 2000 miles away'.[3] And there was traditional deference, both in the desire to secede from Australia but remain within the British Empire, and in the eventual meek acceptance of British rulings that secession was constitutionally impossible.

It is true that the recent past had also brought notable improvements in communications with the outside world. Railway links to the east, completed in 1917, were supplemented in 1929 by a regular air service to Adelaide. An overseas airmail service soon followed. Although direct telephone contact with the United States was not available until the very end of 1941, calls to eastern Australia had been possible since 1930 and to London since 1932.[4] That same year saw the beginning of radio transmission by the Australian Broadcasting Commission. By the end of the decade its two Perth stations,

*(West Australian Newspapers)*

6WF and 6WN, were also providing the programmes for country transmitters in Kalgoorlie, Wagin and Geraldton. Among commercial stations, while 6KY was broadcast exclusively in the metropolitan area, 6IX had sister stations in Katanning and Merredin, 6PM in Northam and 6PR in Dardanup.[5] Although all of these—and the ABC in particular—used recorded material from overseas sources, reception was often poor, even in the substantial south coast town of Albany, where people struggled with varying success to pick up transmissions from Perth.[6]

Important though they were, these changes in communications had not been sufficient to break down a parochialism that could be simultaneously convinced of its virtuous difference from the rest of Australia and fearful of its loneliness in a threatening world.

Closer to the Dutch East Indies than to the great cities of eastern Australia, the state's population was concentrated in the south-west corner, and especially in a metropolitan area itself remote from the northern outposts of Wyndham, Broome, Port Hedland and Exmouth Gulf, which were to be directly threatened by Japanese attack in 1942. Out of a state population of 467,000, some 228,000 lived in the metropolitan area of Perth, Fremantle and their immediately surrounding suburbs.[7] The small port of Geraldton, the only significant population centre north of Perth, had a mere four to five thousand people, numbers roughly similar to those in the two other major centres further south, Bunbury and Albany.

Perth itself had far more inner city residents than was the case later in the century. But despite the rattle of trams along Murray and Hay Streets and the hiss of trolley-buses down Wellington Street, it was also much more like a large country town. Residents on the south side of Adelaide Terrace could look down across a huge paddock, covered annually by wild nasturtiums, with no buildings in Terrace Road to obstruct their view of the Swan River. Further west the foreshore was a tangle of bamboo scrub stretching for hundreds of yards either way behind Government House.[8]

North of the river, Subiaco, Nedlands, Dalkeith and Claremont were well established, as was Cottesloe on the coast. Further north Scarborough was more a beach playground than a residential suburb, with holiday cottages, cheap shops and open-air entertainments. Access to an almost undeveloped City Beach was along a single-track switchback road of wooden planks, widened in places to allow converging cars to pass each other. Development had begun immediately to the south, with the new subdivision of Floreat Park boasting 'splendidly planned and sensibly restricted' blocks selling for the bargain price of as little as £40 apiece. Long before this, less affluent families had settled further away from the city, in Wembley to the north-

*One of Perth's beach playgrounds on the eve of the war*
(Mask Productions, Perth)

west, Tuart Hill to the north, and Carlisle, Bassendean and Midland Junction to the north-east. South of the river, suburbia stretched little further than South Perth, Victoria Park, Applecross and Melville.[9]

In an era of still limited private vehicle ownership, these residential patterns were largely a reflection of the network of public road and rail communications. Canning Road became a bitumenised 'highway' in 1930 and the Canning Bridge was finally opened in 1938. It was fortunate that the Fremantle Bridge was rebuilt in the following year, connecting with the newly renovated Perth–Fremantle Road (later named Stirling Highway), as the older thoroughfare would not have handled the increased traffic of the war years. Relatively cheap and efficient buses ran along these two highways, the forty-minute journey between Perth and Fremantle costing sixpence. Trains ran from the city to Midland Junction and Fremantle, and trams from the city to Subiaco. Trolley-buses took twelve minutes to reach Wembley and also ran south of the river to Victoria Park.[10]

Access to Perth's closest southern suburb, however, was still by ferry. The construction of a bridge across the Narrows was delayed for many years because the Town Planning Commissioner was of the opinion that 'South Perth was one of the most beautiful suburbs he had ever seen, and he would not like to see it spoiled by the dust, din and danger which a bridge and the consequent traffic would bring to it'.[11] Until the bridge was built in the 1950s, many Perth people viewed Fremantle as a distant, almost separate, community.[12] This was a perception that would be reinforced, rather than broken down, during the war.

The Swan River may have been a barrier to easy communication between northern and southern suburbs but it was also a playground for children and adults alike. Numerous sailing and rowing clubs included several close to the city centre, along the Esplanade near the foot of Barrack Street. One man, who was to develop a close association with American servicemen in one of those clubs, recalled a carefree childhood in Como, learning to swim from the jetty, playing in boats of many sizes and walking the foreshore to collect small bath-loads of crabs or prawns.[13] On the broad northern bays of the river, which would soon be home to American flying boats, there were designated swimming 'baths' at Nedlands, Crawley and Claremont. While the baths were discreetly segregated into male and female sections, they were the scene of serious swimming. At Crawley one young woman, who would eventually spend much of her life as a war bride in America, trained for the long-distance 'Swim through Perth'. Her first attempt ended when she discovered that the Narrows were also shallows by accidentally touching bottom and being disqualified.[14]

Away from the seediness of the Fremantle waterfront, the metropolitan area was generally seen as a safe environment, where houses were left unlocked and young people moved around unsupervised and unchauffeured. Although it was overwhelmingly suburban, Perth also had typical urban institutions, ranging from churches, a university and theatres to trotting and racecourses, football grounds, dance halls, a zoo, a Luna Park amusement area at Scarborough and a notorious inner city street of brothels. Its educational, social and artistic life showed enthusiasm but also the limitations of a small isolated population in a climate favouring a leisurely outdoor life-style.

The local theatre scene had thrived in the interwar years. The Perth Repertory Club offered the public traditional, commercially orientated theatre that was well patronised. More radical plays were performed by the Perth Workers' Art Guild, which was established by Katherine Susannah Pritchard and Keith George to encourage 'working-class' art and culture, and foster leftist drama. Small in membership, the Communist Party had a high public profile, publishing a newspaper and operating a bookshop under the Horseshoe Bridge in Perth, its activities legitimised by the support it received from such prominent local people as Pritchard and Paddy Troy.[15]

There was great local pride in The University of Western Australia, founded in 1913, which was unique in the nation in providing free tertiary education. It had its limitations, not least in its lack of a medical school, which meant that would-be doctors were obliged to study in the east or overseas. But its small academic staff enjoyed considerable local prestige as cultural arbiters and expert commentators on increasingly troubling events in the outside world.

While some women received a university education, there were no opportunities for them to pursue academic careers and very few openings commensurate with their abilities in other areas of employment. As they found outlets in voluntary work, they were joined by many non-graduate women who also had the motivation and leisure to take them beyond the purely domestic sphere.

With no large-scale manufacturing industry, Perth may have escaped the urban degradation of many other cities but not all of their problems. As some male social casualties were inconspicuously drinking themselves into oblivion in the scrub on the river foreshore close to the city, there were females prostituting themselves nearby at rates half those charged in Roe Street, near the city's railway station.[16] Virtually all such indigents were white because the Aboriginal population was even further out of sight in rural segregation.

Denied working opportunities by economics and convention, middle-class women were prominent among those who expressed concern for the plight of such people. No doubt some were moved as much by the threat to the moral climate as by compassion for the disadvantaged. But it was probably their social consciences and activism more than anything else that prepared Perth for the disruption that war would bring. The Women's Service Guild's prolonged campaign against the unofficially tolerated brothels of Roe Street expressed outrage at the associated 'crime and corruption'. It insisted that the registration and compulsory medical examination of prostitutes, far from reducing the incidence of venereal disease, merely promoted 'a false sense of security in men', thereby encouraging 'a most sordid and brutal form of sexual promiscuity'. Yet accompanying this moral indignation were enlightened demands for free and confidential treatment of venereal disease, sex education for boys and girls, social assistance for destitute females and the employment of women police officers.[17]

The Guild was also notable in these immediate pre-war years for its campaign against the mistreatment of Aboriginal people, especially women and especially by the police. Few others matched its public outrage at the evidence of more than a century of exploitation, which had seen Aboriginal people everywhere succumb to disease and demoralisation under policies officially labelled 'protection'. While virtual slavery ruled the lives of many on the cattle stations of the north, those in the southern half of the state were excluded from most urban areas and segregated in squalid settlements, of which Moore River, to the north of Perth, was the most notorious.[18]

Significant though women's activism was, there is no evidence that it had a major impact on the predominant racism of the times. In 1941 complaints were made to the Tramways Board that a number of Aboriginals, who were camped near the Fremantle Cemetery, were travelling to and from Perth on the board's trams:

It was resolved that a letter be sent to the Department of Native Affairs calling attention to the fact and intimating that the presence of these natives on the tram cars is objectionable to passengers and the board will be glad if they will take action to prevent this.[19]

Racism was expressed not only in denial of civil and political rights to indigenous people but in support for the White Australia Policy. Hostility to Asian immigration was accompanied by suspicion of those who, in Anglo-Saxon eyes, just avoided being coloured. Small southern European communities were by now well established but still far short of ready acceptance, as the Italians especially were to discover through ostracism and internment as 'enemy aliens'.[20]

None of the varied activities of Perth's social elite—women's activism, higher education, left-wing journalism or live theatre—had the popular appeal of sport. Racing and trotting attracted considerable numbers of spectators, as did football and cricket, which both also involved many younger men as participants. Cricket, however, served to reinforce impressions on both sides of the Nullarbor that the West was scarcely part of Australia. Distance prevented the state team in this one truly national sport from competing in the national interstate competition, the Sheffield Shield. It was particularly difficult to attract other state teams to Perth. From 1930 to 1940, while Western Australia played twelve matches in the eastern states, only six interstate matches were played in Perth. International teams were seen only when outgoing Australian and incoming English touring teams paused briefly to show the flag at the Western Australian Cricket Association ground.[21]

Important though sports were to social life, noneof them, or even all or them together, matched the mass appeal of the movies. A visit to the cinema was a chance for affordable, escapist entertainment. Australians saw more movies per capita than people anywhere else in the world during this era, and Western Australia was no exception.

People of all ages flocked to makeshift and more permanent facilities in numerous country centres, to ten city cinemas in central Perth and Fremantle and to at least fifteen others, many of them modern 'luxury theatres', in the suburbs. A number of theatres had outdoor screens adjacent or, as in the case of Subiaco's Regal Theatre, across the road, where patrons could recline in deckchairs to enjoy the mingled delights of a Perth summer evening and a Hollywood fantasy.[22] Despite national quotas intended to enforce the screening of a certain percentage of Australian-produced films, cheaper and more popular American 'flicks' dominated local programmes.

It was from these mass-produced Hollywood images that Western Australians' preconceptions of the United States and its people were largely derived — images of Americans, especially men, as glamorous, handsome, wealthy and successful. Most Western Australians had no opportunity to test these images with direct experience of the United States, of expatriate Americans or even of other forms of commentary on American life. There were no direct air links between America and Australia in the early 1940s, and American newspapers were difficult to obtain and invariably out of date. Few American books were imported because of a longstanding agreement that only British books would be brought into Australia.[23]

*(West Australian Newspapers)*

Ignorance about America can also be attributed to the failure of the state education system to incorporate American studies into school curriculums. The United States was considered relevant only as part of the study of broader themes about Australia and its relationship with the British Empire. It was an attitude that extended even to the higher reaches of education. It would be another forty years before

The University of Western Australia offered a course in the history of the United States. Associate Professor Fred Alexander, a specialist in international relations, was in demand as a public commentator on American issues in 1941, not because of expertise in American history, but because he had recently visited the United States.[24]

The rarity of such contact with the United States was in no way balanced by a significant American presence in Western Australia. Some might boast that a former American president, Herbert Hoover, had gained youthful—and possibly useful—experience in the Goldfields, but it was hardly evidence of a trend. Far more revealing was the fact that the United States had opened its Perth Consulate so recently. A 'consular agency' had operated from 1886 to 1930 and then for the next eight years Western Australia had been included in the consular district of Adelaide. The decision to establish a full Consulate under a career officer had been made on the grounds of the state's potential rather than its current importance. The routine work of the office when it opened in May 1938—such as the documentation of merchandise and the issue of passports and visas—did not justify its existence, according to a State Department memorandum. Political reporting was not of 'transcending importance', although the state's unique position in relation to others 'makes it interesting and it is tending to become increasingly influential in Commonwealth politics'. But the state was Australia's largest and in natural resources one of the richest, presenting 'tremendous possibilities for after-the-war expansion in both trade and industry'. Trade promotion, a relatively undeveloped field, 'presents a prolific sphere of activity for exploitation after the war has ended'.[25]

In the mean time, before and during the war, consular reports confirmed the impression of an undeveloped backwater. In 1942 a request by the State Department to all United States consulates to compile a list of companies in Australia in which American capital was invested brought the reply from Perth that 'it appears that the only company incorporated in this state in which American capital is directly invested is Big Bell Mines Limited, 47 St George's Terrace'. Its major shareholder was the American Smelting and Refining Company of New York and there were also six large individual American investors. Big Bell in turn had a 20 per cent share of the Geraldton Oil Distributing Company. Apart from these investments the only other American presence was through a number of local branches of United States companies incorporated in other Australian states, such as Colgate Palmolive, Kodak, Ford, Columbia Pictures, General Electric, Goodyear and Vacuum Oil.[26] Nearly all these subsidiaries were under the management of Australian nationals.

In other ways the consular records confirm how limited the opportunities were for Western Australians to meet real, live Americans. At the beginning of 1940 the Consulate could report only fifty-seven United States nationals in the state, and only an extra three a year later.[27] Most of these local Americans were active or retired mining engineers, whose work had taken them far from the major centres of population. One man emerged from obscurity in the gold-fields to volunteer for the United States forces, claiming extensive construction experience on the Golden Gate Bridge in San Francisco and the Boulder Dam in Colorado. Others in the total included several Italians never suspected of being American until they claimed United States nationality in attempts to escape internment. Francesco Violi complained from Laverton in September 1940 that, despite spending twenty-eight years in the United States, he had been forced to register as an alien and had been interned on Rottnest Island for a time. He received no comfort from the Consul, who pointed out that even if he was American (which was unclear) he would still have to register as alien.[28]

Although this comment avoided the essential point that as an American the man would have been in no danger of internment, there were other Americans who would have argued that Western Australian bureaucratic paranoia had made conditions almost as bad for them as if they had been behind bars. Captain V. H. Walker was the spokesman for five Americans who had arrived in Australia with Wirth Brothers Circus and had been trapped by the outbreak of war. Somewhat irked by their treatment in the eastern states, they were enraged that officialdom in the west made them leap through bureaucratic hoops as often as they performed in the travelling big top. They had been required to report to the police as aliens every thirty days in Victoria, fortnightly in New South Wales, weekly in South Australia but now daily and sometimes several times per day in Western Australia.[29]

Another transient whose presence said far more about the peculiarities of Western Australia than the realities of America was Mrs Doretta Vera Micko Zinke, an American who, during a trans-Australian train journey to the West, was suspected of being a spy. The *Sunday Times* reported in March 1941 that she was in fact an American ethnologist in Australia to study Aborigines. But this story was doubted by the authorities. She was alleged to have falsified a train ticket to avoid paying a £5 fare and to go to a destination other than the one at which she had stated she would study Aborigines. Even worse, she had been rude to F. I. Bray, the Commissioner of Native Affairs in Perth. The Australian Defence Department told the American Consulate in Perth that it had been concerned for some time about Zinke's case. It wanted to prevent her travelling to Darwin 'in as much as her intention to study aborigines appears doubtful'. She both confirmed and confounded these official attitudes by reaching Darwin and taking a job in the Victoria Hotel. Despite this unusual mode of studying Aborigines, the American authorities were less suspicious than the Australian, listing Mrs Zinke as an ethnologist in their records and taking some trouble to expedite her later request for passage home to the United States.[30]

Eventually the war would flush out several other unnoticed Americans, arguing United States nationality to resist call-up for medicals for military service in the Australian forces. Yet the eighty names listed in the Consulate's return for 1942 did not represent an increase significant enough to counter the impression that real Americans were close to being an unknown species at a time when artfully manufactured images of American life were familiar to all Western Australians. These images, however, were a distortion of reality.

It was ironic that the United States itself was a good deal more insular than Western Australia. The world-wide dispersal of Hollywood movies—and of other forms of commercial imperialism—was not accompanied by any general attempt to understand or adapt to other societies. While isolation for many of the 467,000 Western Australians meant constantly looking elsewhere for cultural as well as physical reassurance, the United States, with its 131 million people, was big enough and diverse enough to be a world unto itself.

A long history of isolationism in foreign policy had been interrupted by belated and brief involvement in the First World War. But the policy had been resumed with a vengeance, the 'return to normalcy' of the 1920s having been accompanied by restrictive quotas on immigration. These were designed to end the mass southern and eastern European immigration, which had fuelled America's industrial revolution but, in the eyes of many, threatened its social cohesion. Neither these restrictions nor the country's massive industrial power had saved it from the problems of depression, which reinforced a demand for escapist entertainment.

The images that Hollywood presented to Americans and to the world may often have been violent, with gangsters confronting the forces of law and Indians giving way to the forces of progress, but there was much more celebration of the consumer boom of the 1920s than commentary on the disasters of the 1930s. Moviegoers saw little of the huge regional, social, racial and educational variety of a society under stress and little of the armies of white unemployed who would also be among the first to enlist. There was no sense of the poverty, illiteracy and naivety soon to be disguised by uniforms, haircuts and a modicum of training.

The ignorance and innocence of Western Australians about the United States did nothing to restrain, and indeed probably intensified, their sense that here was the powerful friend that was needed to replace an embattled Britain. That was a need of course that was eventually expressed on behalf of the whole nation by Prime Minister Curtin. But long before he made his famous statement, on 27 December 1941, that Australia was looking to America, the same message had been pushed relentlessly in Western Australia by the *Fremantle and Districts*

*Sentinel.* The newspaper's stridency partly betrayed indignation that few shared its fears. But at least its year-long campaign had made its ideas commonplace.

As early as 16 January 1941, at a time when Australia was happily despatching its troops in their thousands to Europe and the Middle East, the *Sentinel* was doing its best to convey to local people the urgent need for overseas friends to offset the indifference of eastern Australia. The arrangements that were allowing the United States to use naval harbours in various parts of the British Empire offered

> an unique opportunity to invite 'Uncle Sam' to utilise Cockburn Sound—now idle—and it would present a pretty picture to see the 'Union Jack', the 'Australian Flag' and 'The Stars and Stripes' waving in the breeze at our magnificent naval harbour, Cockburn Sound, the 'front door' to Australia.[31]

No doubt aware that most Australians would have no idea where this front door was, and convinced that the west was simultaneously 'under the thraldom of the Eastern States' and yet abandoned by them, the *Sentinel* proclaimed in its next edition:

> Eastern Australia is well defended, BUT NOT SO WA. This is not a parochial matter; it is an EMPIRE matter, and what a grand picture it would make to see the 'Union Jack', the 'Stars and Stripes' and our own 'Federal Flag' flying together for the protection of Australia.[32]

A month later—still long before the Japanese advance seemed a real threat—the paper sounded almost desperate in its search for salvation:

> What must we do to be saved? And what can we do to be saved? Give the Americans the rights—YES! Give Uncle Sam the Right to use Cockburn Sound. And fly the Stars and Stripes there as a warning to our ENEMIES and HER Enemies.[33]

*23*

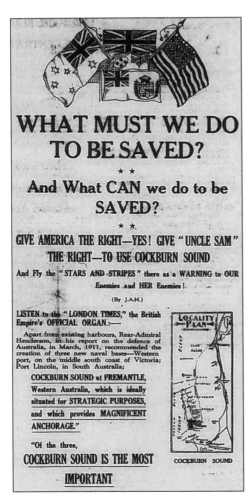

(Battye Library Newspapers)

The *Sentinel*'s message was insistent and almost incessant in embracing the United States without spurning Britain. Giving a new twist to the secessionist yearning of eight years earlier, it sought refuge in a great new empire. A leading article in March insisted that 'a movement has been started for bringing about the political union of English speaking peoples'. The paper's immediate contribution to 'The Greatest Political Move in the History of the World' was two versions of a name for 'the proposed super-state'—the 'United States of Brit-America' and 'the United States of America-Britt'.[34]

Later in that same month of March 1941 the *Sentinel* was ecstatic at news of the arrival of a flotilla of American warships on a visit to Sydney and Brisbane. Insisting that 'the people of Australia are greatly pleased at Uncle Sam's expeditious way of doing things', the paper was equally confident that young Western Australians shared its enthusiasm for flags. Under a headline 'Stars and Stripes Wanted by our Children' it reported that 'school children everywhere are asking when a distribution of America's flags is to be made. This is only natural and they won't be satisfied until they get them.' This was in contrast to their elders: 'Wake up! people of WA, before you are blown to pieces. And get the Stars and Stripes here. You've been fast asleep long enough, and the geese are cackling, stretching their necks and warning you.'[35]

By August, as Japanese expansion became more menacing, a further visit from American naval vessels was actually a source of concern to the *Sentinel*:

> The quiet way in which the American Cruisers arrived at Brisbane, without notice and without the breath of suspicion on the part of anyone that such a thing was about to happen, should serve the purpose of illustrating how easy—very easily possible—it would be for others not so friendly, to suddenly present themselves at an Australian port, and instead of friendly greetings, present us with a few bombs.

The only reassurance that would satisfy the paper was the thought of an American presence in the west: 'It would be just like Christmas' to have them in Perth.[36]

It has to be acknowledged that the *Sentinel's* obsession with the Americans as potential saviours was not necessarily representative of local opinion. Indeed some of its strongest language was directed at the failure of the 'Perth press' to share both its sense of urgency about the state's vulnerability and its sense of destiny about the potential for global Anglo-Saxon union. It had begun its campaign in January 1941 by asking indignantly: 'Why is the Perth morning and evening Press editorially silent on the big question of AMERICA having the right to use our naval harbours on the WA Coastline?... And further, why do these papers hesitate to publish letters on the subject. Why? Why? Why?' The only explanation it could think of was that 'there is a "screw loose" somewhere'.[37]

By March the paper was simultaneously demanding that 'these up-to-date Americans' be invited to visit 'the finest naval harbour in Australia...Cockburn Sound' and sneering:

> And what has our Perth daily press got to say about it? And what are our local governing bodies doing? Are we all fast asleep?

Wouldn't it help business? Wouldn't it be a pleasing sight to see the 'Stars and Stripes' in our midst? Wouldn't it put the wind up against any nation that has nefarious designs upon any part of Australia.[38]

Yet if the *Sentinel* was extreme, it was not alone in its concerns and hopes. In July 1941 Associate Professor Fred Alexander sent to the United States Consulate in Perth the typescript of an article he had written for the *Bulletin*, entitled 'Aid to Russia—From the United States Angle'. In a covering letter he expressed the hope that 'our navies will meet again in the not too distant future'. Thanks to his visit to the United States, Alexander was in demand. His radio talk on 6WN on 22 August 1941, entitled 'American Snapshots—A Democratic National Convention', offered impressions and information that in a later era would have been regarded as commonplace to the point of banality. But, in the mixture of ignorance and expectancy that prevailed in the months before Pearl Harbour, anything he could say with the authority of an academic and the novelty of first-hand knowledge was keenly received.[39] A lecture he gave to the Adult Education Board on 'Australia and the United States of America' aroused such interest that the Fremantle City Council invited him to repeat it to local citizens: 'We think that our people down here would appreciate hearing the impressions gained by you during your visit to that great country, more especially as the two countries mentioned have recently become more and more interdependent on each other [sic] in a very real sense.'[40]

Hopes of exploiting that perceived 'interdependence' were not confined to the metropolitan area. In late October 1941 a member of parliament reported to Prime Minister Curtin on a recent visit to Albany. 'Certain leading citizens' had suggested that 'in the event of conflict in the Pacific, Albany might be considered by the Government as a suitable base for our expected Ally', the United States. Curtin replied immediately that the 'representations in this connection have been noted'. If it was far from reassuring that even a Western Australian Prime Minister could be so non-committal, it was probably as well for local susceptibilities that the Department of the Navy's reactions—'badly placed strategically'—were contained in a dismissive handwritten and uncommunicated scrawl on the original letter.[41]

The *Fremantle and Districts Sentinel* might well have agreed with this last sentiment, for its advocacy of its own 'front door of Australia' never wavered. On 4 December 1941 the paper was confident that the Americans would need bases in Australia: 'The State Government should encourage the U.S.A. to the utmost, and give her every information about all our harbours from Esperance to Darwin, but not try to put a "wet blanket" over Cockburn Sound.'[42] Four days later the prayers of the *Sentinel* and other Western Australians began to be answered.

On the morning of 8 December 1941 Mason Turner, United States Consul in Western Australia, became increasingly annoyed as the waitress in the dining room of Perth's Esplanade Hotel seemed more interested in crouching over a radio than producing his breakfast. Impatience turned to amazement when, inquiring as to the reason for this priority, he was told irritably that the Japanese had attacked some American base called Pearl Harbour.[43]

Appointed officially in July as successor to the first American Consul, Charles H. Derry, and his temporary Vice-Consul, Lloyd Himmel, Turner had seen the isolation of Perth as a safe haven for family life. By the time he arrived on 15 September from his previous post in Lima, Peru, the Japanese advance was beginning to make it seem less safe. Now, as he abandoned breakfast and hurried to his office on the fifth floor of the CML Building in St Georges Terrace, he knew that his immediate future was likely to be quite different from his expectations when he had accepted one of the least significant postings in the American diplomatic service.[44] Over the next two months Turner sought out office space in Perth for the military personnel he was secretly told his country would eventually send.

While Mason Turner was quite consciously preparing for the arrival of American servicemen, the Perth metropolitan area had been doing so unconsciously for the previous two years. The Americans would eventually be welcomed by a city scarred by the recent past as well as scared by the immediate future.

# FLEETING ATTRACTION

*Chapter Two*

## UNWITTING PREPARATION

As THEY WAITED ANXIOUSLY in their threatened outpost for a modern version of the US cavalry, Western Australians were already affected by a war that the Americans were only now entering. The absence of husbands, sons, fathers and lovers was emotionally traumatic but also an opportunity for many women to take on public roles barely dreamed of in peacetime. A more dramatic, but short-lived, social upheaval had taken place as men in uniform poured overseas through the maritime gateway of Fremantle. Troopships from Sydney, Melbourne and elsewhere in the east had introduced transient but troubling violence, with the authorities impotent to protect property or ensure personal safety on metropolitan streets.

The Japanese threat made real by Pearl Harbour meant that an American arrival would be welcomed with starry-eyed ecstasy by some and gratitude by virtually all; but the previous two years' experience meant that official and voluntary organisations were better prepared to meet a friendly but potentially unsettling invasion.

It is almost a cliche that the Second World War at first seemed 'far removed from the tranquillity of Western Australia'.[1] Remoteness for a time certainly made for leisurely, almost casual, defensive pre-cautions, both military and civilian. But the war had produced major upheaval and, if there was indeed tranquillity, it was at least partly the result of war's inevitable companions: censorship and security surveillance. For the first two years of the war these two functions were more closely allied, and more closely linked to military control, in Western Australia than elsewhere.

The national Security Service was a civilian organisation. There was nothing unusual that the Deputy Director, as the head of the state branch was known, was a military officer, Colonel Moseley, nor that his staff was a mixture of seconded military and police personnel and civil servants. But it was a typically Western Australian arrangement that they worked in the same building as Military Intelligence and Military Censorship, Yorkshire House in St Georges Terrace. As a 1943 report by investigators from the service's 'head office' eventually noted, 'the close relationship existing between Security Service and Army and

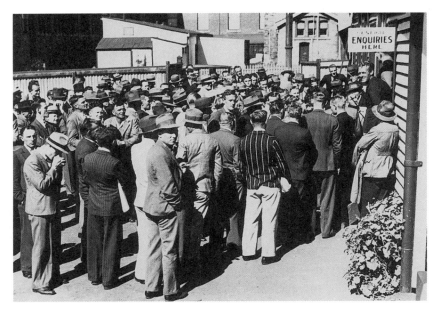

*Early tranquillity—volunteers in September 1939*
(West Australian Newspapers)

the harmonious relationship which obviously exists between the two organisations is no doubt partly due to the fact that Western Australia is so isolated from the eastern States and that they have to rely to a considerable extent on each other'.[2]

It would be easy to question the capacity of the Security Service to monitor subversion in one third of the Australian continent with a staff of twenty-four sharing one motor car and one motorcycle. And equally easy to question the value of that close and harmonious relationship when the motorcycle broke down and the army replaced it with one just as bad.[3] But there is strong evidence that, especially through a network of informers in the country and city, which included such pillars of the community as bank managers, the service was able to conduct an impressively far-reaching surveillance of threatened subversion. If its most notorious results were the internments of aliens long resident, and even in some cases born in Australia, these were a tiny fraction of its intrusions into the lives of the civilian community. In one twelve-month period its staff completed 1730 security investigations, which resulted in 314 prosecutions, 16 Restriction Orders and only 9 internments. There were 'at all times an average of 90 to 100 files on hand in the [Investigations] Section for inquiry and [sometimes] averaging as high as 200'.[4]

No doubt the Security Service felt that it was making a major contribution to the 'tranquillity' of the West. Probably in any circumstances the wartime atmosphere would have brought wide public support for the investigation, prosecution, restriction and internment of people whose views or nationality could easily be branded as threatening. But another factor was the wartime control of news, preventing any possibility of journalism critical of the erosion of civil liberties. In this respect Western Australia was part of a national system, in which the press in each state was subject to censorship under the overall supervision of a Chief Publicity Censor, a civilian public servant in Canberra. But the state was also unique in that the State Publicity Censor's office in these first two years of the war was controlled by the Department of the Army.[5]

This arrangement was deeply resented by local journalists and not particularly liked by Chief Publicity Censor E. G. Bonney in Canberra.[6] In January 1941 a deputation from the WA District Journalists' Association complained that the incumbent, Major Corbett, was 'not qualified for the position of Chief Censor'. Although they described him as 'too old for the post', they also resented his lack of sympathy for the problems of journalists.[7] The problem for Bonney was that he could not induce any of them to take on the job. He was able to draw on the local knowledge of Prime Minister Curtin, who told him that G. L. Burgoyne, editor of the *Daily News*, was 'easily the best'. According to Bonney, the stumbling-block was that the salary of £600 did not attract Burgoyne.[8] Judging from other confidential material in the Chief Publicity Censor's records, however, there was much more than money involved. Both before and after the army finally relinquished this civilian censorship role, with the appointment of Walter James as state Deputy Publicity Censor in February 1942, the *News* editor was a relentless critic of the system. As James himself soon noted, 'Mr Burgoyne is not a good player and is apt to be arrogantly resentful of censorship interference'.[9]

Essentially, however, neither reasoned criticism nor intemperate rage had any impact on a system dedicated to obliterating from public view anything that might help the enemy or dismay the community. Censorship in December 1940, for instance, insisted that there should be no public discussion of criticisms that the Perth Civil Defence Council was inactive, especially 'in regard to the evacuation of children'.[10]

To judge from the rigour of the decisions made in other states, it probably made little difference that censorship was under military control for so long. But certainly, with Major Corbett in charge, there was no chance that there would be wide reporting of events and trends much closer to the surface of community sensitivities than the plight of foreigners and other potential subversives. The *Fremantle and Districts Sentinel* in December 1941 gave prominence to threats by the military authorities to fine and imprison those guilty of breaches of security. In doing so it cited National Security Regulations that applied everywhere, under which 'persons are prohibited from obtaining, recording or communicating any information with respect to the number, description, armament, equipment, disposition, movement or condition of any arm of the services...'.[11] This was a prohibition of particular relevance in the West and one that makes the pages of the *Sentinel* and every other local newspaper extremely inadequate guides to the social impact of mobilisation in the first two years of the war. Only in the files of the censorship authorities, and other government records released long after the war, can one find the evidence to qualify the notion of dream-like tranquillity in these early years.

While the fighting seemed far away, the effects of the war were quickly felt, even though barely reported in the press. Throughout Australia the rush to join the second AIF (Australian Imperial Forces) meant the disruption of normal working and family lives. Mixed feelings, ranging from grief to euphoria, excitement to foreboding, marked the departure of these troops to the Middle East in 1940 and 1941, including the first Western Australian contingent, which left Fremantle, after seven months training at Northam, on 3 January

*Departure of the first Western Australian troopship*
(Australian War Memorial, Negative No. 1530)

1941.[12] Yet the Perth metropolitan area was affected by much more than the private emotions of local individuals and families. For thousands of troops from the eastern states, shore leave in Fremantle and Perth was the last contact with Australia. For the citizens of this usually isolated community their presence brought an even greater air of abnormality, verging on unreality, than had been experienced by their counterparts in the east.

Blanket censorship could not conceal from the country's largely seaboard population that many of the world's great passenger liners, sometimes alone, sometimes in huge escorted flotillas, were sailing from Australian ports. A soldier's letter, impounded by the military censors in Perth in February 1941, told of his departure from Port Melbourne on the *Mauretania* at the end of December:

> Between 5 and 6 pm on the Monday, we picked up with our convoy which consisted of the 'Queen Mary', 'Aquatania' [sic] 'Awatea' and 'Dominion Monarch' escorted by the Australian cruiser 'Canberra'... (probably the most costly convoy afloat consisting of 200,000 tons and 20,000 troops)... I shall post this in Perth under a plain envelope so keeping it from the eyes of the censor who scans everything written aboard. I have no scruples in sending this information to you as the 'secret' sailing of the 'Mauretania' was witnessed by hundreds of Sunday visitors to the beaches who were taken on pleasure cruises about our ship...[13]

This was not the only assemblage in Australian waters of near-legendary vessels normally plying the Atlantic crossing. Another intercepted letter told of an embarkation on the *Queen Mary* in May:

> On our way round from Sydney to Freemantle [sic] we picked up the rest of the convoy and when we were all together there were the 'Queen Mary', 'Mauretania', 'Aquitania', 'Empress of Britain', 'Empress of Canada', 'Empress of Japan', 'Andes'. Seven of the largest vessels in the British Fleet, and they were a truly magnificent sight.

*Great liners as troopships—Fremantle Harbour, January 1940*
(Fremantle City Library, Print No. 1696)

The writer revelled, perhaps a little naively, in the luxury of his accommodation: 'My steward told me that it was the suite Mrs Simpson, or should I say the Duchess of Windsor, used when travelling to England. This was my home for the next 44 days.'[14] Another indiscreet writer was equally impressed with the public appointments of his unnamed 'real luxury boat':

> Our Messing Hall for instance has marble slab pillars and marble slab walls. Row on row of concealed lights, several big paintings, we have several lifts on board, a grand lounge with big deep chairs, a big foyer which we use for Reg. Orderly rooms, wonderful wooden pannelling [sic] in the corridors, some good carvings in wood, plenty of showers etc.[15]

Those on the *Queen Mary's* several voyages had no opportunity in Western Australia to relieve the tensions of departure and an uncertain future: 'Freemantle [sic] was our only Australian port of call, but as the Queen was too big to get anywhere near the shore we had no leave...', complained one letter writer.[16] But for many others Fremantle and Perth offered brief respite from a physical and psychological atmosphere that could be oppressive even on the great liners. The censorship files hint at festering resentment and actual violence suppressed from the news outlets of the day. 'There is things I would like to write but can't', wrote one soldier, as his ship pulled away from Fremantle in June 1941. He was right to be cautious, for his letter, addressed to a woman in South Australia, was found in a bottle on the Western Australian coast and passed on to the authorities for disciplinary action. Even so, he had said much more than the authorities wanted the public to hear:

> If I had my chance to leave the Army I would get killed in the rush. We are in Fremantle now. There is about 8000 of us on board this boat not counting what's on the other four. We heard that we only get two pounds till we reach the other side. We sleep in hammocks here.[17]

If the huge capacity of the famous liners meant that large numbers experienced at least a hint of unwonted luxury, for others novelty meant squalor. An officer wrote in April 1940 of the cramped miseries of 1204 troops on 'an old regular British Army Transport', with makeshift sleeping accommodation and food prepared in galleys awash with the overflow from adjacent latrines:

> The disparity between the saloon accommodation provided for the officers and sergeants, and the troop deck accommodation for the men, is so great as to cause embarrassment to those occupying the better accommodation. I should be much happier myself if I lived on a troop deck and shared the hardships of the men.[18]

It may have been from such a ship that another intercepted letter, from a soldier to a woman in New South Wales in August 1941, told a far more sinister story of hardship and malevolence than had emerged from the bottled message in June: 'Seven men have already died on board. Two were sergeants who were thrown overboard by somebody or other. Another NCO was locked up in the steam room for three days without any food and is in a pretty bad way.' Almost as an afterthought, because he was writing to his fiancée, the soldier added plaintively: 'I didn't have anything to do with any of it...'[19]

Variously unsettled, frightened and even exhilarated by recent separations from familiar people and surroundings, by the spec-

35

tacularly unfamiliar manner of their departure, by the novelty and tensions of shipboard life and by the uncertainty of the future, the transit troops were determined to make the most of their last moments in Australia.

The authorities were not totally unprepared for problems. Proposals were put forward in 1940 to close hotels at 6 p.m., a practice that would eventually become general until long after the war. Boy scouts were mobilised, in the words of their motto, to 'be prepared' to lend assistance with information and directions. And the inevitability of sexual activity on a grand scale was acknowledged by extensive plans to combat venereal disease, through lectures and the wholesale distribution of condoms on board ship and the establishment of 'Blue Light' treatment facilities ashore. These plans proved inadequate, and the red lights of Perth's brothels shone more steadily than the blue of Wellington Street and Fremantle.

The military authorities complained angrily in late September 1940 that 'considerable confusion and upsetting of troops occurred', when a promised Blue Light station on the Fremantle wharf had not been in place at a time when at least 250 men, returning from shore leave, had required treatment: 'It was necessary to expand the "Blue Light" Depot on the ship and the medical officers and personnel had to work until the early hours of the morning to give treatment to those reporting.'[20] More upsetting to the ladies of the Mothers' Union than the diseases that the troops might be taking away from Perth's notorious Roe Street was the way its booming business threatened social decorum. Asking for a hoarding to be erected to screen the street from the view of children travelling to school, the mothers discussed 'how visiting soldiers were informed about Roe Street' and were told of 'a lady who reproved a soldier for asking a boy scout to direct him to the place'. Feeling that 'it would be a pity to interfere with the work the scouts are doing when the convoys are in port', but that this was scarcely the work for which they were supposed to be prepared, the ladies resolved 'that all scout masters instruct boys in regards to the use and dangers of the houses of ill-fame and in so far as possible guard them against being brought into indirect contact'.[21]

*Chaos on the wharf as troops leave in 1940*
(Australian War Memorial, Negative No. 7314)

Censorship has kept many of the specific details of violent incidents out of the public record. But it could not hide the general awareness that the presence of transit troops at times made the streets unsafe for the general public. The Fremantle City Council responded to the requirements of censorship by referring to troop ships as 'hospital ships'.[22] This phrase recurs in a great deal of the correspondence from the Town Clerk's office in the months immediately before the arrival of American troops. There can be little doubt of its true meaning considering that it occurred so often in conjunction with the campaign to introduce six o'clock closing in hotels. The Town Clerk was not responding to the mayhem caused by speeding wheelchairs or flailing crutches when he urged the state Premier to put a stop to the 'disgraceful scenes which occur in the streets of Fremantle every time a transport or hospital ship arrives in our Port'.[23]

Nor were 'disgraceful scenes' confined to the waterfront of the port city. Throughout much of the metropolitan area drunken violence was common, public and private property was damaged, and transport services were disrupted. In the dying days of the war in 1945 J. J. Simons, editor of the *Sunday Times*, was to plead for the retention of social and welfare facilities until all naval and troop movements had ceased. To abolish them

> is to give an open invitation for a return of that disorder which marked the transit of troops in the early stages of the war before adequate amenities were provided for the entertainment of men in uniform. Perth has some very unhappy memories of the first year of the war when troops virtually took possession of the City. It is not merely a coincidence that these scenes disappeared with the establishment of places wherein healthy diversions could be provided.[24]

Fifty years later Mrs Pat Catt, a teenager at the start of the war, recalled some of those scenes of pandemonium with more affection. The Ninth Division were, said Mrs Catt, wonderful men:

> I'll never forget going in to watch those boys march when they
> went away. They were the finest lot of men you could ever see. The
> trouble was, we'd just gone through the depression years and these
> men had no money. They had nothing and so they all joined up.
> They really were the pick of our country.

But, she admitted, 'they really went to town… What they didn't do to
the city was nobody's business.'

> They just took over the town. They went into Boans [department
> store]; they just took things. They didn't buy them—I can assure
> you of that—or at least I don't think they did. They went up into
> the ladies' department and took corsets, bras and God knows what;
> and they took their coats off and put them on over their uniforms
> and walked up the street in this women's clothing. You've no
> idea—they just went *crazy*.

Craziness spread to the trains, where soldiers took over and tooted the
horns: 'They tooted them all the way between Perth and Fremantle.'[25]

Mrs Marjorie Ward remembered the chaos of the era rather
differently. The 71-room Derward Hotel she managed with her
husband was packed beyond capacity. It was common to put up
stretchers in its roof-garden as makeshift beds for servicemen, who
looked 'so pathetic that you felt you had to do something for them'.[26]

The authorities had begun to respond to the lessons learned from
scenes both outrageous and pathetic towards the end of 1941, when
the growing Japanese threat saw troops stationed in the metropolitan
area at Swan Barracks. Volunteers had opened a buffet in Barrack
Street in premises owned by the Quinlan Estate, and the search had
begun for hostel accommodation for troops. By the time the first
Americans arrived in March 1942 both officialdom and various
volunteer groups were much better prepared to welcome them.[27]

Those voluntary efforts may have involved a great deal of public
leadership by the male-dominated local governments of Perth and
Fremantle, but overwhelmingly the work was going to be done by

women. And, again, long before the arrival of the Americans it was the changed circumstances of women, as much as the emotion-charged departures of local troops or the violence of those in transit, that gave the lie to the notion that for almost two years the war was a remote irrelevancy.

In late January 1942, almost two months after Pearl Harbour—and with the American descent on Australia a matter of fervent hope rather than confirmed reality—an article entitled 'Women and War Work' appeared in the *Dawn*, the journal of the Women's Services Guild. Its extensive list of occupations being filled by women was recognition of their contribution to the war effort but, implicitly, also a commentary on the extent to which large numbers had quickly moved beyond their normal domestic roles.

Women were prominent—and more numerous than ever—in traditional voluntary agencies such as the Red Cross and the St John's Ambulance Nursing Division. They were in the Australian Army

*War gave new opportunities for women in traditional areas*
(Mask Productions, Perth)

Nursing Service, the Women's Australian National Services, the Women's Air Training Corps, the Australian Army Women's Service, the Cycle Corps and the Emergency Service Companies, and they acted as naval ambulance drivers. As members of Voluntary Aid Detachments, women might be used at home or abroad as nurses, clerks, cooks or theatre orderlies. The Country Women's Association was placing women in the Land Army for a wide variety of agricultural work. WAAAFs (members of the Women's Auxiliary Australian Air Force) were in full-time service in Australia as wireless telegraph operators, office orderlies, mess women, mess stewards, tailors, drivers, clerks, fabric workers, dental orderlies and clerk accountants.[28]

The reminiscences of one WAAAF hint at the emotions that must have been felt by many, especially middle-class, women as they found themselves in new situations. As a twenty-year-old public service clerk without permanent position, and recently transferred from her favourite Forestry Department to a position she found quite boring,

*War also gave new roles to women*
(Mask Productions, Perth)

service in the WAAAF offered welcome novelty to Avis Grounds-Weston. Yet initial training at the Karrinyup Golf Club also brought a threatening invasion of privacy. Communal showers with twenty other women were distressing not only because of the miserable trickle of water but because this was the first time she had seen other adults completely naked.[29]

Much the same mixture of emotions attended her induction and training as a radar operative. To join fifteen other Western Australian women as the first trainees for this highly secret new weapon of surveillance at Richmond in New South Wales was exciting and an honour. But she had to begin by enduring the rigours of a seven-day journey aboard a troop train. While segregated compartments protected her from the profanity of the male passengers, meal stops were an ordeal of dust, extremes of temperature and minimal hygiene. For the first time she saw Aboriginal people in numbers, frequently clasping scraps of discarded food into the recesses of ragged garments. For the first time in her life she had to cope with something as small and yet troubling as human hairs in a cup of tea.[30]

Avis and her fellow-trainees were of course entering a totally new field. Yet although most females entered occupations, such as nursing and clerical work, that were already recognised as 'women's work', the January 1942 edition of the *Dawn* could also celebrate the notion that Western Australia had 'made history': the State Arbitration Court had confirmed an agreement between the Amalgamated Engineering Union, the Australasian Society of Engineers and the Boilermakers' Union to admit women into the engineering trades.[31]

This was still very far from a recognition of equality, for the pay rates for women were not much more than half those for males. But in the atmosphere of war there was no clear feminist agenda. The March edition of the *Dawn* reported the Federal Government's announcement of equal pay for women doing work usually done by men (with 60 per cent of that rate during training). Yet the same edition gave at least as much prominence to the news that more than two thousand people had attended a rally run by the Six O'Clock Closing Campaign on the Perth Esplanade, an event very much in keeping with activist women's traditional role of moral guardians.[32] Clearly, in spite of the vastly increased opportunities for female employment in both military and civilian occupations, there was still a great reservoir of middle-class women ready to respond as voluntary workers to the further dislocations of war. Eventually there would be as many as three thousand of them in Perth administering to the needs of servicemen in the social, welfare and recreational facilities that were put in place as a result of the sometimes painful lessons of unpreparedness.[33]

Of course by this time, in early 1942, the war was making an impact, not simply through the social upheaval it introduced, but as a very real military threat. Remote though the fighting may have seemed in the first eighteen months, from the latter half of 1941 the citizens of the metropolitan area were being compelled to confront the possibility of attack and even invasion.

# FLEETING ATTRACTION

## Chapter Three

## OUT OF THE BLUE

IF PEARL HARBOUR had raised hopes of an American presence, the following two months brought nervous uncertainty as the Japanese threatened and then overran Singapore and the Netherlands East Indies. While censorship kept the population figuratively in the dark, with suppression of all news of American troop movements, the authorities in Western Australia attempted to do the same in a literal sense with the consolidation of blackout procedures. A light-hearted response to this and other air-raid precautions suggested that the metropolitan population at least was still not convinced of the imminence of attack. But there was no doubt about the gravity of the war situation in official eyes. Serious plans were made to evacuate Geraldton and surrounding areas, and the Fremantle waterfront was the scene of brutal sanctions against Chinese merchant seamen whose industrial actions were threatening attempts to send relief supplies to northern Australia.

The American Consul was privy to all the anxieties of the period, as he dealt with American refugees from the north. Although he had more certain knowledge that American help was on its way, he was as surprised and elated as the local population with the dramatic suddenness of its arrival.

In a sense the American military influx to Australia was in motion even before the United States declared war on Japan. Seven ships had sailed from San Francisco on 21 November 1941 to carry supplies and troops to the Philippines. Joined by the US Army Transport *Holbrook* on 30 November, the convoy, instead of sailing west from Hawaii, was sent south-west to avoid Japanese naval concentrations. On 13 December, in the aftermath of Pearl Harbour, the ships were diverted to Australia. The convoy arrived at Moreton Bay, Brisbane's outer harbour, about noon on 22 December 1941, followed over the next week or so by six other transports bringing more equipment.[1]

At this stage, of course, the United States was very much on the defensive. As the Philippines came under irresistible pressure from the Japanese, the headquarters of the United States Asiatic Fleet were established at Surabaya in the Dutch East Indies. On that same day — 1 January 1942 — General George Brett took formal command of all United States forces in Australia; two days later he established his headquarters in Melbourne, and on 4 January he was in effect co-opted onto the Australian Chiefs of Staff Committee.[2]

Censorship kept these developments out of the press, but it could not prevent some people from being aware of them nor the spread of rumours that American forces would soon be arriving in large numbers. On 5 January, the same day that the *Holbrook* was discharging its troops in Darwin[3] — and at much the same time as a few American airmen and ground staff were arriving secretly in Broome[4] — the officials of voluntary organisations in Sydney and Melbourne were vying with each other to be recognised by the Prime Minister as organisers of hospitality for anticipated large numbers of American personnel.[5] Two days later an inter-office memorandum was circulating in the Australian Broadcasting Commission about the need to broadcast an American newsletter each week for 'American executives, soldiers, technicians etc. in Australia'. It was impossible to say how many Americans there now were in the country, but it was believed the number was fairly large 'and it will increase considerably in the near future'. Within ten days a further memorandum was confident that 'in the next two or three weeks about 20,000 additional American people will arrive in Australia'.[6]

These expectations would have been no comfort to Western Australians, even if they had been privy to the secret deliberations of officialdom or the rumours circulating in the offices of the ABC. Adopting the defensive strategy to become notorious as the 'Brisbane Line', the Chiefs of Staff had determined that the vital part of Australia was the area centred on Sydney, from Port Kembla in the south to Newcastle one hundred miles to the north. While this major centre of population and industry was held, Australia could continue to fight the war. Protection of Western Australia, the Northern Territory and North Queensland would require a division in each of these areas. If this distribution were made, virtually no troops would be left in the vital area. For psychological reasons it was decided to leave one brigade in each of the three remote regions and concentrate the remainder of the available force between Rockhampton and Melbourne.[7]

Although General Douglas MacArthur, on assuming supreme command in the region in late March, would criticise the 'Brisbane Line' as defeatist,[8] the earliest American presence had done nothing to modify the policy. A secret conference on 4 January, involving the Australian Chiefs of Staff, representatives of the British and Netherlands East Indies forces and an American delegation under General Brett, had discussed the 'location of Primary and Secondary Bases of U.S. Forces in Australia' without mentioning Perth or Fremantle. The same was true of two subsequent meetings on 13 and 19 January.[9]

An eventual indignant Australian riposte to MacArthur, in the safer circumstances of mid-1943, showed how remote the western third of the continent was from the minds of Australian military strategists:

> The facts were that early in 1942 there were so few trained or semi-trained troops in Australia and so little equipment that the east coast was wide open. We concentrated on the defence of Sydney, and there were small forces, nowhere of the strength of a division round Brisbane and north of Brisbane: only after Coral Sea could the centre of gravity be shifted further north.[10]

Certain knowledge that 'the centre of gravity' was never likely to shift westward was confined to official circles in the aftermath of Pearl Harbour. For this reason many of the public in the Perth metropolitan area were slow to take seriously the precautions against possible invasion now being implemented by the authorities. Even for them, those precautions may have still had an air of unreality back in September 1941, when the first trial blackout was made. But by 18 December, in the wake of Pearl Harbour, there was a real sense of urgency.

The director of Civil Defence, L. E. Shapcott, reported that a Central Control Headquarters had been established in Perth and extensive blackout plans partly implemented. All floodlighting under the control of municipal councils and all conspicuous neon signs had been extinguished. So had foreshore lighting at North Beach and

*Blacking out street lighting*
(West Australian Newspapers)

Scarborough. Floodlighting of war memorials was to be extinguished, those in Fremantle having already been dealt with. Street lighting at Fremantle and the Richmond Trotting Ground lighting were now under control. Householders were to be responsible for the blackout of their own houses, with external lighting to be switched out altogether. Drivers of cars and other vehicles were instructed to pull into the side of the road in an alarm and switch off all lights, so as to leave the road clear for military and emergency traffic. The dimming of car and vehicle headlights was under consideration, and householders were being advised to dig trenches in their own yards.[11]

Within a week it was decided these measures were inadequate. Beach lighting had been extinguished but it was found that the glare from street lights could be seen fifteen miles out to sea. Because increased numbers of ships were seeking refuge in the harbour, the Fremantle Defence Committee asked civil defence authorities

> to forthwith extinguish all street lighting and other conspicuous grouped lights, such as Luna Park at Scarborough, from North Beach to South Fremantle extending to a depth of 3 miles from the coast. All Harbour wharf and other lighting, except that essential for working ships, will also be extinguished.[12]

Even these measures were insufficient. On 2 January 1942 it was decided that there was still far too much glare caused by uncontrolled house lighting. The civil defence authorities were asked to order 'a complete black-out of the Fremantle Defended Area, to be effective as soon as possible; some delay must be accepted in order that the Authorities have time to promulgate the necessary instructions and to enable householders to purchase suitable materials for blacking out'.[13]

On 13 January a trial blackout and half-hour air-raid warning were held throughout the metropolitan area. Practice sirens were sounded at 10 a.m. in both Fremantle and Perth to familiarise people with the trial twelve hours later, when trains and trolley-buses were halted and motor vehicles expected to pull off the road.[14]

Even now not all the public was convinced that these measures were serious. According to the *Daily News* next day, the blackout had been 'successful', but its report—headed 'Second Blackout Suggested'—related 'success' to the efficiency of organisation rather than public response. While 707 breaches of the blackout had been reported,

> thousands of people switched off their house lights, sat on verandahs or on footpaths, yarned and joked... Radios blared, people sang, and community songs by groups of householders helped tide away the thirty minutes.[15]

Similarly, on 23 January the Fremantle Defence Committee recommended a permanent complete blackout of the Fremantle area. Another trial blackout had failed 'owing to the fact that householders had not attempted to black out their houses but had simply turned out their lights'.[16]

Even members of that committee were at odds about the need for a permanent blackout of the Fremantle and Cottesloe areas and whether all moving traffic at night should be fitted with permanently screened headlights. There was also criticism that sirens had been used for a test blackout when they should have been reserved for actual air raids. There were, however, two things that committee members could agree about: they should not be required to telephone the Commissioner of Police in Perth for permission to sound the sirens, even if there was an air raid; and it was necessary to remove 'enemy alien fishing craft from their present anchorages at Fishmarket Jetty, Fremantle'.[17]

It should have been possible to see that a few Italian fishing-boats in Fremantle had little connection with the Japanese onslaught to the north. But this was a nervous period for authorities who knew quite well that, while the West had been marginalised by defence strategists, it was hardly remote from the war, even in the distant south-west corner. One product of the desperate military situation—and one sign that local official nerves were on edge—was an ugly affray on the Fremantle wharf on 28 January. Attempts were being launched from several Australian ports to provide relief supplies to the beleaguered American forces in the Philippines. Great difficulty was experienced in obtaining crews for two ships, the *Yochow* and the *Hanyang*, which were being loaded at Fremantle with supplies shipped from Brisbane and Melbourne.[18]

For some time the Chinese crews of these and four other ships of the China Navigation Company in Fremantle had been demanding higher wages and better conditions, but agreement had not been reached. Finally the crews of both ships imprisoned the master of the *Hanyang* in his cabin and threatened him with violence unless he agreed in writing to their demands. An intervention by the WA Seamen's Union, advising the Chinese crew to return to work, seemed to have resolved the dispute on 26 January. But when the crew walked off the ships the next day, the authorities sent in a military detachment from the 5th Garrison at Swanbourne on 28 January, and in the ensuing violence two Chinese were killed.[19]

According to the Australian Army authorities, the military guard was under orders to avoid using force if possible but to 'fire if necessary'. Immediately rushed by the Chinese, the soldiers fired 'about six shots'. After the killings the crews were removed from the ships. Most were placed under guard at the Woodman's Point quarantine station. About fifty crew members, 'who were regarded as trouble makers were transferred to the detention barracks at Fremantle'. The Army's account concluded: 'The Prime Minister, who was in Perth at the time...acquiesced in the action which had been taken regarding the crews.'[20]

After making its own inquiries the Chinese Legation produced a quite different version of events. Its protest to Dr Evatt, the Minister for External Affairs, insisted that, although there had been disputes on the vessels, 'no serious disturbance of any kind had occurred and no life was threatened' until the sudden arrival at the wharf of scores of fully armed soldiers and two ambulances. While many of them stood guard on the ships and at the gangways, others rounded up the seamen on shore.[21] Believing they were going to be coerced to work, the crew tried to force their way out:

> The shooting was started by a military officer and, in an instant, bullets flew here and there, with the result that the quarter-master (Tong Youn Tong) was killed on the spot and that a fireman (Yu Ping Sang, aged 25) belonging to the crew of the s.s. HANYANG was fatally hit and died immediately afterwards.

Others were injured by firing and one through 'a fall caused by severe beating from the soldiers'.[22]

At the subsequent inquest the coroner found it 'regrettable that these men should have been shot', but he was sure that 'the Naval and military authorities must have had a very excellent reason for taking these drastic steps and it is probably wise that the reasons are not disclosed'. If the pressures of war explained this less than probing investigation, the Sydney *Daily Telegraph*'s background briefing to its report on the inquest suggested that the racism of the period was also a factor. The military escort had shown great restraint. It was not until the Chinese tried to seize arms that firing took place. An attempt to stop Tong by bayoneting him in the thigh had failed, so 'he had to be shot to prevent a riot'. The report concluded: 'Tong's appearance was fanatical.'[23]

This report, three weeks after the shootings, was the first time the incident had found its way into the newspapers. Until then it was subject to the censorship that was carefully shaping public awareness of the war and, especially, suppressing news of American troop movements.[24]

By February this continuing official secrecy greatly concerned some of those with privileged information about the commitment of American troops to Australia. On 15 February the fall of the 'impregnable' fortress of Singapore, including the capture of fifteen thousand Australian troops, was a shattering blow to national morale. The Prime Minister's response was to call it 'Australia's Dunkirk': 'It will be recalled that the fall of Dunkirk initiated the Battle for Britain. The fall of Singapore initiates the Battle for Australia.'[25] But the Prime Minister's earlier recognition of the irrelevance of Britain, as he turned to the United States, seemed more important to those concerned to boost morale.

The celebrated film-maker Ken G. Hall, then Producer-Director of the Sydney-based newsreel company Cinesound Productions, wrote to the Department of Information in Melbourne on 16 February:

> Now is the time, above all others, to break some detail of the American aid to Australia in the interests of public morale. I know the problems you are faced with and I know where the restrictions are coming from, but I do sincerely suggest that every possible ounce of pressure should be brought to bear to get out something that will uplift the public at the present time when their morale is drooping quite heavily. In my own opinion it is of paramount importance. I have an interview with Admiral Leary. This is what he says:
>
> 'I am very proud to be here and to take command of the Anzac Force. You all know that Anzac stands for fighting—and that's what we need today.
>
> 'The most cheering news that we have today is that lots of our boys are coming over to join you, and before long there will be so many Americans here it will be hard to tell whether this is a part of America or a part of Australia.'[26]

Not at all alarmed at the threat to Australian identity, Hall thought that this story, from such an authentic source, had 'a tremendous kick'. But it was 'a foregone conclusion that when the Censor sees it, it will come out. Can you do anything to help keep it in?'[27]

The official reply on 19 February was negative: 'The question of morale is not, as you say, of paramount importance in this matter, but the security of Australia... The public does need lift but, for the present, has got to "take it".'[28]

On that very day—while Perth cinema audiences were being offered *That Uncertain Feeling* with Merle Oberon and *Out of the Fog* starring Ida Lupino and John Garfield[29]—what the public of Darwin was having to take was a feeling far stronger than uncertainty as Japanese bombs arrived out of the blue. And what the Western Australian public was being urged to accept, more urgently than ever, was that the speed and scale of Japanese expansion made black-outs, slit trenches and air-raid warnings more than childish games or excuses for impromptu parties.

Calling the bombing 'the biggest news since Japan started the Pacific War', the *Daily News* followed its headline of 'Thirty-Nine Darwin Casualties' with another, 'Things are Moving on the Home Front': 'Realisation of their danger has come at last to West Australians and they are preparing in haste against it... There is work for all... Some people are saying that invasion seems inevitable.' An editorial insisted that 'every adult is a soldier' and that 'Australians can take it — not by apathetic stoicism divorced from action but from coming out — fighting'.[30]

(West Australian Newspapers)

Another way to come out, it suggested, was with a pick and shovel to 'dig a slit trench now':

> The expression 'It can't happen here' should never be used in Perth now, for it can happen here and it may happen soon... This weekend should be used by all family men who have not done so in preparing a shelter trench for their families.

As well as offering instructions to individuals, the paper also reported that 'public air raid shelters (slit type)' were to be built in Supreme Court Gardens. 'Trenches for Nedlands' announced similar excavations alongside bus routes in that inner western suburb.[31]

A regular all-night blackout was instituted in the metropolitan area on 21 February, two days after this first attack on Darwin.[32] Five days later the *Daily News* reinforced its message of urgency by reporting that a man had been sentenced to one month's imprisonment with hard labour for refusing to put out his light when asked by police. It also printed—'to cut out and keep'—a series of pictures and instructions on how to stop bleeding: they 'may help you to save a life if the Japs bomb Perth'.[33]

The bombing of Darwin on 19 February was the prelude to regular attacks there and on the north-west of Western Australia, including Broome and Wyndham, over the next few weeks. Although these were areas far from the state's major centres of population, the attacks gave substance to the warnings in the press. Feelings of vulnerability were not soothed by the weakening of the Bickley heavy artillery battery on Rottnest Island, as men were transferred from there to Darwin,[34] making local military and civil defence authorities painfully aware that little could be done to resist invasion, a contingency that had come to be taken increasingly seriously over the previous two months.

In late December 1941 a detailed army reconnaissance had been

A suitable indoor shelter can quickly be arranged and in fact at all times left prepared with materials on hand in your own home. Select an inner room for preference at least two walls between room and outside, and against the wall furthest from window place a strong dining room table. Fit up as diagram.

Site for a covered trench should be at a distance equal to half the height of the closest building. Trenches should be 5 to 6 ft. deep and up to 3ft. 6in. width. A trench should be rendered as weather-proof as possible by covering with iron and 2ft. of earth. See diagram.

*(West Australian Newspapers)*

undertaken of the area 'from Gingin to Moore River Estuary thence across country to Moore River Bridge finishing at Mimegarra':

> It has been submitted that in the event of a landing in force at Jurien Bay which under certain circumstances is not difficult, approach to Perth could take either the route inland via Dandaraga and Moora to the Midland Railway or direct along the line of the Old Stock Route to Moore River bridge thence to Gingin...[35]

By early February plans were being made at a meeting of representatives of various rural companies, such as Elders, Dalgety and Westralian Farmers, for the evacuation of stock from 'agricultural areas embraced by Northampton, Geraldton, Irwin, Mingenew, Mullewa, Morawa, Greenough, Perenjori, Upper Chapman and Three Springs

*Digging slit trenches at Subiaco school*
(West Australian Newspapers)

*(West Australian Newspapers)*

Road Boards'. This was a region that contained 675,000 sheep, 10,000 cattle and 11,000 horses. It also contained people, but for the moment the emphasis was on removing all female sheep, 'as these are the basis of the industry'. Removal could not possibly be commenced without military authority, and cooperation with the Railways Commission was vital. It was important to begin sooner rather than later, 'in case of emergency, when trains are being used for evacuees or military purposes'.[36]

Evacuation on a voluntary basis had already begun from Geraldton, as some families chose to send their children—sometimes accompanied by mothers—either further inland or further south. The five thousand people of this coastal town naturally felt more immediately threatened than those in the metropolitan area. They had already seen the removal for internment of several local Japanese families, pioneers in the tomato-growing industry of the district but sufficiently integrated into the community for one woman to be a well-liked local barmaid. They had also seen the arrival of the fleet of pearling luggers from Broome, moved south to a 'safety' that was belied by urgent defensive preparations: the building of block-houses at the harbour entrance and the partial destruction of the railway jetty to forestall an easy landing of Japanese. The 'bush telegraph' suggested to Geraldton people that the damage and casualties in Darwin were on a much greater scale than reported in the press. Fears of bombing were acute because of the presence of a large Shell depot full of high octane fuel.[37]

The military presence in Geraldton was active enough to remind locals of the dangers of their 'forward position', three hundred and fifty miles north of Perth, without in any sense offering reassurance about its defensive capabilities. The so-called 'Geraldton Garrison' of veteran volunteers had two big guns, mounted on a sandhill at Bluff Point. People were warned to keep their windows open during practice firings: if they were left closed, they were liable to be shattered, even as far as three miles away. Although on these occasions star shells could be seen bursting far out to sea, locals were well aware that there was no real capacity to resist or pursue invaders and raiders. The local airport was currently used only by training aircraft, which, thought the locals, could be shot down 'with a pea-shooter'. In these circumstances the public needed little encouragement to dig slit trenches and accept a far more rigorous blackout than in the metropolitan area.[38]

While the people of Geraldton and Perth remained in the dark as Singapore fell, Darwin was bombed and the Dutch East Indies were overrun by the Japanese, hopes of an American presence in the near future were at last being given substance in official circles. On 11 February 1942 the District Naval Officer, Western Australia, was told by the Naval Board 'to convene a sub-committee to deal with all matters connected with the transport and movement of all outgoing and incoming American defence stores, equipment and personnel in Western Australia'.[39] On the following day the Collector of Commonwealth Customs and Excise in Fremantle wrote to the Department of Interior in Canberra:

Without quoting any authority I wish you to know that in the near future the port of Fremantle will probably be used extensively by the U.S.A. Navy, its transports and store ships.—Whether U.S.A. or local Navy Officers will control the movements of those vessels on arrival in port remains to be seen, but it can be assumed that the vessels will be sent away on their various missions without reference to this department.[40]

Because no American Army officer was yet available for the sub-committee, the American Consul was asked to act in his absence as a member of the new sub-committee.

This was probably a task Mason Turner could have done without in the midst of a hectic schedule. If the numbers of locally resident Americans were small, their decision about whether to stay or attempt to return home was a difficult one, and one with which the Consul could readily identify. He was himself uncertain whether to send his wife and two children a hundred and twenty miles inland to the presumed safety of a sheep station or keep them in Perth to wait for information about sailings to the eastern states. But advising others faced with similar dilemmas was a demanding task. After spending a morning in Fremantle with Charles O. Thompson, a United States Consul, and two other officials evacuated from Singapore, Turner returned to his office in Perth to find there had been fifty-two telephone calls and nineteen personal callers during his absence.[41]

Thompson's assignment as a temporary Vice-Consul in Perth for the remainder of 1942 was timely,[42] as his arrival coincided with an influx of civilian American refugees. Most were employees of such companies as Standard Oil, Caltex, General Motors and Goodyear, but there were also a number of missionaries and their wives.[43] Their presence was not confined to the metropolitan area. Writing to the WA Railways to arrange transport to the eastern states for a hundred United States citizens, Turner pointed out that seventy of these were recent evacuees from Java who had been billeted in Bunbury.[44]

As he advised his compatriots on the war situation—and eventually arranged the passage of all the refugees back to the United

States[45]—Turner experienced typically Western Australian frustrations. Quick contact with the eastern states was proving virtually impossible, thanks to telephone facilities that made conversations almost inaudible. A combination of these technical faults and the needs of security made even liaison with his own Consulate-General in Sydney awkward. Perhaps irked by being asked to serve on the new sub-committee at Fremantle, he wrote on 12 February expressing his surprise that no representatives of the US Army or Navy had yet been appointed, 'as everything seems to indicate that a United States Military or Naval Detachment might descend upon this district at any moment'.[46]

Turner was right. Annoyed on 18 February to receive no support from Sydney as he searched for vacant office space,[47] on the 24th he was reporting to his superiors that 'the situation has changed completely'. Advance contingents of army machine-gunners, the 197th Coast Artillery, had arrived out of the blue; a huge wireless mast had been erected in the grounds of The University of Western Australia; and 'both the United States Army and Navy have established bases here, the Army having its headquarters in the R.A.A.F. building, and the Navy has, very naturally, established its headquarters at Fremantle'.[48] Turner could have added that the Americans had put up anti-aircraft guns on the Fremantle wharf, and that D Troop of the 197th Regiment, which had arrived on USS *Pinegrove*, had headed straight for Rottnest to augment the depleted Bickley Battery with their 50 millimetre anti-aircraft guns.[49]

The Consul's obvious relief might have quickly subsided had he interviewed some of his newly arrived compatriots. From his New Hampshire home fifty years later, Fred Wood recalled his arrival in Fremantle with the 197th Regiment armed with a new rifle but no training in its use.[50] But all that mattered at that moment, to Mason Turner and many locals, was that Americans had indeed arrived— with amazing speed and in considerable numbers. On the same day as Turner wrote to Sydney, he was being greeted heartily by the Treasurer of the RAAF Comforts Fund, an organisation run by 1914/18 airmen and their wives:

About 1,500 American airmen—all excellent lads, made use of our
RAAF Rendezvous National House William Street during the week
end. It was a pleasure to see them, welcome them and help them.
We will be glad to see many more. These 'up and at 'em' boys will
do a good job.[51]

Most of the airmen quickly passed through to the airfields that
the Americans hastily built or improved in the south-west and in
places as remote as Corunna Downs near Marble Bar and Forrest on
the Nullarbor. In the same period more Army and also Navy personnel were pouring into the metropolitan area.

Although 22 February 1942 marked the arrival of American
troops in the settled areas of Western Australia, a more important date
in the state's social history was 3 March. The Army would move on
within a few months, but the latter date saw the beginnings of a

*Anti-aircraft guns on Fremantle wharf*
(Battye Library, 622/5)

United States Navy presence that was to remain until the end of the Pacific War in August 1945.

Whatever they did for local morale, these first American arrivals had little immediate impact on the military situation. The newly recruited Army unit had travelled under heavy escort across the Pacific and then from Brisbane and Sydney. By contrast the Navy was arriving battle-scarred and in retreat from a Japanese advance that was now directly threatening north-western Australia. The American Asiatic Fleet had been based in the Philippines, but was forced to retreat after heavy Japanese bombing of Manila Bay and the imminent fall of Java. The initial plan had been to set up new submarine operational headquarters in Darwin, after Surabaya was deemed unsuitable, but when administrative staff arrived they found the communication links with the rest of Australia and America unreliable, and the roads connecting it with other capital cities poor and subject to flooding. There were no rail links between Darwin and the rest of Australia, the harbour had a high tidal range that was not suitable for submarine activities and it was within range of Japanese patrols.[52]

By now the fate of the vessels at the centre of the violence a few weeks earlier in Fremantle was symbolic of a desperate crisis. The *Yochow* had eventually sailed on 17 February and was at sea when Darwin was bombed on the 19th, the day before the *Hanyang* left Fremantle. Further difficulties with the crews—including suspected sabotage to the engines of the *Yochow*—prevented both of these vessels from proceeding beyond Darwin, where their cargoes of foodstuff were unloaded. A third ship, the *Don Isodoro*, which had departed Fremantle for Corregidor on 4 February, was bombed by aircraft and beached on Bathurst island on the day of the attack on Darwin, losing its cargo of ammunition and 550 tons of rations.[53]

While these events confirmed the unsuitability of Darwin as a base for the retreating US Navy, consideration was briefly given to the use of Exmouth Gulf. On 28 February 1942 Rear Admiral Purnell arrived there by air to examine the area. An inspection convinced him that it was unsuitable for a major submarine base; and on the same day he embarked for Fremantle in the USN Submarine Tender

*Holland*. The arrival of the *Holland* on 3 March signalled the inauguration of Fremantle as the site for the new American submarine base and repair unit in the newly defined South West Pacific Area.[54] It was considered ideal for the purpose, being sufficiently outside the range of land-based Japanese aircraft to be safe from continuous bombardment, and having adequate support facilities in terms of food, medical and energy supplies. Although many improvements to the port were needed, Fremantle had accommodation, transport, communication networks and entertainment facilities that would not have been available in Darwin, even if the strategic situation had permitted that more northerly location.[55]

Typically, it was three days later, on 6 March, that this unilateral American decision to use Fremantle as the base for twenty fleet

*US submarine in Fremantle Harbour*
(Mask Productions, Perth)

submarines and five light 'S' Class submarines was announced to Commonwealth authorities. Meanwhile, the USN Auxiliary *Black Hawk* and the US Submarine *Stingray* were assigned temporarily to Exmouth Gulf to service southbound submarines of the US Asiatic fleet. And on 13 March the Americans decided to establish a second submarine base on the south coast of Western Australia. Two days later the tender *Holland* and five submarines sailed to Albany, escorted by the destroyer USS *Parrot*, two minesweepers and the tender *Childs*, which was to provide maintenance facilities for Catalina patrol aircraft.[56]

While the submarine base in Fremantle was to be the most important American presence throughout the remainder of the war, other arrivals in late February and early March were important. As Chapter 5 will show in some detail, more than two thousand Army personnel passing through in a relatively short period of time had considerable impact. Less numerous but of longer term significance were the Catalina flying boats from the United States Navy Patrol

*Catalina flying-boat on the Swan River*
(Currie Hall, UWA)

Wing Ten. Three arrived from Java in March, going first to Albany. After some three weeks, bad weather persuaded the Americans to move them to what was to be their permanent base for the next two and a half years: Crawley Bay on the Swan River. Nine more reinforcements were to follow in April.[57] From their base in Perth, and using advance bases at Geraldton, Exmouth and Port Hedland, the Catalinas patrolled the Indian Ocean and the waters of Northern Australia.

# FLEETING ATTRACTION

*Chapter Four*

## 'THANK YOU, PRESIDENT ROOSEVELT!'

UNHERALDED BECAUSE OF CENSORSHIP, the arrival of American forces in Western Australia in late February and early March 1942 was almost universally welcomed. For a full month before their presence was officially acknowledged, the newcomers were offering reassurance and excitement to a population with mixed reactions to military trends but predisposed to idealise Americans. They arrived when the Japanese surge through South-East Asia was already threatening the state's north-western outposts and giving a sense of urgency to civil defence preparations in Perth, Fremantle and the agricultural districts to their north. Friendly, well-mannered, stylishly uniformed and with money to spend, the Americans were everything most people wanted and, thanks to Hollywood, more than half expected.

By the end of that first month small business was booming, taxi drivers were overcharging to their hearts' content yet being tipped for the first time in their lives, and Perth women were in love, in bed and even on the verge of marriage with the glamorous newcomers. Over the next few months unwanted pregnancies, hasty marriages and heart-breaking separations marked a brutal end of happiness for some women. For the community as a whole, harmony lasted much longer.

Lessons from the turmoil created by transit troops in previous years meant that the Americans were greeted by improved facilities and a coordinated official response. And many private offers of hospitality implicitly recognised that young men far from home might want surrogate families as well as romance and sexual adventure. It was a honeymoon that could not last forever, but it did last for most of 1942.

There can be no doubt that, when the Americans arrived in February and March 1942, Western Australia was in an extremely vulnerable position. Fully trained Australian troops were all overseas with the AIF, leaving home defence in the hands of only partially trained and equipped troops and volunteers. An AIF Corps was on its way back, but none had arrived. The collapse of resistance in the East Indies was freeing the Japanese to concentrate massive forces on an Australian invasion.[1]

*Fully-trained troops were all overseas in early 1942*
(West Australian Newspapers)

Against an estimated five to six hundred available Japanese aeroplanes, Australia had in training three squadrons of fighters, two of dive-bombers and one of heavy bombers. It was believed that in the month of March the Japanese could have at least three divisions ready to attack the north-west coast. Invasion would involve forces landing in the Broome and Wyndham areas and a simultaneous attack east of Darwin. Since the initial raid on 19 February, Darwin had been bombed almost daily.[2]

Although the situation was undoubtedly critical, there was not a uniform response in the populated south-west. Some were more frightened than at any time in their lives; others regarded warnings of imminent Japanese invasion as a joke. Such differences can be tentatively explored, but no general explanation can rest simply on varied circumstances of age, location, gender or class.

The contrast is extreme between Michael Papadoulis of Northbridge, who had no later recollections of fear, and Joy Anderson (née Gawned) of Wembley, who remembered the era as one of unrelenting anxiety. But was it the wisdom of years that gave Joy, aged ten in 1942, greater awareness than the seven-year-old Michael? Perhaps Joy's anxieties flowed from her family's grief at the death of a young male relative in the overseas war and from the fact that her own father was serving overseas, leaving her mother to support the family by opening a small shop in Wembley. Maybe her recollections were shaped by the knowledge

*(West Australian Newspapers)*

that for some months her mother took her and her sister to the country. Michael's contrasting indifference to the Japanese threat may have reflected the continuous presence of his father, running his city fruit shop. It may have been the product of a Greek immigrant family's failure to follow closely the wartime trends in the English-language media.[3]

Exploration of many more individual reactions could only extend the range of hypotheses. Children even younger than Joy and Michael could not possibly understand the potential of danger: all they might eventually recollect was the absence of fathers before the advent of friendly men in uniform dispensing sweets, chewing gum and affectionate hugs. Boys some ten years older than Michael might be impatient to follow fathers and brothers into uniform. And even the ten-year-old Joy was well aware that girls not much older than herself were missing, and even already mourning, departed boyfriends.

All that can be said with certainty is that, whether people were fearful of the future, depressed or even elated by the present, all were pursuing work and leisure in an environment drastically changed by official responses to the unfolding crisis.

The newspapers of the era reveal the same range of attitudes as the memories of individuals. Censored though they still were, they now conveyed the sense of imminent danger felt by the authorities. But they also revealed very mixed public reactions.

On 3 March censorship prevented any newspaper reference to the inauguration of the Americans' Fremantle submarine base. But the *West Australian* warned: 'It must be fully realised in Australia that the major battle, not merely in the air but in all phases of physical impact is but one step removed from our own shores.'[4] On that same day Broome was bombed by Japanese forces, causing the destruction of four million dollars' worth of Allied equipment including seven American planes and three flying boats as well as thirteen other Australian, British and Dutch aircraft. The majority of casualties were evacuees from Singapore and Dutch military personnel, as most Australian civilians had been transported out of the north-west after Darwin had been attacked a few weeks earlier. Those who remained in Broome were totally unprepared for the attack. Although an ideal military target, with a refuelling station catering for many Allied aircraft and a recently upgraded aerodrome, Broome's primary defence was a Voluntary Defence Corps organised by a Gallipoli veteran, equipped with less than a hundred rifles.[5]

On the day following this first bombing of Broome the *West Australian* concluded:

> We in Western Australia have to face the fact that our North Western coastline is now vulnerable to enemy raids…and that in consequence our more southerly coasts may soon engage the attentions of an audacious, skillful and relentless enemy… The danger of similar attacks much farther southward becomes a more imminent possibility.[6]

The press offered no reassurance to those reared on notions of Anglo-Saxon superiority over myopic, slant-eyed Asiatics. On the contrary, it invoked the racism of fear implicit in the myth of the 'Yellow Peril'. Articles described the skills and bravery of the Japanese soldiers, detailing battles where they had been successful, with commentary on their tactics and courage. 'The Japanese have proved themselves to be original, skilful and formidable fighters.'[7] 'Japanese bomb aimers, even from tremendous heights, are uncanny in their accuracy.'[8]

On 7 March the *Daily News* printed a map of shelter locations in the city in case of air raids. On 11 March it announced that all road direction signs within a twenty-mile radius of the coast were to be removed. Two weeks later a complete blackout of the Fremantle and Cottesloe areas was implemented.

Yet in those same two weeks there were signs that many did not take the blackout seriously. While advertisements invited the public to 'Laugh in the Dark at Luna Park',[9] air-raid wardens complained at the excessive lighting still being used there.[10] As the blackout was extended to the northern end of Waterman's Bay, the Scarborough amusement park was closed down at night, although still drawing big crowds during daylight hours at weekends.[11]

**Laugh in the Dark at**

# LUNA PARK

**Tonight and Every Night.**
Special Matinee Today, 4 p.m. Free.        Matinee Sunday.

(West Australian Newspapers)

In this same month of March 1942 the blackout was contentious for other reasons. There was growing concern over the 'grave risk of serious accidents' unless the 'standard mask' on car headlights was reviewed.[12] The nerves of bus drivers, in particular, were said to be frayed by the frequency of near misses.[13] Many individuals were irked at having to find and put in place blackout materials in their homes. For a hotel proprietor this was irritation on a grand scale. 'Blackout? Don't talk to me about the blackout', said one of them fifty years later. 'We had seventy-one blinds we had to paint black.' There was also a large area of glass in the hotel's ground floor dining-room, some of which had to be screened and the rest painted black.[14]

Even officials found the blackout irksome. On 14 April the Fremantle Town Clerk wrote to his counterpart in Northam:

> You would hardly know Perth and Fremantle with its shelters and boarded-up windows, and at night the blackouts are getting on our nerves... Believing that our Town Hall is a target we had the glass removed from the whole of the 48 windows and we are working entirely with the electric light during the day and we are all suffering from eyestrain.[15]

Slit trenches were at least as controversial as the blackout. Those digging them faced such unpleasant surprises as the 'recovery of human bones at Wellington Square in East Perth'.[16] Those who failed to dig them were chastised by a press that was simultaneously a mouthpiece for authority and a commercial enterprise prospering from excitement. It was 'Not Good Enough', the *Daily News* told its readers on 16 March, that only two hundred men had answered a call for volunteers to dig trenches on the Esplanade over the weekend. People had to realise that such trenches would prevent the enemy from landing planes there: they would not stop families having picnics.[17]

Despite this lethargy, very many shelters and trenches were dug. But the authorities kept the pressure on the public by complaining about their misuse. On 20 March it was announced that 'people who use public air raid shelters except for their proper purpose will soon be liable to immediate arrest'. The public was probably irritated to be told that some people were 'Shelter Pests' without ever learning exactly what they were doing. It was one thing to be told that the 'conduct of some people in shelters is outrageous and must be stopped'. But it was quite another to be sure what was causing the caretaker of a park now criss-crossed with trenches to protest: 'What goes on here is unbelievable! My job has become a revolting one!'[18]

The thought of stumbling into something improper, outrageous, unbelievable or revolting could only add to the problems of women already faced with a fashion dilemma. Slacks were the most appropriate garments for a sudden plunge below ground: 'Those who can afford it buy a man-tailored coat to match. Others get a bright woollen jumper', reported the *Daily News*. But the shops could barely meet the surge in demand for this new wartime wardrobe.[19]

Continuing Japanese attacks, even though in the distant north, were good material to make people take air-raid precautions seriously. When the *Daily News* announced 'Bombs on Wyndham' on 24 March, it also claimed that South Perth residents were uneasy that bombs on Perth might lead to a break-out from the Zoo, involving 'six lions, tigers, a black panther, leopards, bears, buffaloes and boa constrictors'.

The *News* gave no indication of how widely it had canvassed local opinion to reach this conclusion. Certainly some of those who were responsible for ushering the public to safety in central Perth felt that few people were living in fear of airborne attack. The chief air-raid

*Air raid shelters outside the Commonwealth Bank, Murray Street, Perth*
(West Australian Newspapers)

warden for the Plaza Arcade and the portion of Murray Street westward along to Barrack Street was well trained for his duties. For some time he had attended lectures and practice sessions on Sundays and in the evenings at the old Prince of Wales Theatre on the corner of Murray and William Streets. In his spare time he used to 'climb all round the Plaza Arcade in the roof, carrying buckets of water, pumps and other gear'. The first time he was called into action by a siren sounding the alert, he grabbed his helmet, whistle and armband from his first-floor workshop above Murray Street and tore downstairs, ready to usher everybody in the vicinity into an air-raid shelter at the back of the Savoy Hotel.[20]

The barber on the ground floor wasn't ready to be ushered anywhere, saying 'Oh, bugger it, I've got to finish this shave first'. Leaving barber and soapy customer to their fate, the warden then ran up and down the arcade 'like a mad dervish', blowing his whistle to absolutely no effect: 'I had as much chance of herding the people into the air raid shelter as herding a wild bull through a cyclone fence—everybody stood in the middle of the road, looking up in the air, saying "where is it?".'[21]

Further along Murray Street to the east a hotel proprietor turned air-raid warden twice responded to alerts by leading his guests into a shelter next door. On the second occasion the tally of people in the shelter was one short of the number of guests in the hotel. Returning bravely to the hotel, the proprietor found one old lady making a very leisurely response to the danger: 'She didn't know how long she would be in the shelter, so she thought she'd take a bath first.'[22]

On the other hand, air-raid precautions made a deep impression on the young Joy Gawned. Fifty years later she had vivid memories of being issued with a disc imprinted with her blood group; of air raid drills at school; of being issued a hessian hooded cape to wear in the trenches, its pockets containing barley sugar, a rubber cork to bite on and a whistle. Joy also remembered 'quite elaborate' backyard air-raid shelters in the suburbs: her aunt's was well equipped with food, books and bedding.[23]

Similar preparations made a quite different impression on the seventeen-year-old Pat White in Subiaco. Her father had built an underground backyard shelter and her mother stocked it with food—'and of course we couldn't have cared less'. An alarm one day was marked not only by a siren but by an American arriving in a jeep from the nearby base, yelling to women talking in the street: 'You bloody women out in the street—get off the street!' The Americans were sufficiently alarmed by the rumour of enemy planes at this period to have begun moving torpedoes from the base out into the bush. But it was not just the women who ignored him, preferring to stand in the street gazing into the air. On a nearby verandah Pat's grandfather refused to consider a descent into the shelter: 'If I'm going to die, I'll die in my rocking chair.' And he went on rocking.[24]

However mixed the attitudes in Perth in early 1942, three hundred and fifty miles to the north there was a far stronger sense of danger. There were 'slit trenches everywhere', recalled local Geraldton resident George May, and the blackout was absolute, not the

*For some, air raid precautions were a game*
(West Australian Newspapers)

'brownout' he later encountered on a visit to Perth. Air-raid warnings were frequent after the attacks on Broome and the evacuation of most of its civilian population, and naturally everybody was nervous.[25]

When the sirens sounded one night at ten o'clock, George, knowing his mother was sick and alone, ran home for a quarter of a mile in the pitch dark, miraculously dodging people and hurdling slit trenches. He secured his mother under an upturned couch, as he had been instructed, and then sat back to observe and listen to a huge exodus of cars, with headlights shining, towards Perth. The next day he could have bought nearly every house in nearby streets. The family doctor told him that he had made seven pre-arranged house calls and found nobody home.[26]

In contrast to George May's vivid memories of an embattled Geraldton, most evidence would suggest that Albany—deep on the south coast—was understandably more relaxed. It was 26 June before the local newspaper announced a 'Shelter Trench for Albany' to be built by the council.[27] Even after this—and even though there was the worthy aim of providing one metre of trench space for every local citizen, as trenches were dug along Stirling and York Streets[28]—there was some doubt about how seriously the threats of air raid and invasion were being taken.

Air-raid wardens were remembered for being as officiously strict in Albany as anywhere else, policing not only the blackout but also the painting of white lines around the wheel arches of vehicles. Whether such measures had a real chance of preventing people from being run over in the gloom was as uncertain as the meaning of the siren at Middleton Beach. The beach was guarded with barbed wire and machine guns, which were certainly intended to repel human invaders. But whether it was air-raid warning or shark alarm that periodically woke the locals only became clearer when the siren was moved to the centre of town.[29]

Young David Bird's problem as air-raid messenger was solved only by the failure of any raids to materialise. It may have been casualness rather than callousness that led the authorities to give the vital task of running messages through falling bombs to a twelve-year-old. To David, however, it was a hollow gesture to be given an allowance of a single rubber tyre, for he was neither a skilled unicyclist nor even owner of a bicycle.[30]

Yet even in Albany—as far away as it was possible to be in Western Australia from the Japanese attacks that had so far occurred—at least one resident had fears very similar to Joy Gawned's in Perth, even though she was an adult rather than a ten-year-old. The arrival of women evacuees from Singapore via Broome made Phyllis Vaughan very conscious of the threat in the north. Accommodated in holiday cottages, especially around Middleton Beach, but without the servants they were used to, these 'completely useless' white women now had to be taught how to cook on a wood stove. As Phyllis built up a large stockpile of canned food in her laundry in preparation for the worst, she had a recurrent dream that a Japanese invasion would catch her without a can-opener. By the time those fears faded she had five of them in the laundry.[31]

Phyllis was certainly ahead of her time when she pulled the heavy woollen blackout away from her windows one morning in mid-March, well over a month before the local authorities were demanding such precautions.[32] Overnight the majestic Albany harbour had filled with almost seventy warships. Her first reaction was to rouse her sister Molly with the news that the Japanese invasion might have begun. The fear did not prevent the two jumping into Molly's 'very small car' and using some of its 'very small petrol allowance' to rush to the corner of Grey and York Streets. There they discovered to their immense relief that the new arrivals, already pouring ashore 'with their white caps turned up', were 'Americans!'[33]

It was late March 1942 before Prime Minister Curtin announced officially that 'there are very substantial American forces in Australia... There is in this country a feeling of deep gratitude to the President and people of the United States... We will not be left quite alone.'[34] This statement followed publicity of a similar nature in American newspapers, although by American orders no information as to the strength or location of the units was released. The appointment of General Douglas MacArthur as Supreme Commander of the South West Pacific Area (SWPA) was announced simultaneously and all Australian combat troops were placed under his command.

Curtin considered MacArthur's appointment to be indicative of the importance America ascribed to the safety of Australia.[35] Both this assumption and the delay in the announcement of the American arrival flew in the face of reality. The presence of the Americans was well known long before Curtin's announcement and was as widely applauded, whether or not people saw that they had come, not to save Australia, but to use it as a vital base for their own war in the Pacific.

Most of the press had played the official game of pretending that the Americans had not arrived. To people in the metropolitan area it must have seemed odd that the *Daily News* on 5 March should proclaim 'Yanks in London' but not mention that they were also in Fremantle, The University of Western Australia, Rottnest Island and the local pub. When the first American death occurred on that very same day, all the paper could say of the unfortunate William Lucion Glover, who had been run over by a train at Fremantle Station, was that he was a sailor, 'a married man', and 'had no relatives in Australia'.[36]

While the *Geraldton Guardian* also referred to the presence of American troops in England and Ireland in early March, without mentioning their presence in Western Australia,[37] the *Albany Advertiser* was even more coy. A day after the announcement by Curtin it was still referring to Americans as 'visitors [who] recently came within the precinct of this town'.[38] And even a week later, while it was prepared to admit that Americans were in Australia, it could still offer only a nudge and a wink about their presence in the town, by printing a comprehensive conversion table of 'American Currency Values' to coincide with the opening of a local Allied Service Club.[39]

By contrast, from the start the *Fremantle and Districts Sentinel* was unable to contain its excitement. On 26 February, within four days of the arrival of the first troops, it was defying censorship under the heading 'The Anglo-Saxon Race. America and Australia Unite':

> The Americans are well-liked here, and on all sides favourable comments can be heard. The recent arrivals are a fine type of men, particularly well set up, and also smartly uniformed. The absence of heavy drinking, and also the fact they have friendly manners: these things are winning for them much appreciation. These men are certainly a good type, well paid and mostly skilled men...

In early March the *Sentinel* was jaunty in its optimism about the immediate future, extravagant in its hopes for the longer term and militant about its moral right to publicise the American presence. A front-page insistence that 'public opinion should not be suppressed on great national questions' went on:

> Incidentally, we also want to see millions more 'YANKS'—as we Australians call our American friends and helpers—in Australia,

especially at the old historical port of Fremantle. And somehow we think our wish will soon be an accomplished fact… It is pleasing to note the good relationships between the Anglosaxon peoples of the world everywhere are proceeding very satisfactorily indeed, and this is particularly noticeable with regard to Aussies and the Americans everywhere… This paper wants to see the Americans in Australia, not in thousands only, but in many millions, bringing with them their business acumen and their wealth, and making Australia forge ahead like a second Canada.[40]

A week later the paper seemed momentarily to have come down to earth with the report of a disparaging remark overheard in the street:

'Yes, I have been looking around', said an unassuming, quiet observer. '[Perth] is very quiet and slow, and is about the size of the New York cemetery, and just as dead, I think…'. Of course, 'Sentinel' readers will understand it was an American visitor that said these things.[41]

By the end of the month, however, it was clear that editorial attitudes were unchanged, as its front page greeted MacArthur, his wife and 'four year old precocious son', while an 'Aussie Girl' said 'Welcome, Uncle Sam' in extended verse proclaiming that '…we are not afraid/ We know the Yanks will hear our calls'.[42] And by the middle of the year, in a logical finale to eighteen months' idolatry of the Stars and Stripes, the *Sentinel* was calling for a referendum to support Western Australia's incorporation into the United States.[43]

The *Sentinel* was a very unusual newspaper. Probably more convincing evidence of the welcome is to be found in the files of the American Consulate. Several young men were inspired by the new-comers to offer their services to the United States forces. One, seeking to enlist in either the Navy or the Merchant Marine, claimed to speak for 'half a dozen' other Australian boys, all over seventeen.[44] There was no chance that such offers could be accepted by the Consulate and even less that another youth would be referred, as these were, to the

US Navy base in Fremantle. Offering himself as plumber, carpenter, electrician or photographic technician to the US Navy, the young man was eager to photograph 'Jap or Nazi ships'. Confident that, if allowed to do this, 'I will be famous because it will be history', he finished pathetically: 'I am deaf.'[45]

Such individuals were of course typical of nothing except the sad frustrations of the young and the medically ineligible. By this time, after two years of war, it was inevitable that young men would be far outnumbered in the welcoming chorus by females of all ages.

'President Roosevelt. Dear Sir,' wrote June Birt of Methodist Ladies College, Claremont, 'I want to thank you for sending your soldiers, sailors and airmen to help Australia. I am only an Australian school-girl, but when I see the American men and planes I feel more secure.'[46] She concluded her letter with a request: 'Since you are such a great statesman, I hope you would not mind if I asked you to send me your *autograph, please.*' Temporary Vice-Consul Thompson was grateful for but unmoved by her 'generous sentiments'. 'It is sincerely regretted that it is contrary to the practice of the President to comply with requests for his autograph.'[47] Sweetly innocent though the young girl's request undoubtedly was, it was typical of Perth's welcome for the Americans in the way it combined genuine relief, gratitude and admiration with a touch of opportunism.

Within a few weeks of the American influx what a later era would call the 'hospitality industry' was booming. All rooms in the city's hotels, reported the American Consul, were occupied by his compatriots: the '[picture] theatres are now literally jammed at all times' and 'most dance halls are currently either given over exclusively to the entertainment of the armed forces or are largely preempted by service personnel'.[48] If Turner's report had been more specific, it would doubtless have identified the particular popularity of the Embassy Ballroom, mentioned that the roller-skating rink in Hay Street was always full of Americans, and acknowledged that so were the nightclubs, because, unlike their Australian counterparts, the Ameri-cans could afford to buy drinks there. Indeed a number of new nightclubs—or cabarets, as they were more often called—had already popped up like mushrooms in the blackout.[49]

Not all entertainment was commercial. Dances and parties were organised by the Red Cross, and the Student Guild of The University of Western Australia gave permission to Americans based on the grounds to use the Refectory for dances, providing there was no alcohol and all festivities ceased before midnight.[50] A number of organisations emerged specifically to provide entertainment for the servicemen. In Fremantle, this was mostly financed by the Mayor's Patriotic Fund, which received donations from a variety of sources, but predominantly operated from the profits of Saturday night dances held by the East Fremantle Football Club in the Town Hall.[51]

Underlying all these activities was one common factor. While organisations were offering hospitality, and while local businessmen were seizing new economic opportunities, the Americans were seizing local women in an embrace of immense mutual pleasure.

On 14 March 'Loves a sailor' addressed an urgent query to 'Mary Ferber', the 'agony aunt' of the *Daily News*: 'Would you please tell me…if it is possible to get in touch with a sailor in the US Navy if you only know his name?' The curt reply—'Apply to the Secretary of the Navy, Washington'[52]—may have been a sign that the column was toeing the censor's line in pretending that there were no American sailors nearby. But it might just as well have been a snort of impatience that the young woman was such a slouch. For on the previous day, under a heading 'Met, Wed in One Week', the *News* had announced that Roma Coombe, 27, of Nedlands, who had been introduced to Ensign William Owen of Washington, DC, one week previously, was to marry that night.[53]

A week later, immediately after the American presence had at last been officially acknowledged, the newspaper attempted, under the headline 'Dean Warns of Marriage Pitfalls', to remove the blinkers from girls galloping towards matrimony with a home in America as the ultimate prize. Anglican Dean R. H. Moore offered 'a word of warning to all those Australian girls (and their parents) who contemplate marriage with our gallant allies'. Marriage did not bestow immediate American citizenship; therefore entrance to America would not necessarily be easy. There were as yet no arrangements for the Paymaster of the US forces to pay allotments to new wives, and it could take four or more months for such payments to be organised. Finally, in a comment not likely to restrain those already in the final sprint to the altar, the Dean pointed out that US divorces would not necessarily be recognised in Australia.[54]

On 30 March the *Albany Advertiser* exclaimed: 'Now Girls, Go Easy!'

> Judging by the favour shown by the many girls and women of the usually quiet little burg to the sons of Uncle Sam during the past week or two, it can only be surmised that they are to some extent falling for the boys from 'The States'.

Warning local young women against rushing into 'summer-time marriages', it implored them to 'look before you make the final leap!'.[55]

Such warnings had little effect. By mid-April 1942 Mason Turner was writing in some consternation to the Consulate-General in Sydney about 'the present situation wherein numerous members of the American armed forces have contracted marriages with Australian women'.[56]

Instant attraction and rapid transaction did not of course mean permanent devotion. Some romances withered as quickly as they had blossomed. On 30 April the *Albany Advertiser* was reporting 'Love's Young Dream Shattered'. Four weeks previously a young US sailor had married a seventeen-year-old girl in Perth. The girl had just appeared before the Perth Children's Court after being found drunk and in the company of several soldiers; the husband now wanted a divorce.[57] If this was an extreme case, already by mid-1942 there were more than a few local women complaining of fickle lovers, unwanted pregnancies and uncertain finances.

Yet at this early stage, when Americans were still pouring in and out of the metropolitan area in numbers, such emotional casualties were the unlucky exceptions, their complaints largely confined to private letters. And while there were undoubtedly some local men already in anguish over errant wives dazzled by American charm or unsettled by American largesse, it is hard to find evidence at such an early period of the violent male jealousy that would be aroused in the longer run by American relationships with local women.

Strangely absent from the public record and private recollection is any evidence for the violence at this period referred to by John Hammond Moore in one of the few references to Western Australia in his book *Over-Sexed, Over-Paid and Over Here*. Moore quotes from the recollections of Joseph C. Harsch of the *Christian Science Monitor* about events following immediately after the arrival of the first submariners in early March:

> The next morning the men of that squadron came ashore and took the town. But the following day one of the big Empress liners arrived in Perth with the Australian Sixth Division aboard. There ensued the unrecorded 'Battle of Perth'. I would be fascinated to know what the casualties actually were from the action in which the Sixth lads did their best, with indifferent success, to reclaim the girls of Perth from the U.S. Navy.[58]

While it would be foolish to dismiss the possibility of the kind of brawling that had already occurred, and would occur again as troop-ships passed through Fremantle, this hint of major conflict cannot be allowed to stand unchallenged. It is based solely on reminiscences from Harsch in letters to Moore 'three decades after the event'.[59] There is no doubt that Harsch and other American journalists were bitter about the strictness of Australian censorship. Yet, even when freed from those shackles, in writing about the Australian scene for an American audience on his return to the United States, Harsch never referred to this incident.[60] At the same time there is no record, of the kind so common in the files of the censors, about the need to suppress reporting of any such violence at this time. It is also interesting that Daniel and Annette Potts, in their *Yanks Down Under*, quote US Admiral Lockwood's comments from Perth to his wife in July 1942 about the violence already commonplace in Brisbane and elsewhere:

> As you may have read, scraps between U.S. & Aussie troops on the East Coast are worrying authorities there. Gen. Bennett and I are taking steps to prevent the entrance of the serpent in our garden. Relations have been very excellent here.[61]

Whatever transient violence may have broken out, in the continuing absence of large resident contingents of Australian troops general approval of the American presence was broadly based through the local community. Romance and sex may have topped the agenda for some, but it would be a distortion to present the Americans simply as an insensitive army marching through the bars, ballrooms, brothels and bedrooms of Perth and Fremantle. An editorial in the *Australian Women's Weekly* on 2 May 1942 urged Australian families to extend hospitality to Americans: 'Invite Them to Dinner…a dinner with a dinkum Australian family can do more to bind the ties of friendship between two countries than one hundred plenipotentiaries.'[62] The consular files show that such exhortations were quite unnecessary in the Perth area. Long before this, offers of meals, accommodation and every kind of hospitality had flooded in.

On 20 March—still a week before the American presence was officially acknowledged—a Highgate woman wrote to the Consul: 'There are, at present, a great many U.S. Army, Navy and Airmen in this City and whilst most of them are quite capable of making their social arrangements there are quite a number who fail to do so.' Offering home hospitality from other families as well as herself, she was a little concerned her motives might be misinterpreted. She insisted that her 'intentions, like those of the penguin in the story, are really quite good and offers made in all sincerity'.[63] So too, no doubt, were the intentions of a North Cottesloe man who offered a weekend at his beach flat for any Americans 'who have no friends in Perth' and offered the services of his daughter to 'pick them up in town'.[64]

Some of the offers showed a touch of anxiety and, again, a hint of opportunism. A Nedlands man, fearing that there would be enforced billeting of troops, rushed in quickly, hoping for 'some chance of having desirable men, rather than having to take in anybody under compulsion'. He wanted men of 'moderate habits' who wouldn't overwhelm his septic toilet system.[65] A Victoria Park woman also had standards. Her husband, shell-shocked from the First World War, had fits, and wouldn't be able to cope with 'men who came in *drunk*'. But she had confidence in the Americans. 'Your men appeal to me,' she told the Consul. 'They always appear to know how to behave.'[66]

The public welcome was as warm as the private. In mid-March Albany women made dinner for a hundred and fifty 'visitors' before they could be named publicly as 'Americans'.[67] A few days later the *Albany Advertiser* was commending the way the 'ladies of the various Albany Organisations and the younger set' had formed themselves into 'one comprehensive body in their endeavour to carry out a very laudable object, the securing of a suitable building' to be used as a social facility for 'soldiers and sailors of various Allied countries, as well as our own forces...should they happen at times to be hereabouts'.[68] The countries involved were not especially 'various', for the 'Allied Service Club' was opened at the beginning of April to the strains of the American and British national anthems, while 'Major Vaughan...jocularly remarked on the fact that the visiting naval men were acting up to the best traditions in their immediate popularity with the fair sex'.[69]

In Geraldton, where an advance Catalina base was only just being established, it was left to the local newspaper to prepare the public for an American presence that would always be small. Under the heading 'Allied Co-operation' it reported that 'money is being poured in to establish the Americans in suitable bases, to enable them to train and be trained, to give them every facility to carry on the battle for Australia'. 'An added value' of the millions of pounds received—with 'millions more' to follow—was that Australians and Americans were fast becoming 'buddies', enjoying 'mutual appreciation and respect'.[70]

In Perth, officials of every conceivable organisation fell over themselves to welcome the Americans. The West Australian National Football League told the American Consulate of its wish to set aside two dates in its schedule of fixtures for the coming season 'when it is hoped arrangements can be made for demonstrations of American football and baseball, proceeds to be handed over to Patriotic Funds...'.[71] This was a slightly odd offer, since the *Daily News* had announced on 26 February that League football was to be suspended for the duration of the war.[72]

Soon sporting clubs of every kind invited all American servicemen to join them, an offer qualified only in one instance by the feeling that supplies of tennis balls were about to run out.[73] On the Esplanade waterfront the Australian Natives Association rented half its sailing club premises to American chief petty officers.[74] Nearby, at the foot of Barrack Street, rowing facilities were offered by the Lord Mayor of Perth.[75]

Inevitably the Americans were keener on some offers of hospitality than others. A Presbyterian minister from Victoria Park wrote to the Consulate twice in May, puzzled that he had received no response to his offers to entertain American troops.[76] The Dalkeith secretary of the Guild of Young Artists was initially elated at the report that a US serviceman had been seen buying music by Bach. But her follow-up invitation to all Americans to attend the Guild's concerts[77] was less appealing than the various sporting opportunities, to say nothing of the sensuous delights of the Embassy Ballroom and other palaces of pleasure.

Underlying many of the welcoming initiatives, in addition to spontaneous enthusiasm and gratitude for the American presence, were the lessons learned from the earlier days of the war, when Australian transit troops had brought chaos to the metropolitan area. The Lord Mayor, Thomas Meagher, had been a key figure in the establishment of a Citizens' Reception Council (CRC) to coordinate the activities of thirty-two organisations, including all religious denominations except the Methodists. Eventually the recollections of George Nelson, the long-time chairman of the CRC, and of *Sunday Times* editor J. J. Simons—who was also chairman of the Young Australia League (YAL)—were not entirely favourable to the authoritarian tendencies of the Lord Mayor and the Australian military command. More importantly, they showed indirectly how much better prepared Perth was to receive the Americans than it would have been a year earlier.

When the need for hostels and other troop facilities became urgently apparent in 1941, recalled Nelson,

> we were chasing buildings in this town. The State Government could not help us. The Church of England offered us the ground outside St George's Cathedral and Mr Simons threatened to run me out of town if we built on it. Mr Gordon Dunleavy then broke his lease behind the Adelphi and our first hostel was opened just in time to take the refugees from Singapore. We went to the RSL to help us with entertainments. The Perth Sub-Branch gave us Monash House at the corner of King and Hay Sts. for Sunday nights. This was inadequate. I rang the Lord Mayor and asked him to do something—he said we could have the Town Hall—very expensive proposition. Prior to 1942 we found that feeding was necessary for the troops and we opened a buffet in Barrack Street, the premises for which were provided by the Quinlan Estate.[78]

The CRC had been trying unsuccessfully to take over the Young Australia League Hall in Murray Street, Perth, for twelve months, after the military authorities decided that all existing facilities were inadequate. In early 1942 the YAL headquarters and adjoining YAL apartment house were requisitioned under National Security Regulations and handed over to the CRC 'for use as a Hostel and for recreation purposes for members of the Allied forces'. In May 1942, after the arrival of the Americans, 'to honour the womenfolk who had been working very hard for two years, the centre was given the name of the Chairman of the Catering Committee...and called the Phyllis Dean Service Club and Hostel'.[79]

By the time all these facilities were in place, Lord Mayor Meagher was acting not only in reaction to local experience and needs, but as part of a coordinated national response to the American presence. In January 1942 the Australian–American Co-operation Movement and the Australian Comforts Fund had both sought official recognition from the highest levels of government as organisers of hospitality for the imminent influx of American servicemen. The Department of Defence Co-ordination decided that 'in order to ensure the success of such a movement it is essential that its organisation be undertaken by the Lord Mayors in the various cities, as by that means the assistance of the numerous interested bodies can best be welded together'.[80]

It was also in response to national trends that in June 1942 the Lord Mayor called a public meeting to form a Western Australian branch of the Australian–American Co-operation Movement, which was already established in Sydney, Melbourne, Adelaide and Brisbane. Its object was to foster mutual understanding, especially by stimulating appreciation of President Franklin Roosevelt's post-war policy of international cooperation, as expressed in the Atlantic Charter and the Lend Lease agreements between the United States, Great Britain and the Soviet Union.[81]

The United States authorities were far from passive participants in all the expressions of mutual goodwill that marked the first few months of their presence in Western Australia. Military and consular representatives were in ready attendance at official and semi-official cocktail and supper parties.[82] They were equally ready to respond to requests for the loan of a seventeen-foot-long US flag to the Busselton and Districts War Fund,[83] for a military band recital at the Capitol Theatre in support of the Free French Forces Fund,[84] and for 'a detachment or two of United States Troops, Marines or Naval Men' to take part in a fundraising parade through the city to Forrest Place, organised by the Victoria League Camp Comforts Fund.[85]

In July 1942 the first four months of an overwhelmingly harmonious relationship were marked appropriately when the Premier's Department helped to organise a public party to celebrate United States Independence Day at the Perth Zoo.[86] Over the remaining months of 1942 there would be many further official expressions of mutual regard as well as unofficial ones, especially between the women of Perth and the American visitors. But increasingly the notion of American independence had a special local meaning. Very quickly after their arrival the Americans were bringing with them the resources and the organisation to provide for their own needs. On 17 July the consular staff were in polite attendance at the official opening by Sir James Mitchell of an Information Bureau for all Overseas Men in Uniform at Padbury House in St Georges Terrace.[87] This was a facility that was going to be needed much less by the Americans than by other overseas troops—from Britain, New Zealand and the Netherlands—and even by Australian troops as they returned from the Middle East. As the next few chapters will show, while Americans were a pervasive presence for the next two and a half years in the metropolitan area, and even some places beyond, they wanted virtually nothing that the host society could offer except the warmth of human contact, especially with women but also with children and whole families.

# FLEETING ATTRACTION

*Chapter Five*

## A PERVASIVE PRESENCE

IT IS VERY MUCH THE ARGUMENT of this book that one reason why the American interaction with the people of Western Australia was different from the situation in the eastern states was that the Americans themselves were different. They were Navy personnel rather than the Army GIs discussed exclusively by John Hammond Moore and largely by Annette and E. Daniel Potts. Neither those authors nor perhaps most contemporary Western Australians are, however, aware that for a time, even while that Navy presence was being established, there was also a significant Army presence, especially in the Perth metropolitan area. Before the distinctive impact of the Americans on the local scene can be discussed, it is necessary to establish more precisely the locations of both Army and Navy personnel.

The American Army presence in Western Australia was significant for only a few months of 1942. Base Section 6 of the United States Army Forces in Australia (USAFIA) consisted of the whole state, except the Kimberley (which was part of the Darwin-centred Base Section 1). Its first commanding officer, Lieutenant-Colonel James C. Mann, who had arrived alone and unannounced on 25 February 1942, established his headquarters in the ANA building in Perth. The arrival soon afterwards of the 197th Coast Artillery and the 699th Signal Reporting Company was a sign of the Base Section's essentially defensive purposes at this stage. Further indication of the gravity of the military situation came on 23 March, when 20 officers and 143 other ranks disembarked from the *Queen Mary* at Fremantle 'for permanent station' as the 5th Station Hospital.[1]

Grave though the circumstances and hurried the arrival, it was already clear that the Americans were virtually self-contained. Hearing of rumoured plans to open an American hospital, Mary Mears of the local Red Cross Society wrote to the American Consul four days after the arrival of the medical unit to offer her services as a nurse. After consulting Major Wiltrakis, the medical officer in charge, Mason Turner replied that if such a hospital were opened the nursing staff would almost certainly be American Army Nurses.[2] This was a slightly disingenuous reply because there were already thirty American nurses in the newly arrived medical unit.

The immediate sense of crisis soon subsided. By mid-April the official announcement of the 'Mission, Organisation, and Methods of Operation of Base Section 6' described a support role. It was 'to operate a service command for the administration of the several base sections, ports and camps...to receive and assemble all US troops, supplies and equipment...[and] to perform supply and administrative functions for combat troops to enable them to move freely and with minimum of delay'.[3]

Numbers of personnel were at their peak in May, June and July, when the strength of the Base Section comprised 119 officers, 2038 warrant officers and enlisted men and 30 nurses. As numbers of Australian forces steadily grew to some fifty to sixty thousand over the rest of the year, the Americans were redeployed to more critical areas in the Pacific war. By late July there were a mere 21 officers and 171 enlisted men, as the 197th Coast Artillery was removed and the 5th Station Hospital transferred to Canberra. The departure of the Station Hospital's nurses meant that, for the remainder of the war, the American services' presence was to be exclusively male. When the 699th Signal Reporting Company was pulled out in November, Base Section 6 was reduced to a token force of 3 officers and 22 enlisted men.[4]

Over these same months the US Army's Air Force was laying the foundations for a much more far-reaching and longer-lasting presence. By 30 June 1942 fighter aerodromes had been built or upgraded, or were under construction, at Arrimo, Moora and Northampton, bomber aerodromes at Corunna Downs, Cue, Tammin, Narrogin and Wagin. Fuel storage facilities had been installed at Merredin, Kalgoorlie, Northam and Narrogin. Activity on this scale was a major part of the Americans' war effort in the region and an important source of the growing sense of security their presence had brought to Western Australia. But although work was carried out under American supervision, surveys were undertaken by the WA Lands and Surveys Department and paid for by the Commonwealth Department of the Interior, while airfields were constructed by the WA Main Roads Board.[5] For these reasons, and because of the distant, sparse populations in most locations, the immediate social impact of Air Force activity was much less than that of the Army in and around the Perth metropolitan area.

Short-lived though this army presence was, it was characterised by intense activity. Within two weeks of arrival, commanding officer Mann was pressing his headquarters in Melbourne for urgently needed equipment to upgrade port depot facilities at Fremantle, including twelve mobile cranes, eight forklifts, twelve stackers, twenty-four tractors, a floating crane and a truck with power hoist. Deciding that the army needed more storage space, Mann quickly acquired a 30,000-square-foot warehouse from the West Australian Wool Company, half a mile north of Fremantle on the highway to Perth.[6]

With equal urgency Guildford Grammar School was taken over to accommodate the 5th Station Hospital, its seven buildings considered suitable for a 250–300 bed facility. At Perth's Karrakatta Cemetery a plot was set aside, consisting of 1256 graves, with an adjoining area reserved for a further 3000, for burial of United States Army, Navy and Marine Corps personnel. Fortunately neither of these facilities was much used. Following the withdrawal of 5th Station Hospital, Guildford Grammar was handed back to be partly used by Australian forces as a military hospital.[7] And none of the handful of graves taken at Karrakatta were needed for war casualties. In 1942 only four American soldiers and thirteen sailors died: two in train accidents, three in car accidents, one in an accident at Victoria Quay, Fremantle, two by drowning, three of illness, two by self-inflicted gunshot wounds and four unspecified.[8]

Numerous private and public buildings were also needed for only a short time or not at all. But their speedy acquisition marked a much greater intrusion into the lives of the community than activities in the secluded surroundings of a cemetery or a private school on Perth's periphery. Between 25 March and 19 April 1942 at least forty properties were requisitioned for the use of the 197th Coast Artillery, the vast majority of them in Fremantle, but stretching also into adjacent suburbs on both sides of the river. These included the regimental headquarters at the Hillcrest Salvation Army Maternity Hospital in Harvest Road, North Fremantle, a dispensary and hospital in Canning Highway and regimental supply stores at the Claremont Drill Hall. The first battalion headquarters were at the Richmond Park raceway, and its various batteries at several sites in Fremantle as well as Bicton, South Perth, Jandakot and Cottesloe. Second battalion headquarters were at the Salvation Army Aged Women's Retreat in Harvest Road, North Fremantle, its officers' quarters at 25 Herbert Street, and batteries throughout Fremantle and on Rottnest Island. Regimental motor transport facilities were in Canning Highway, East Fremantle, and at Mosman Park.[9]

Although many men were temporarily accommodated in tents and Quonset huts at Fremantle, Melville and even the Ascot racecourse, arrangements were also made to billet both officers and enlisted men in privately owned property. In the early stages this could be a rather cavalier process, as a US Army report eventually suggested: 'Owing to objections raised by landlords, it was later decided to introduce a new form of contract with slight modifications, this form consisting of letters making and accepting the offer.'[10]

Such difficulties, however, were far too minor to disturb the mood of grateful welcome that prevailed throughout the period of the US Army's passage through the metropolitan area. And no such misgivings emerged in the one rural location where there was a significant but largely secretive American presence.

In late March 1942 Gingin farmer Ian Edgar was puzzled to find strange tyre tracks as he rode around the paddocks of his property 'Strathalbyn'. When he arrived back at his house an army jeep containing two American officers was waiting for him. They were looking for a site to establish an observation post overlooking the coastal plain. Climbing into the jeep, Edgar directed them to the top of Sunday Hill, half a mile to the west of his house, from where there was an uninterrupted 180-degree view from north to south, and west to the coast. He then showed them a suitable camping area on the east side of the hill and offered them a supply of pipes to bring water from a nearby well to the camp. A few days later, on 31 March, a convoy of trucks arrived with some fifty servicemen and supplies to establish a camp.[11]

In many ways the story of the interaction between Americans and Australians in this unique location is typical of the period of the US Army's presence in Western Australia—and typical also of the good relations over the same months of 1942 between the US Navy and the civilian population. To Mr Edgar, who had dutifully followed civil defence instructions and built a backyard bomb shelter a few months earlier, and to the rest of his household—wife, two daughters and two female domestic helpers, Hazel and Edna—the American arrival was tangible evidence that the West was no longer almost defenceless. It also brought the stimulus of novelty, the prospect of friendship and even a sliver of economic opportunity. Hazel and Edna were encouraged to set up a canteen for the Americans in an empty cottage on the farm. Within three weeks they were able to repay Mr Edgar the £10 he had lent them to stock up with groceries.[12]

The relationship was much more than commercial. The two American officers enjoyed numerous free meals with the family, while many of their men dined without payment in Edna's kitchen. Mutually enjoyable also was the need to hide from the officers the many occasions when enlisted men paid unauthorised visits to canteen and kitchen. While Edna provided clandestine meals, Hazel openly catered to the men's musical needs. More than fifty years later Mr Edgar could recall among his happiest memories of the period the many occasions when groups of Americans surrounded piano-playing Hazel, singing 'You are my sunshine, my only sunshine!'.[13]

Despite this warmth, there were also clear boundaries between professional and social spheres. The newcomers established an observation unit on top of Sunday Hill with the speed and thoroughness which had marked the American influx as a whole. But they were secretive about its purpose, and Mr Edgar could only guess that they were operating one of the still quite new radar systems.[14]

As well as efficiency there was self-sufficiency. Gingin had no power, so the Americans brought their own generator to supply the radar unit and their living quarters in tents among a clump of trees. The new canteen attracted them much more for the human contact than its menu, since supplies were delivered to the Americans two or three times a week in a truck that also looked after the needs of a similar unit in the hills at Kalamunda. The Edgar family sometimes benefited from its visits, tasting spareribs for the first time in their lives and enjoying pork, which the Americans insisted on having in preference to the local 'sheep meat'.[15]

American self-confidence was in no way undermined by the presence of Australian forces at Gingin, two miles away from the Edgar farm. Visiting an Australian camp one night for dinner, the American officers were amazed at the primitive facilities and no less surprised that their hosts were able to bake cakes and other delicacies in two mud-covered forty-gallon drums. Yet self-confidence did not breed obvious arrogance. Regular visits by the Americans to the local pub and attendance at dances produced so little friction that the locals wondered whether they had been hand-picked for their good behaviour.[16]

The Americans were in Gingin long enough to leave lasting good memories and the youngest Edgar daughter with a temporary

American accent. But they left after a stay of only some five months.[17] Probably their departure was the result of the diminishing threat to the south of the state. But although Geraldton became a more important centre for radar surveillance, a very similar base to the one at Gingin was operated through most of the war in Perth's Darling Range.

The First Signal Corps, United States Marines, operated a secret base somewhere between Kalamunda and Mundaring. Personnel spent ten days at a time camped in the bush, followed by periods of leave billeted at the Claremont Showgrounds. But they also spent some off-duty time in Kalamunda. They attended dances at the Kalamunda Hall and frequented the Braeside Tea Rooms, from where the proprietor's daughter invited them to musical evenings in her home. Like those in Gingin, they impressed locals as 'a wonderful crowd', who nevertheless were largely self-contained.[18]

Whatever the underlying operational reasons, the departure of the small Army radar unit from Gingin had been in keeping with wider trends that made the American presence in Western Australia overwhelmingly naval. On 30 November 1942 Captain Walter R. Gottschalk began the process of dismantling the Army's Base Section 6. His appointment in September to replace the higher ranked Lieutenant-Colonel Mann had itself been a sign of the base's diminished importance. Now his report that there were pending a mere twelve actual, and eight potential, claims for damages submitted by Australian citizens was testament to the relative smoothness of the Army's relations with the local population. On 11 January 1943 Gottschalk announced the closing of the base in fourteen days' time. All personnel were to be transported by ship to Sydney—scarcely a major exercise, as there were by now only two officers and seventeen enlisted men remaining.[19]

While the impact of the US Army on the Perth metropolitan area was intensive but short-lived, that of the Navy was intensive and sustained. As the American Consulate formally reported at the end of the war, 'American Naval personnel, enjoying either protracted residence in Perth or Fremantle, or frequent shore leave in those cities, at its maximum numbered over four thousand'.[20] The focal point of this pervasive presence, in an operational though not necessarily a social sense, was of course the port of Fremantle.

The decision that had been quickly made in March 1942 to place the main submarine base as far south as Fremantle had not meant abandonment of hopes that Exmouth Gulf would become a major base as the war situation improved. The arrival there on 19 May of the tender *Childs* was acknowledgment of 'the need for an advanced base on the NW coast to reduce the distance between base and patrol areas'. Known as 'Operation Potshot' the base never fulfilled the hopes pinned on it. A heavy swell in the Gulf waters, produced by north-westerly winds, meant that submarines could not be satisfactorily serviced alongside the tender. To this climatic deterrent was added a military one. Even though by early 1943 the Allies were regaining control of the area around the Dutch East Indies, and even though the Exmouth Gulf area had fixed anti-aircraft defences and an RAAF fighter sector headquarters, Japanese air raids on 20 and 21 May forced an American withdrawal. As the American tenders sailed for Fremantle at the end of the month, the continuing need for a fuelling station in the area was met temporarily by a Dutch tanker, pending the installation of fuel tanks ashore at Onslow. But these various diffi-culties had convinced the Americans that the area was too vulnerable to be a major base: Fremantle's continuing importance was assured.[21]

In addition to the long-term presence of the submarine base, there were temporary visits to Fremantle by other units of the Asiatic Fleet throughout the war years. Accommodation for naval personnel varied according to length of stay and rank. The Fremantle Old Women's Home was the American Receiving Barracks for the duration of the war, with a capacity to accommodate almost seven hundred men. Those whose visit to Perth was transitory were billeted in various warehouses around Fremantle or the Quonset huts that had been erected on North Quay. Others stayed upstairs in the old Fremantle fire station, or slept in tents on East Fremantle or Claremont oval or in the camping areas at South Beach and Melville. Private homes were requisitioned for the use of officers and their staff. Other servicemen

*Fremantle: activity at the submarine base*
(Mask Productions, Perth)

who had wives and families were allowed to rent privately.[22] Mrs J. Balcombe, eventually a war bride, recalled submariners living in apartments near Westgate in Fremantle, at a house in Safety Bay and in Myola Hall in Claremont.[23]

Even fifty years later some individual families maintained their indignation at having property requisitioned,[24] but this did not happen on a large enough scale to have a general effect on attitudes to the Americans. Immediately before they arrived there was a flurry of press criticism of the acquisition of what proved to be their main Fremantle barracks. On 19 February, under the headline 'Scandal of Old Women's Home' the *Daily News* complained that sixty-nine old ladies had been evacuated to an old house with inadequate facilities. It was too old and too small and still undergoing renovations: 'However urgent the shift may have been, there is no possible excuse for the disorganised manner in which it was carried out.'[25] But the issue quickly faded a couple of weeks later when it was realised that the home had been acquired for the Americans.

Although the submarine base was in Fremantle, the submariners also found accommodation in central Perth. The American Consulate considered that only two hotels in Perth—the fifty-room Esplanade and the fifty-four-room Adelphi in St Georges Terrace—'could be considered as suitable quarters for commissioned officers'. But from March 1942 for the duration of the war Americans completely monopolised all of the city's modest hotel accommodation: in addition to the Esplanade and the Adelphi this included the forty-seven rooms of the Savoy in Hay Street and the twenty-seven-room Australia in Murray Street, the Wentworth on the corner of Murray and William Streets, the Palace at the corner of Barrack Street and St Georges Terrace, as well as many smaller hotels, both licensed and residential. They also took over the Ocean Beach Hotel at Cottesloe and were prominent at the Oceanic in Mosman Park and the Captain Stirling in Nedlands.[26]

The submarine base had a major store in Hay Street, Subiaco. Some personnel lived on the premises, others in private accommodation nearby.[27] The Subiaco Hotel became a favourite social centre, while the Americans also organised entertainment for themselves and the locals at the King's Hall in Rokeby Road.[28]

Although these western suburbs acquired a distinctive American flavour, in some of them, and particularly Nedlands, the Americans were not submariners. Between March 1942 and August 1944, at any one time there were upwards of two hundred personnel flying and servicing the US Navy's Catalina flying boats at Crawley. Although, like the submariners, they tended to move into hotel and other private rooms in the city, as they became familiar with Perth, their main accommodation was at The University of Western Australia, in the riverside suburb of Crawley.

Early in 1942, the Vice-Chancellor, G. A. Currie, gave his permission for a number of rooms in the Engineering and Agricultural buildings to be occupied rent-free by the Americans, providing all depreciation, maintenance and damage costs were covered by the visitors. The Americans' dentist had his own suite in the University's Engineering Building. The Americans were allowed to erect Quonset huts in the grounds near the river and also opposite the University on

*UWA: Americans at work in the Engineering building*
(Lt. Wiegand, USN, Matilda Bay Catalina Base 1942–43: UWA Archives)

Stirling Highway, as accommodation for enlisted men. In this latter location, the site of the University's present-day Currie Hall, there was also the Bachelor Officers' Quarters. On the Swan River foreshore the University's Boat Club became the headquarters and mess for this unit, Catalina Patrol Wing Ten. Riley Oval, on the University campus, was used as a parade ground.[29]

To the west, in the next river bay, the Nedlands Park Hotel (Steve's) was taken over as barrack accommodation for some of the Catalina personnel and there were also messing and sleeping quarters at the adjacent Pelican Point, the southernmost extremity of Crawley.[30] Local resident E. V. Taylor, who was seventeen at the start of the war, had vivid recollections of American officers who were billetted at Steve's, of others who rented the house opposite his home on the corner of Hillway and Melvista Avenue and of Americans taking over the petrol station at the corner of Stirling Highway and Broadway.[31]

*UWA: on parade on Riley Oval*
(Lt. Wiegand, USN, Matilda Bay Catalina Base 1942–43: UWA Archives)

Although certainly outnumbered by the submariners, in many ways the six hundred Catalina personnel, who served in successive tours of duty between March 1942 and August 1944, had an equally important social impact. While the vital contribution of the submariners to the naval war was taking place secretly and mostly far away from their home base, the departure of the flying boats on equally far-flung patrols across the Indian Ocean was a daily occurrence, which maintained over a long period the sense of security and comfort that the Americans had brought with them.

Reminiscing fifty years later, Mrs Marjorie Ward felt that latterday protests against the visits of American ships were the work of people who could not possibly understand the 'huge relief' engendered by the American arrival out of the blue in 1942. People who hadn't lived through those years would not understand the pleasure she got from seeing American uniforms in the street and, especially, from seeing the flying boats on the river. From the city hotel she managed in Murray Street she would take her children up to Kings Park to see the planes

UWA: an assembly of Catalina personnel
(Mask Productions, Perth)

coming back from their daily run up the coast: it gave everybody 'a nice feeling'. One man, age fifteen in 1942, recalled with similar warmth that the reassuring sound of the planes warming up on Crawley Bay could be heard as far away as Cottesloe.[32]

Although most Americans were in Perth and Fremantle, the Navy also had personnel in a number of country centres. Their arrival at Spring Hill, near Northam, to establish a major explosives store came literally 'out of the blue' as far as seventeen-year-old Gwen Anderson was concerned. Working at the local telephone exchange, she was almost deafened by the unexpected arrival of an American plane. This was the start of a lengthy presence in which Americans lived and played, without serious friction, in close proximity to much larger contingents of Australian soldiers. They were well behaved and did not get involved in serious fights or drunkennness on visits to Northam pubs and dances. Probably the most destructive effect they had on the community was their eventual removal of no fewer than nine local women as war brides.[33]

The Americans were also an attractive and reassuring presence, in very different ways and for different periods, in the coastal towns of Albany and Geraldton.

The US Navy's second submarine base at Albany remained operational for just under a year from the time of its establishment in mid-March 1942. In that period virtually no shore facilities were established, although the Americans built an observation tower at the Princess Royal Fortress. The submarines, based at Deepwater Jetty, were maintained by tenders, first the *Holland*, then the *Pelius*. With some hundred and fifty men on each of the five large submarines and over a thousand on the *Pelius*, the great majority of men, both submariners and support crews, lived on board ship, but a deadline of 11.59 for returning to ship every night gave them ample opportunity to make their presence felt in town.[34]

A few officers rented houses—one in Golf Links Road, another overlooking Middleton Beach—and many others, both officers and enlisted men, were given hospitality by people in town and by local farmers. Rest and recreation leave took groups of them regularly inland to Bolganup and Karribank and sometimes even as far away as Williams. In Albany itself the impact of sheer numbers was very great in a town of some four thousand people, and it is little wonder that a woman as nervous as Phyllis Vaughan had been about the Japanese threat would feel 'very much safer' after she had first glimpsed their white caps.[35]

In different ways, and even though numbers of personnel were vastly smaller, the Catalina flying boats brought similar reassurance further north. The mission of these low, slow-flying planes was to patrol the western coast of Australia: if they spotted Japanese submarines, they would either call in surface vessels to attack them or would drop bombs and depth charges themselves. They took off from Crawley Bay and flew ten, twelve, sometimes as many as fourteen hours before returning for overnight refuelling stops at one of several northern advance bases. There could be little social interaction at such desolate outposts as Shark Bay and Potshot, where refuelling was from tenders. Although some crews ventured ashore for such authentic Australian experiences as kangaroo shooting, others rested aboard their planes.[36]

*An authentic Australian experience*
(John Antonides, Sun City, Arizona: UWA Archives)

Geraldton was altogether different. Advance Base Baker provided food and housing, and medical treatment if needed, while planes were serviced and checked for safety. Planes would usually arrive at night, the same crews taking off next morning to fly a day's patrol north or west of Geraldton, returning for another night there before going back to Perth. Sometimes crews would spend as long as three days at the Geraldton Base before returning to Perth.[37]

The base had a commanding officer, executive officer, doctor and some twenty to twenty-five support personnel. These included radio operators, who maintained twenty-four hour contact with aircraft and with the Crawley headquarters, crew for a tender and four African-American Navy cooks. There was also crew for a large torpedo boat. Accommodation for base personnel was in two requisitioned private facilities. Enlisted men were in a girls' boarding school, sleeping six to eight in each room, while officers enjoyed greater luxury in a doctor's residence in Marine Terrace on a large block complete with tennis court. On the western end of the waterfront, where a long stretch of firm white sand was fronted by cottages and beautiful pine trees, the Americans built a small jetty. Here, with their section of the beach surrounded by barbed wire, the Catalinas would be towed in for refuelling by the small tender which could also winch damaged aircraft ashore for repairs.[38]

The personnel of Advance Base Baker offered comfort to local people out of proportion to their small numbers. Outnumbered from the start by the Geraldton garrison and, within a few months, by up to forty thousand Australian troops in the surrounding countryside, they nevertheless promised something different to a population unnerved by the disasters unfolding to the north in Darwin and Broome and familiar with the defensive routines of blackouts, slit trenches and air-raid warnings. American Catalinas could pursue the Japanese planes that some locals claimed to have seen already circling overhead in daylight; they could hunt the Japanese submarines undoubtedly lurking off the coast.[39]

Relief at the American presence meant tolerance of American bravado. Local resident George May was more excited than annoyed by the regular 'daredevil' flying of pilots passing a mere three feet above the mast of his small boat. It was an excitement reinforced by at least three crash landings of Catalinas. It was sheer bad luck that one landing aircraft struck a piece of debris, probably timber from one of the sections of the old railway jetty, which had been demolished to retard an enemy landing. It was no doubt unfamiliarity with local conditions that saw another pilot unable to cope with the strength of an easterly, as he barely cleared the breakwater before crashing into the sea. But, however unaware of local conditions, it was surely a breach of all the basics of flying when a third pilot attempted to land with a thirty knot southerly buster behind him. Bouncing for three hundred yards, his aircraft smashed the mast and rigging of a fishing boat, one of its occupants avoiding disaster by leaping overboard, the other by crouching flat.[40]

Fortunately none of these accidents caused death or serious injury. Neither did the weekly antics of the pilot of a small sea-plane, who brought the Americans' paymaster up from Perth. Sometimes Catalina men were forced to dive into the water as he skimmed their jetty. On one occasion it was George May and his friends who had to lie flat on the top of a wheat bin. It was no surprise, but almost disappointing, when the thrills dried up for two months after the pilot was grounded for flying through a hangar in Perth.[41]

This was not the only piece of showmanship in the metropolitan area. Here, gratitude for the visible reassurance provided by the Catalinas persisted long after the welcome for Americans was otherwise wearing a little thin. In 1944, when three Catalinas 'wrapped' many of the buildings of central Perth with toilet paper, the Lord Mayor was 'seriously disturbed', according to one of the pilots. But 'most Aussies thought it was great', even before the Americans deployed a truck to clean up as much of the mess as they could find.[42]

Although this was an unofficial prank, swiftly addressed by the American authorities, it was in many ways typical of a self-confidence, bordering on arrogance, widely welcomed and tolerated in the difficult circumstances of 1942 but, as we shall see in later chapters, the source of some disillusionment in the long run.

The American push for a dominant role in wartime Perth and Fremantle was most strongly resisted, not in the army or naval spheres, but by those concerned with control of merchant shipping. And the resistance came much more from British than Australian authorities.

At the beginning of 1942, immediately after the arrival of the first convoy carrying American personnel and Navy, Army and Air Force stores, urgent consideration was given to the control of ports during the expected huge increase in maritime activity. A meeting of the Overseas Shipping Representatives' Association (OSRA) in Sydney on 9 January decided that in each major port there should be a committee, consisting of a representative of Sir Thomas Gordon, who headed the British Ministry of War Transport in Australia, and the chairman and two or three principals of OSRA. Mixed in with the desire for efficiency was a concern to maintain British and Australian control:

> It will be necessary to see that no effort is spared to give the best possible service in order to avoid our American friends setting up their own organisation... Under present arrangement it will be possible to see that all vessels, i.e. British Ministry of War Transport vessels, also American vessels, are all given a fair deal and handled to best advantage in the common interest. Without this organisation and under divided control the position might easily arise under which either British Ministry of War Transport vessels or American vessels would be seriously prejudiced. While it is urgent for all American convoy vessels to be handled to best advantage, this of course does not mean that urgent British Ministry of War Transport vessels are to be prejudiced.[43]

The hope of resisting an American push for independent control of their own shipping was short-lived. On 9 March Perth Consul Turner received a letter from Charles E. Brown, announcing both that he had been appointed as the 'Representative of the United States War Shipping Administration, Anzac Area' and that he in turn had appointed Mr W. C. Canty 'as my representative in Western Australia'.

Canty was to supervise 'all matters pertaining to the handling of American ships and American controlled vessels'.[44]

This appointment did not mean inevitable friction with British and Australian authorities. As he established himself in an office on the premises of Dalgety & Co. in Fremantle, Canty was instructed by L. D. Causey, US Navy Commander, to cooperate with locally based American civilian and military authorities and with the representatives of the British Ministry of War Transport:

> It will be your duty to see that tonnage is used to the best advantage and dispatch facilitated. You are not authorised to charter U.S. owned or chartered ships to other services, but you may, in case of urgent necessity, make available for military use, for short periods, such tonnage as, in your judgement, is necessary.[45]

In the immediate future the 'urgent necessity' was for the Americans to acquire, rather than release, ships. From late April 1942 there were considerable tensions between American and British War Transport authorities over two ships, the MS *Centaur* and MS *Gorgon*, which the British were about to remove from Australian waters and which the Americans insisted should be retained because they were 'peculiarly adapted to service on the west coast of Australia' and their threatened loss 'further slows up our deliveries of supplies'. After initial refusals from the British, it took intervention at the highest level — by General MacArthur and Prime Minister Curtin and through the Australian High Commission in London—before these two ships plus a third, the *Charon*, were released to the Americans on 12 May 1942.[46]

Despite these controversies, Canty was transferred in August to Townsville because the volume of shipping was greater there. But over the next few months, with the submarine base in full swing, with troopships bringing back many Australian soldiers and with a further increase in merchant shipping, conditions at Fremantle prompted the US War Shipping Administration in Sydney in early 1943 to send its Marine Superintendent, Harold P. Petersen, to investigate. He discovered a situation that demanded the re-appointment of a permanent American representative, preferably an engineer—'but a man of Canty's type would be very desirable if an engineer is not available'. Partly this was because of congestion that threatened the war effort but also because 'eighty per cent of the shipping in this port at the present moment is American' and yet shipping was almost completely controlled by Harold Hooper, the representative of the British Ministry of War Transport:

> Mr Hooper is a most able man, as are all of Sir Thomas' men, and has built himself an organisation here in Fremantle that practically controls the port. He is Chairman of the Ship Repair Committee, also Chairman of the Priority Committee and a member of OSRA. Through his position as Sir Thomas' representative, he has an office allocated to him in the Naval Control building and has full access to all communications. He, or one of his men, boards all vessels, ascertains what fuel they need, what repairs, stores etc., they want and he then relays these orders to the agents. The agents could naturally resent this, but as most of the shipping up to now has been other than American, nothing could be done.[47]

Petersen insisted that his relationship with Hooper was 'most cordial', but American resentment at British control of the port was not far from the surface of his report: 'Since my arrival on the scene I have very tactfully conveyed the idea to him that I would take care of all those matters in so far as American ships are concerned and that our agents were appointed for that purpose.'

There was nothing very tactful about the American regime that was put in place in response to Petersen's appraisal. In July 1943 a confidential report by Consul Turner on Samuel H. Richter, the recently appointed local representative of the US War Shipping Administration, was both perceptive and frank about the potential for discord between American and Australian manners. 'When Mr Richter first arrived,' Turner told his Sydney superiors, 'I was disappointed in finding that he was rather aggressive in manner and too much possessed of those mannerisms usually associated with the commercial traveller to make him perfectly suited for service in his new position.' He had since found him to be very hard-working and was convinced he would be well suited to his duties 'if this were an American community':

> We Americans understand his type whereas many Australians, I am afraid, do not. Mr Richter tends to be extremely definite in every expression of opinion and likes to have the last word in any discussion, regardless of the person with whom he may be speaking.[48]

Richter may have been abrasive enough to offend even a fellow-American. But by 1943 many in the host community would have said that his brash decisiveness was typical of American conduct on a broad front. Nowhere had it been seen more clearly than in the determination of American servicemen to secure their own personal comfort in their temporary Western Australian home, the theme of the following chapter.

# Fleeting Attraction

*Chapter Six*

## The Quest for Comfort

FAMILIARITY WITH PERTH AND FREMANTLE in the late twentieth century gives little insight into the social atmosphere of the Second World War. A soaring, shining central Perth business district has displaced solid sandstone elegance in the main thoroughfare, St Georges Terrace. Pedestrian shopping malls, multi-storey car parks and overhead walkways have transformed the grid of streets stretching north to the railway station. Today's office-workers and shoppers inhabit the same Perth streets but an utterly different environment from those who sauntered and staggered from pub to club, from dance hall to movie theatre, half a century ago. The acclaimed restoration of inner Fremantle has been a pastel-coloured gentrification rather than a revival of menacing waterfront seediness. The cappucino-sipping, pasta-twirling customers of its pavement cafes are remote from an era of blackouts, six o'clock swilling and drab cuisine rendered even drabber by rationing.

The Perth first encountered by the Americans may have shocked them with its isolation and provincialism, but it was already much changed by the war. And those changes, it must not be forgotten, included the presence of servicemen of several other nationalities. The

British and the Dutch also had a long-term presence in Fremantle submarine bases. There were more transient British naval personnel throughout the war—and in huge numbers in its final stages—as well as New Zealanders and, most numerous of all from the end of 1942, Australian soldiers.

Outnumbered though they were, the Americans were unique in their attitudes and their impact. From the beginning of March 1942 they were a pervasive, self-confident and largely self-sufficient presence in the metropolitan area and one or two places beyond. Whether at work or play, they knew what they wanted and did not hesitate to take it or, if necessary, acquire it from elsewhere. While they may have occasionally used the now abundant social facilities available to all servicemen in both Perth and Fremantle, they needed them far less than others.

In the crisis atmosphere of 1942 there was little reason for locals to resist the American push for efficiency, comfort and lively entertainment. Through access to a range of goods no longer readily available they gained as much as they gave in their hospitality. And in many instances there was money to be made from an American casualness about cost that was understandable among well-paid men with uncertain futures.

By March 1943 there were signs of irritation with that once reassuringly decisive and refreshingly exuberant presence. Although mercenary motives and much genuine goodwill would survive to the end of the war, the honeymoon was definitely over.

One measure of the quick impact of the US Navy on Western Australia in 1942 is the scale of work carried out on its behalf. By the end of June the Australian Department of the Navy had authorised only one American project for New South Wales (at a cost of £2500), one for Victoria (a mere £45), five for Queensland (£13,815) but thirty-five for Western Australia, costing £22,006.[1]

Although the projects included £1 spent on cleaning a 'cesspool' at the American Admiral's home in Jutland Parade, Dalkeith, most were substantial: £2750, for instance, for construction of a timber ramp and road at Pelican Point. A derrick was also erected there and soundings were taken in the river for the erection of a seventy-five-foot jetty and the laying of six moorings. Important work was done in Fremantle, but much of the activity in these early stages centred on the Crawley area. There were improved sanitary facilities for the nearby Steve's hotel and numerous alterations and improvements to the University's facilities. These included lavatories, showers, kitchens, hot water supplies, laundry facilities, store rooms, refrigerators, stoves and a twenty-bed sick bay and dispensary.[2]

At the same time there was work at locations well removed from the metropolitan area, including the reconditioning of a railway siding at Geraldton. The two largest expenditures were on the inland explosives stores, located at Spring Hill and Spencer's Brook near Northam.[3]

These and other more minor activities—such as the securing of the stores in West Subiaco—were carried out at express speed and with a disregard for bureaucratic niceties that left the Australian Director of Navy Accounts authorising all projects but complaining in a handwritten note: 'The US Authorities should have placed all the above Requisitions through this department. Suggest they be notified accordingly.'[4] Similarly the Vice-Chancellor of the University wrote to the Commanding Officer of the US Navy on 27 April 1942 about rent-free facilities lent to his forces and about the rights also granted to erect other buildings:

> Further, in consultation with myself permission was granted for the erection of huts to house additional personnel between the Institute of Agriculture and the Engineering School as a radio laboratory. Further permission was granted to erect masts for a transmitting station and to use a small laboratory in the Engineering School as a radio laboratory. Excavations have been made in University grounds on the opposite side of the road from the students' boat shed to take oil tanks which have been placed in position (also a sewer cut through, which was a necessity). University insists on correct courtesy, as no approach was made to them on the latter two items.[5]

The Americans' breezy decisiveness is scarcely surprising. MacArthur had insisted on the complete military autonomy of his troops in Australia, who gained a reputation for acting first and then asking permission. Told soon after their arrival in Fremantle that telephones would take at least a week to be installed at their head-quarters, the Americans simply removed the number they required from local telephone boxes.[6] In the same way public boxes in Stirling Highway were plundered for telephones for the exchange established in the Agriculture Building of the University.[7]

A major factor in both the local and national tolerance of virtually independent American activity was the still vulnerable military situation. Several American complaints that shore searchlights were silhouetting their submarines were countered by Australian insistence that it was necessary to verify the identity of the vessels because 'the Americans are not prepared to agree to the submarines entering and leaving port during daylight'.[8] A conference at the end of April 1942 decided that searchlights would be dispensed with in return for a US Navy commitment that its submarines would enter and leave port on an agreed timetable. But a week later the port authorities were complaining that the Americans were not keeping to this arrangement.[9]

Although such sensitivities can seem extreme in hindsight, the very real contemporary fears are illustrated by other concerns of the civil defence authorities. The same meetings that were addressing these problems of blackout and submarine security were also grappling with the security threat posed by 'a huge sign in the form of a yellow dingo on the Fremantle–Perth Highway, which was visible many miles to the seaward and an exceedingly prominent landmark'.[10]

The nervousness that questioned, but then grudgingly tolerated, American operational independence also explained a willingness to indulge American insistence on higher standards of comfort than seemed to be available as they swept into Perth and Fremantle. When the Australian Navy accountants queried the need for extensive painting and other refurbishment of the Base Force Barracks in Fremantle, the reply made it plain that the Americans could not tolerate the conditions endured by old ladies. The premises had been 'formerly the Old Women's Home in that town, owned by the State but vacated just before the US Navy arrived, and then taken over by the Navy. Renovations were essential for the health and cleanliness of the staff occupying...'.[11]

Similarly, heating appliances, 'amounting practically to central heating', were provided in the Messing and Sleeping Quarters for Patrol Wing 10 at Crawley. 'This type of work', the accountants were told, 'is not usually done for Australian personnel, but the US Navy, arriving in winter, apparently found it essential, particularly as all members there arrived in Perth after some two years in tropical climes.'[12]

Central heating was also applied to the ground and first floors of the University's Engineering Hall (now part of the Guild of Under-graduates complex) and electric heating to the University Boat Club building, the operational base for Patrol Wing 10. Individual electric heaters were placed in the Quonset huts erected by the US Navy. The Americans even insisted on part of the Crawley Tea Rooms, which were also on University land, being closed in for protection from the elements.[13]

The Americans showed similar impatience with local amenities by securing a supply of fresh vegetables from their own gardens in Fremantle. In April 1942 their request for permission to plant a vegetable garden in the land adjacent to their base at Arthur's Head received a deliberately discouraging reply from the Fremantle City Council. The soil was choked with couch grass and needed an abundance of fertilisers to overcome its lack of nutrients. Neverthe-less, two full-time market gardeners were appointed and the Americans proceeded with their vegetable garden.[14]

The vegetable garden was largely symbolic, its output totally insignificant among the array of items available to them but not directly to the local population. Perhaps more than anything else it was this abundance of material goods in an era of civilian rationing that made the American presence so distinctive.

Under the Lend-Lease Act of 1942, Australia was to provide the American servicemen with food rations, 'in many cases to the extent of

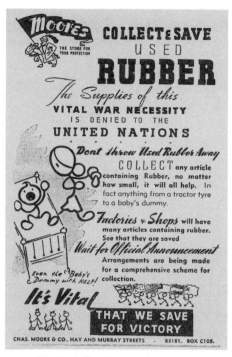

COLLECT & SAVE
USED
**RUBBER**

*The Supplies of this*
**VITAL WAR NECESSITY**
IS DENIED TO THE
**UNITED NATIONS**

*Don't throw Used Rubber Away*
C O L L E C T any article
containing Rubber, no matter
how small, it will all help. In
fact anything from a tractor tyre
to a baby's dummy.

*Factories & Shops* will have
many articles containing rubber.
See that they are saved

*Wait for Official Announcement*
Arrangements are being made
for a comprehensive scheme for
collection.

*It's Vital*

**THAT WE SAVE
FOR VICTORY**

CHAS. MOORE & CO., HAY AND MURRAY STREETS  -  B3181. BOX C108.

*(West Australian Newspapers)*

[Australians] going on short supply ourselves'. United States servicemen in Australia received the same rations as the Australian military forces, resulting in a cut in their ration items from thirty-nine down to only twenty-four. To compensate, however, the Americans were allocated an extra allowance to enable them to purchase additional food from canteen stores which were exempt from duty and sales tax. Throughout Australia over 1.5 billion pounds of foodstuffs were supplied to the Americans by the end of 1944, including fresh fruit, milk, beef, pork, lamb and canned goods.[15]

For the local population, rationing was a major irritation rather than a symptom of severe crisis. Petrol, tea, sugar, butter and meat were all rationed during, and for some time after, the war, while potatoes, canned meat and citrus fruits were generally unavailable to civilians. Shops were supplied with only one carton of chocolate to sell per month.[16] The restrictions were felt by most families and by those involved in public catering. For twelve months, towards the end of the war, the Derward Hotel closed its dining-room for lunch and dinner partly because of such shortages, though difficulties in obtaining staff were also a factor. Before that closure, proprietor Marjorie Ward had found the Americans, who formed the bulk of her patrons, quite undemanding. They were happy to accept whatever was on offer in the hotel dining-room and never attempted to exert an influence on what was served.[17] If this tolerance was the product of good manners, it must also have reflected an American confidence that they could eat much better at their own bases.

University staff, invited to the officers' mess at Crawley, were amazed at the quantities and variety of food.[18] Even the American enlisted men were impressed by the similar abundance available in their own mess hall. As one recalled, 'you could order what you wanted any time of day'—not only hamburgers, hot dogs and ice cream, but all manner of fresh food, including fruit, butter, milk and eggs.[19]

While such resources denoted American self-sufficiency, they were an obvious incentive for many locals to maintain the warmth of their welcome. A cook in the United States Navy remembered the pilfering of food from the kitchens by Americans to be common-place.[20] Much of this was taken to the homes of Western Australian families who offered their hospitality to the Americans, but who would have had difficulty providing extra meals from rationed food. 'As soon as the Americans discovered that ration tickets were a fact of life for us', recalled Phyllis Gurley, 'they supplied us with meat all the time.'[21]

*Issuing ration books: an irritation more than a hardship*
(West Australian Newspapers)

Eggs, butter, canned ham, fresh meat and even flour were gratefully accepted by local families, as were more luxurious commodities such as chocolates and salted nuts. Americans with local girlfriends could sweeten relations with junior family members through gifts of candy. Cigarettes were provided in almost unlimited amounts, while Pat Tully recalled that regular gifts of Raleigh tobacco were the easiest way for American boys to warm the heart of her father.[22]

In Albany the family of David Bird entertained Americans to dinner four or five times a week. They would regularly bring tobacco and sometimes a pillow-case full of tea or sugar. But the American presence was relatively short-lived in the south coast town. When ten Americans arrived one evening with a greater array of delicacies than usual, nothing was said openly but it was assumed correctly by his family that they were about to leave. Ice cream, oranges, tea, Planters' peanuts and steak provided an appropriate gesture of farewell from visitors who had brought such pleasure to one family that David's sister, fifteen in 1942, was still writing to several of them fifty years later.[23]

Apart from natural kindness and perhaps a sense of gratitude, especially for female company, the Americans sometimes had their own ulterior motives for generosity. In Geraldton George May, who kept a boat moored less than fifty yards from their jetty, saw an American acquaintance dumping large quantities of chilled meat into the water. Appalled that prime steak and other delicacies were being discarded at a time when locals could not even get cheese, he was told that if the Yanks did not dump it their rations would be cut.[24]

This was not the last time that George would supply the Americans with a few crayfish in return for meat and other goods which he was able to distribute especially to older people in need. Crayfish were also a useful currency for transactions with the crew of the locally based torpedo boat. There may have been a limited market for the home-made cigars soaked in rum produced by one crew member, but both supply of and demand for American cigarettes, in this town as everywhere else, were inexhaustible.[25]

George May was not interested in the duty-free whisky that was another envied, and frequently transacted, ingredient of American privilege. Nor did he require more than a fraction of the petrol he could have obtained. Small amounts were gratefully accepted for the boat that enabled him to maintain the supply of crayfish. When he asked for a four-gallon drum to be filled, his American friends breezily offered to deliver 44 gallons to his home. With petrol rationing—instituted in October 1940—restricting most private motorists to some fifty miles' driving per month, it would have been easy to sell what he did not need. But it would have been equally easy for the authorities to find out. Although there was probably a modest black market, it was hard to do much in a place as small as Geraldton without being caught.[26]

George's caution was sensible. Fifty years after the war he could not remember many of the Americans by name but had a clear recollection of a friend called Tex. On 7 November 1942 the *Geraldton Guardian* reported that John Carrington had been charged with 'being in possession of one four-gallon drum of petrol', which, he claimed, had been given to him by an American called Tex Corning.

In addition to scarce but familiar items, the Americans also introduced many families to items previously unknown, ranging from canned corn, spaghetti with meat balls and Spam to peanut butter and stuffed olives. The most frequently remembered innovation was Coca-Cola, sometimes taken to families but most often first encountered at parties and dances organised or frequented by Americans.

By some quirk of wartime supply the Americans in Geraldton found themselves without bottled Coca-Cola but with a supply of the vital syrup. Arrangements with a local soft-drink plant to mix the syrup with carbonated water and bottle their own Coke were so successful that the parent company in Atlanta, Georgia, eventually intervened, using its immense influence with the American war machine to suppress this pirate operation.[27]

It was one thing for an industrial giant to cut off supplies of a scarce and secret commodity, quite another for the American naval authorities to exercise controls over the flow of groceries from its stores into civilian hands and mouths. Often the American guard at the gate of the Subiaco base would be impressively erect as he checked those leaving for contraband, his hat concealing two pounds of butter, his pockets bulging with tins of asparagus. In return for these and other offerings, the women of his favourite local family would use their sewing skills to make any alterations he and his friends required to their extensive wardrobe of clothes. Even this gesture brought its own rewards. Sometimes £20 would be casually pressed on the ladies for single alterations by servicemen evidently unaware that this represented more than two weeks of average male wages. And these and other women would take advantage of the apparently unlimited American access to cotton sheets.[28]

There were, of course, rules against all transactions that moved goods from American to local hands. In August 1943 the *West Australian* publicised a warning from US military authorities that civilians had no right to be in possession of American cigarettes unless the packet bore the customs stamp: 'An American soldier...has no right to give even one cigarette to a civilian, and if he were seen to give away a packet of issue cigarettes he would be liable to arrest by the American military authorities.' The *West* went on to publicise a case of pilfering that was on a substantially greater scale. A woman was fined £25 for having unlawful custody of twenty-one sheets, a pair of new American army boots and eight packets of Chesterfield cigarettes, to a total value of £9.10.0, the property of the US Government.[29]

Excessive though these particular acquisitions might have been, and beneficial though the American contributions were in general, it would be a slight to the genuine warmth of the local welcome to put major emphasis on mercenary motives. Reminiscence from the period shows that in some families it was not unusual for children to wake in the mornings to find their fathers had brought up to a dozen American servicemen home from the pub to sleep on the lounge-room floor.[30] Australian families of an ethnic background, such as Italians and Greeks, offered their hospitality to servicemen of similar origins.[31]

It would be no less of a distortion to see American relations with the local population solely in terms of the pursuit of women. Even though the chapter that follows concentrates on this obviously important factor, it is clear that many of the servicemen were also missing family life.

The 'incredible generosity' Americans showed towards host families in Joy Gawned's suburb of Wembley was not simply a matter of dispensing surplus luxuries. They purchased 'amazing' amounts of food at her mother's shop, much of it to be passed on to local people. Joy's lasting memories were of the Yanks' friendliness and fondness of children. She remembered one American sailor who frequently bought such 'goodies', but whose main motive in visiting the shop seemed to be to talk about home, often showing her mother his latest letters and photographs of his two small daughters. Joy's lasting regret was that, as a ten-year-old, she was expected to show good manners, and so was less indulged than her three-year-old sister, who regularly asked for sweets and chewing-gum and was never refused.[32]

Even luckier than that little girl were some of those with sisters old enough to date Americans. For the large Lawson family fruit was a scarce wartime commodity. For five small Lawson brothers and sisters it was a major treat to be taken by their big sister's American fiancé to the local greengrocer and told they could have as much as they liked. Fifty years later Dalveen Timms, one of those children, retained vivid memories of an Italian shopkeeper's desperate efforts to keep track of what the children were eating. His attempt to have them put things in bags to take away was fruitless: his shop almost equally so at the end of their visit.[33]

American warmth and generosity towards children, often in the face of potentially annoying provocation, was indeed one of the commonest recollections decades after the war. While chewing-gum was perhaps most regularly demanded and willingly dispensed, American coins quickly became prize souvenirs. In Albany children rolled them down hilly York Street in a game devised solely as an excuse for cadging coins from servicemen.[34] Submariner Homer White remembered fellow-Americans and himself being chased in both Albany and Perth by children demanding coins.[35]

Yet the overriding impression from sources of both nationalities is of an American tolerance not always shared by adult Australians.

On 2 April 1942 the proprietors of the Hydrodrome Tea Rooms, in South Beach Road, Fremantle, wrote to the Commissioner of Police:

> Billetted on the premises at the present time are about 150 American soldiers and these men are continually being pestered by the children for souvenirs, coins etc. The men are not likely to complain themselves; but the truth is that children are literally becoming little beggars.[36]

Clearly, however, much more than money drew children to newcomers more exotic than the British and more approachable than the Dutch servicemen who were also in Perth and Fremantle. For three and a half years the Americans were central figures in the childhood of Michael Papadoulis. In the 1990s he still kept American coins collected during the war. But they were not a beggar's booty. Mostly brought home from his father's fruit shop in central Perth, they were souvenirs of a time when anonymous Americans laughed and brawled their way through the inner-city streets north of the railway, and when more familiar ones secretly dated his eighteen- and twenty-two-year-old sisters.[37]

For at least one male teenager in Cottesloe the Americans were part of an exciting wartime environment. There were barbed-wire entanglements all along the coast, from Fremantle to Swanbourne, and machine-guns and anti-aircraft batteries along the shore near his home. He spent many happy hours hanging about with the Americans who were guarding these facilities or doing firing practice. One submariner, after spending much of his spare time in his home, eventually married a family friend.[38]

Andy Andersen, another submariner, was typical of Americans who forged permanent connections with local families. Meeting his future wife two or three days after his arrival, he was 'adopted' by her family and never had any reason to stay in the hotels taken over by the US Navy or use facilities eventually established by the American Red Cross: 'I had a family to go to', he said years later. 'That's the main reason I came back [to settle in Perth].'[39] The facilities he spurned were, however, another product of American affluence and independence in the midst of an abundance of opportunities for public recreation and entertainment.

Decades before the modern nightclub and cafe society had been born and christened 'Northbridge', Perth's night-time entertainment was mainly in the central business district. In keeping with this pattern there was only one centre of organised hospitality for servicemen north of the railway line—Locksley Hall at 79 Stirling Street, run by the Toc H organisation, with a hundred and twenty beds. The focal point of interaction between servicemen and civilians was the area south of the railway, bounded by Wellington Street to the north, St Georges Terrace to the south, and King and Irwin Streets to west and east. Here were most of the cinemas and the dance halls that had long existed. And here were the hostels and hospitality centres that had been organised with almost desperate speed by influential men alarmed by the social chaos created by Australian troops in transit, and which were run throughout the war by innumerable, mainly female, volunteers.

Dwarfing all others was the Phyllis Dean Service Club and Hostel on the corner of Murray and Irwin Streets. Open day and night, each day it served a thousand customers three-course hot meals at a cost of one shilling each, the same tariff as for a night's accommodation. At various periods it had between seventy-nine and a hundred and twenty beds and no fewer than four hundred 'shakedowns' or mattresses on dormitory floors. There was dancing every night, in a ballroom which regularly accommodated five hundred revellers, and weekly concerts. Other facilities included a lounge, a reading and writing room, a post office, an information bureau, a billeting office, which organised hospitality in private homes, sewing and ironing rooms and hot showers.[40]

Despite the range of facilities and the numbers of personnel using them, it was only a walk of a few yards west along Murray Street to two other major centres of hospitality. On the corner of Pier Street the Red Shield Hostel, conducted by the Salvation Army, was also open day and night, offering snack bar meals at the higher price of two shillings and sixpence, but two hundred free beds as well as a lounge and reading and writing room. Nearby, at 119 Murray Street, the YMCA provided meals, a hundred beds, reading, writing, postal and recreation facilities and dancing four nights a week.

Around the corner and to the left was the Barrack Street Buffet at number 79, which served light refreshments to fifteen hundred people daily at an average cost of threepence each, and which also offered lounge facilities during its 9.15 a.m. to 9 p.m. opening hours. Half a block away the Perth Town Hall offered similar facilities to a thousand people each day and also dancing on Sundays from 2 to 10.30 p.m. Further on in St Georges Terrace, Dunleavy House was open day and night, providing a lounge and writing and postal facilities, hot showers and a hundred and twenty beds per night at one shilling per bed. Also open day and night was an Information and Hospitality Bureau at Padbury House, 170 St Georges Terrace. As well as offering a lounge, writing facilities, refreshments—including free suppers— and general information, this bureau arranged private hospitality for servicemen in both the city and the country.

Turning right along King Street, and eventually back into Murray Street, servicemen had a further cluster of similar centres in which to relax, spend the night and find cheap refreshment: the two-hundred-bed Friendly Union Hostel in King Street; Monash House, on the corner of King and Hay Streets, where there was dancing every day of the week; and Sportsmen's House on the corner of Queen and Murray Streets, open day and night with a hundred and fifty free beds.

All of these Perth centres were run by voluntary civilian organisations, such as the WA Sportsmen's Organising Council for Patriotic Funds, or directly by the Citizens' Reception Council, which was the overall coordinator. The only exception was an Information Bureau and Cloakroom conducted by the Australian Army near the corner of William and Wellington Streets.

A similar pattern on a smaller scale was found in Fremantle. At the southern end of Cantonment Street the Citizens' Reception Council provided a lounge, buffet and reading, writing and games rooms in Wesley Hall. Next door a hostel run by the Mayor of Fremantle's Patriotic Fund offered recreation and lounge areas by day and, at night, a hundred and thirty beds costing a shilling each. The Army and Navy Canteen in High Street, also open day and night, was conducted by a voluntary committee. In Parry Street the Catholic Welfare Organisation's Service Hut was open on weekday evenings and all day on Sundays. As well as free meals, it offered recreational facilities and dances every day of the week.

The scale of all these operations in both Fremantle and Perth says a great deal about a bustling wartime atmosphere, in which servicemen of all nationalities found entertainment, recreation and relaxation in their off-duty hours. In May 1942, in one of his regular reports to his superiors in Sydney and Washington, the American Consul wrote that the five or six 'acceptable motion picture houses in Perth proper', which mostly showed American pictures, were 'now literally jammed at all times, due to the troop concentrations in Western Australia'. There was no live theatre because of the war, but very much alive were the city's dance halls, which were 'currently either given over exclusively to the entertainment of the armed forces or…largely preempted by service personnel'.[41]

Americans were part of this scene, yet at the same time distinct from it. They were conspicuous in private and public dance halls and in cinemas, much less so in the buffets and dining-rooms run by local charities. Carl Uphoff was rare among the submariners in preferring the facilities run by the Salvation Army to those provided by the American Red Cross.[42] He was almost unique among Americans in caring about the relative costs involved. Most of his compatriots preferred to take care of their own social arrangements and ignore facilities that smacked of welfare.

Two women who worked as volunteers in several of the servicemen's canteens in Perth had no recollection of seeing Americans in any of them, even though both in different circumstances became closely involved with Americans. One, whose sister married an American, had vivid memories of the dances the Americans from the Subiaco torpedo base would regularly organise in King's Hall, Rokeby Road.[43]

The other woman became the girlfriend of Bill Barker, a Catalina man whose social life centred on the mess at Crawley, the Captain Stirling Hotel in Nedlands and, especially, the hotels and cabarets of central Perth. Strolling around that city area half a century later, he could point to the upstairs room in Barrack Street he had rented on his second tour of duty in 1944, in preference to another stay in a Quonset hut on the University campus. Yet this man, who remembered vividly the brawn sandwiches served at the Captain Stirling, and even the salmon patties he sought out every time he flew into Geraldton, was completely unaware of the existence of the many canteens, hostels and servicemen's clubs.[44]

Underlying Bill Barker's particular recollections are some more general trends. It was a sign of American affluence that even an enlisted man could very easily afford his own private accommodation in the city. It was a sign of extremely casual arrangements between officers and men that he should be allowed to do so. The commonest working routine for the Catalina squadrons, in which nearly all officers were active flyers, was a three-day cycle: a day on patrol, followed by a day attending to the maintenance of their planes, followed by a day of recreation. With the middle day's work obviously vital to the personal safety and survival of each man, there was very little need for discipline: Bill Barker scarcely saw his officers and had no idea where the senior ones lived.[45]

American independence showed itself in a different form at Geraldton because numbers were so small. Relations with the local population were cordial, but self-sufficiency combined with the needs of security to minimise the impact. George May's regular commercial interactions with the Americans did not bring any social invitations. The only time he entered their base was when he was called in to help repair the damage caused when his drunken friend Tex had searched for a gas leak with a lighted match. On the waterfront, physical closeness made him only too well aware of security. Fishing near the wharf one night, he snared a sixty-pound mulloway, which dragged his small boat close enough to the boundary of the American base for him to be exposed to a searchlight and far from friendly challenge from a guard who knew him well, leaving him convinced that he would have been shot if he had trespassed.[46]

The recollections of Johnson Head, Executive Officer of the Geraldton Base, reinforce the impression of a friendly but more self-contained American presence. For the most part the base organised its own entertainment for personnel stationed there and for the crews flying in and out. This would consist of card games and regular games of softball, especially on summer evenings when there would be time for a few innings after the flights came in for the night.[47]

The Americans in Geraldton were not hermits. Although their black cooks catered for them well, they also ventured into town for meals and had no hesitation in defining their demands. In a December 1942 article, headed 'Cooking Steak the American Way', the *Geraldton Guardian* reported that the 'doughboys' didn't like thick, tough steak, so they took a restaurant manager to the butcher's and showed him what beef to buy, how thick to cut it and how to cook it: 'One of these

*UWA: maintenance of planes every third day*
(John Antonides: UWA Archives)

American soldiers [*sic*] owns what he calls a "steak palace" in the USA, and says that he is going to start one in Australia after the war.'[48]

The aircrews, who frequently flew in and out, regarded it as 'a great liberty town: everybody liked to stay in Geraldton'. Both they and the personnel of the base camp were as likely to visit local hotels and as interested in meeting local girls as Americans everywhere else.[49] But the parties they held in their own premises were exclusive occasions to which few locals were invited, except favoured young women. The need for female company soon led to invitations from the officers to the nurses of the local hospital. In an era of almost military discipline for nursing staff, it was considered something of an achievement to win the agreement of the matron for the young women to attend parties and dances—on condition that they would return to their quarters by 11.30 p.m. The innovation proved so successful that the nursing supervisor also became a regular participant and proved 'an excellent dancing partner'.[50]

There was some socialising with senior officers of the Australian Army in Geraldton, both in the base dining-room, which could comfortably hold twelve to fourteen people, and in the Australians' mess. But in nine months at the base Johnson Head could recall only one large party, held at the local yacht club, to which civilians, other than female dancing partners, were invited along with the military personnel—and they were the mayor and people of comparable eminence in the community.[51]

Social arrangements were entirely different in the months the Americans were in Albany in large numbers. In contrast to their minuscule numbers in Geraldton, they dominated the town's social life. Home hospitality was common, said Phyllis Gurley, because the Americans were very likeable and also because they provided excitement for people who had previously been 'bored to tears'. With most local men away at the war, she had grown used to playing Chinese chequers. After the Americans came she never played it again.[52]

The American officers who came regularly to his house had a few strange customs, said David Bird, such as putting jam on everything, including roast meat. But they were 'gentle, peaceful men', who enjoyed themselves in a domestic situation—where they taught his whole family to dance—or at the community concert every Tuesday in the Town Hall. Here a packed house of three hundred people revelled in singing and dancing, hoping during the floor show that Sergeant Bob Anderson had lost none of the skills that had made him world record holder for Indian club swinging.[53]

Naturally the presence of so many Americans was an opportunity for local business. The response of the sex industry, in Albany as elsewhere, will be given some attention in the following chapter. A less controversial exploitation of the American sex drive was the speedy opening of Albany's first florist's shop. Others catered for different appetites with varying success. One publican had filled a cellar with spirits and bricked it up at the start of the war, awaiting just the opportunity that now presented itself. But Australian customs officials arrived before American customers and confiscated the contents.[54]

Fast food was a more legitimate initiative. In June 1942 advertisements in the *Albany Advertiser* promised the imminent arrival of 'American style hamburgers at Manea's Strand Cafe'. But if a rival was to be believed, this was emulation rather than innovation. Claiming that his 'American Spot' was the first in Australia to sell such hamburgers, Pop Layton was advertising for two hundred eggs a week and 'a strong girl' for his kitchen.[55]

Many Perth people would regard Pop Layton's claims as presumptuous, for the institution most widely associated with the American presence—indeed one of the very few relics of the era that modern Perth people could easily identify—was 'Bernie's', the late-night fast food eatery down below the city of Perth in Mounts Bay Road. The longevity of Bernie's as a fast food outlet was unchallenged anywhere in Australia by the time its closure was foreshadowed in late 1994.

Bernie Hardwick, raised in an orphanage but a veteran of innumerable jobs and small business ventures from the age of thirteen, had battled through the Depression as a vendor of crayfish at the Perth Royal Show and numerous country shows and, especially, as purveyor of cooked prawns, hot dogs and other delicacies to crowds leaving Subiaco Oval and other football grounds. He finally established a small hessian stall, on the site that would remain 'Bernie's' for another fifty-six years, in January 1939.[56]

Selling at first crayfish rolls, cooked prawns and crabs, and coffee—and later steak as well—the business was well established by the time the Americans arrived a little over three years later. But they transformed the enterprise. It was their demands that led Bernie to mince some of his steak and discover American-style hamburgers. It was their patronage that ensured the success of the self-service barbecue facilities till then virtually unknown in Australia but common in the United States. Above all it was their free and easy attitudes to money that enabled Bernie to charge the Yanks prices that horrified many locals: very few of the visitors, one woman recalls, bothered to reclaim the hefty deposit charged for plates. Bernie's, much more than official servicemen's facilities, was the favoured place for a late night snack for male drinkers at nearby pubs, for romantic couples strolling from city movie theatres and dance halls and for many travelling from parties further afield by taxi. Although it was a frankly commercial enterprise, Bernie's in many ways symbolised the mutual self-interest which bound together so many Americans and Western Australians in the war years.[57]

The mixture of motives—among both nationalities—that made the American presence refreshingly welcome in its early stages was shown particularly clearly when American submarine chief petty officers decided they wanted their own social club in Perth.

Not long after the Navy's arrival a group of these men rented part of the Aquatic Club of the Australian Natives Association (ANA) for one night. This was one of several rowing and sailing clubs strung along the waterfront, with a base for the Water Police in their midst, near the foot of Barrack Street. A wild night brought complaints from the police and a dilemma for club secretary Syd Harvey. His problem was not the threat to warm friendships with the local constabulary —who had long since developed an annoying habit of raiding the club for breaching the liquor licensing laws—but the threat to an emerging economic opportunity. The Americans had so much enjoyed their party that they were asking to rent half the premises indefinitely, a request that promised to breathe new life into a moribund organisation.[58]

The double-storey ANA premises were large and impressive, hosting a sailing club, rowing club, river swimming pool, debating club and licensed bar. But the organisation had debts of £600 when Harvey took over its management in 1939 and was now on the verge of closure, partly because of loss of members due to the war, partly because of those licensing laws and the imminence of six o'clock closing.[59]

Fortunately, nodding acquaintance with Commissioner David Hunter and support from a taxi driver enabled Harvey to smooth things over with the police. If his ambit claim for £150 per week rent was outrageous, the figure of £85 eventually bargained for was 'bloody good money' by any contemporary Australian standard. It enabled the club to stay open for the rest of the war. And, as its American half flourished, so did the fortunes of many more taxi drivers, a breed most adept at plucking the American eagle to feather their own nests.[60]

Led over a long period by one known mainly as 'Mac', the petty officers transformed the American section of the club into a haven of totally un-Australian luxury. Perth may have been too cold for winter arrivals, but by summer it was altogether too hot to sustain American life without artificial assistance. The very few Australian men, and rather more women, who saw past the new curtains to the innards of the refurbished club encountered air conditioning for the first time in their lives, not through one unit rattling away in a window-frame, but through at least twenty distributed strategically on tables to cool the brows of gamblers and other species of American party animals.[61]

The Australian club members had long since perfected a system of signals and awkwardly placed doors to slow down a police raid long enough for glasses and bottles to be hurled into the swimming pool at the rear. But a meagre wartime allowance of a few kegs of beer and half a dozen bottles of wine per month made this an expensive process until the Americans arrived with an unrationed abundance of alcohol. If the Australians ran out of beer they found their neighbours willing to offer relief, even though they largely excluded local men from their quarters. As the only Australian invited to their opening ceremony, secretary Harvey tasted Coca-Cola for the first time and, combining novelty with urbanity, achieved vulgarity by mixing it with genuine French brandy. A beer drinker by all previous inclination, he had the misfortune to spend the rest of the war swallowing this offensive cocktail every time he socialised with his American friends.[62]

A regular visitor even more affected by American innovation was a local character, Gus Jensen, an old Swede well known locally as a man who ferried mail to Rottnest Island in his ancient boat. Gus developed the habit of visiting the club regularly on Sundays to take advantage of the extravagant dregs left by the Yanks in discarded bottles. The proportions of whisky, cherry brandy, advocaat and other potions available on any particular day may have been unpredictable, but not so the twisting wake of his boat as it pulled out into the river after every Sunday visit.[63]

In their early stages the club renovations dealt one serious blow to the image of effortless American competence. Deciding that the aged dance floor had to be replaced, Mac's working party from Navy headquarters in Fremantle ripped it up but then found their pride bent as drastically as their nails, and even their hammers, as they tried to replace it with Western Australian hardwood. Tradesmen imported from a boat-building enterprise near the Causeway took two days to finish a job that conservative local assessments suggested would have taken the Americans 'forever'. But ridicule was kept well under control by workmen who earned £4–£5 a day at a time when their weekly wage was probably only about £5.[64]

There were more than simply mercenary reasons why the locals remained either willing participants or understanding observers of the American quest for comfort. True, association with the 'Yanks' gave access to alcoholic and gastronomic luxury, and even novelty in the shape of previously unknown steak sandwiches. But it was well understood that these were men, often with a harrowing recent past and always with an uncertain future, who were living for the present moment. The first-comers had escaped recently from the Philippines. They and their successors would embark on long tours of submarine duty from which they knew they might not return. It was easy to be amused rather than appalled by the volatility of a man like Mac, who on one occasion responded to a gambling loss by heaving the table through the window into the river.[65]

As worrying to the newcomers as the rough-hewn dance floor were the primitive sanitation arrangements in their new club. They might have been deflected by local timber, but there was no way they were going to crouch over malodorous pans when they had the money to buy the biggest septic tank in the metropolitan area. When the bureaucrats flatly refused permission, the Americans installed it anyway. With sometimes upwards of two hundred people partying in their premises, and perhaps a similar number of Australians next door, the tank remained undetected by human eye or nose. In the 1990s it was still there, hidden by a concrete capping with a park bench on top. As they cuddle on the bench, latterday lovers are oblivious to the dark history beneath them, and unaware of what took place half a century earlier in a clubhouse that survived the onslaught of wartime international friendship but was burned to the ground in the early 1960s. The only remaining visible relic of the American presence—but one unacknowledged by any plaque or notice—is a small horsehoe-shaped bitumen drive to the east of the Barrack Street jetty, which the Americans paid £500 to install, in this case with the permission of the city engineer.[66]

The chief petty officers' club was an unofficial piece of private enterprise. But, even in the period it was being established, the American authorities were setting out guidelines for their troops' welfare that were a symbol of self-sufficiency. Amid all the military urgency and logistical complications of the early months of 1942, by June of that year the headquarters Adjutant-General of the US Armed Forces in Australia (AFIA) was informing all bases that, as the American Red Cross Agency 'has been designated by the War Department as the civilian agency to provide recreational and welfare activities for the US Army in Australia, it is necessary that the closest cooperation with this agency be maintained by all elements of

American military forces'. Despite shortages of personnel, the military was to control 'in-camp' sports and entertainment, such as 'concerts, motion pictures, amateur shows, etc.'. The Red Cross was to provide a Field Director for each group of approximately five thousand troops to 'provide advice to military personnel and assistance to the camp recreation hut attendants. The Red Cross will also provide the necessary games, books, magazines, writing papers.'[67]

By the end of 1942 it was being made clear that the Australian Comforts Fund, which had been so proud to welcome the Americans with its services, had a diminished role in American eyes. Its General Secretary was told by the Business Manager of the American Red Cross in Sydney to ignore any requests for sporting equipment that might come from American sources: 'Under our present working agreement with Special Services Department of the United States Army, they assume responsibility for the supplying to American troops of all outdoor athletic equipment such as baseballs, baseball bats, gloves, basketballs, tennis, etcetera.'[68]

The effects of these policies were seen locally as the Americans acquired their own baseball field at North Fremantle and eventually tennis courts at Crawley.[69] If the main general motive of high command in providing such facilities was the maintenance of stability and morale, an important incentive for the men on the spot was the perceived dullness of Perth and, especially, the drabness of Sundays. The very British custom of regarding the Sabbath as a day of rest, and any form of work or commercial entertainment as sinful, was alien to the Americans. It was probably to prevent trouble brewing in idle minds that submariners often had to work on Sundays. For the same reason, the Navy made an occasion out of Sunday lunch, often stretching it through most of the afternoon.[70] It also established a movie theatre to operate on Sundays at its headquarters in the Old Women's Home.[71]

In the host community, not only the cinema but also competitive sport was taboo on Sundays, a tradition perpetuated by institutions such as the Fremantle City Council. Not surprisingly the local newspaper, whose hero-worship of the Americans had begun long before their arrival, was quick to demand changes that would please them. 'Gloomy Sundays Do Not Suit our Yankee Visitors', proclaimed the *Fremantle and Districts Sentinel* in April. 'They are not used to them, and have made out a very good case for reasonable Sunday entertainment for the soldiers and sailors, and we think their requests should be respected and conceded.'[72]

In the following month came evidence that the local council was listening either to the Americans or the *Sentinel*. As it refused a request from the local Christian Brothers School to use a council oval for Sunday sport, it passed a resolution prohibiting organised sports on Sundays, with the proviso that 'such prohibition does not apply to recreational games duly authorised by the Council being played by members of the fighting forces'. A request from the American military to use Fremantle Oval to play football on Sundays was granted under strict conditions: that the matches finished before 4 p.m., that only men in uniform were admitted, and that no admission charges were made.[73]

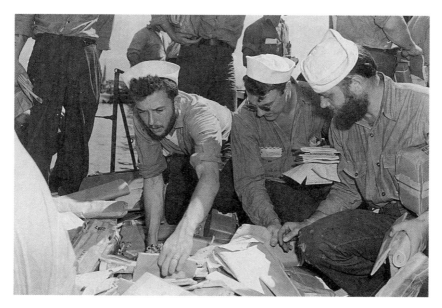

*In isolated WA young Americans were eager for news from home*
(Mask Productions, Perth)

In other ways, too, those concerned to welcome the Americans were bending to the wartime winds of change. All of the many servicemen's facilities in Perth and Fremantle were open on Sundays, most offering meals and other refreshments and several the dancing that was unavailable in commercial venues.[74]

In the eyes of American officialdom Australian-operated facilities, whether on Sundays or throughout the week, were no substitute for those they could control themselves. For a year or so the Navy's Welfare Department organised a number of social occasions for naval personnel, very often at the University. In June 1943 these functions were largely taken over and greatly expanded with the arrival of Jim Purcell as local Field Director of the American Red Cross. The appointment had been made even though the US Army presence in the West was relatively small and short-lived, and Navy numbers fell short of the five thousand specified in the official guidelines for such a post.[75]

With a staff of five, Purcell organised a wide variety of outings, including bus tours to the South West. But by far his most important activity was the establishment of the 'Swan Dive' at the Rowing Club premises on the Barrack Street Jetty. These had been offered to the Americans by the Lord Mayor almost the moment they arrived.

Unlike the unofficial club on ANA premises nearby, which was exclusively for chief petty officers, the Swan Dive was a social club that accepted all Navy personnel. These included men from visiting ships and from the tenders that supplied the submarines, and the administrative personnel permanently stationed in Perth and Fremantle. Even naval personnel of other nationalities were occasionally welcomed as guests. But it was designed for, and mainly used by, the American submariners, who spent up to six weeks a time at sea in very cramped, difficult and dangerous conditions.[76]

The Dive offered a snack bar, rest rooms, a small library, music (usually canned but with live orchestras imported on special occasions) and regular dances, well attended by 'respectable' local young ladies.[77] The snack bar sold such staples of the American diet as hamburgers, hot dogs and milkshakes, as well as beer and other drinks. The club also published a bi-monthly newspaper, the *Porthole*,

*Outside the Swan Dive*
(Pat Tully)

whose pages give a flavour of the efforts that were being made to bring the servicemen into contact with the authentic Australia, with reports of tennis, boating and other sports, and outings to the beach and the bush.

In general, however, despite much continuing goodwill and many individual friendships with local people, American self-sufficiency and self-confidence became less appealing as familiarity grew and the most urgent wartime fears of 1942 faded. An immensely successful facility in the eyes of the Navy and the Lord Mayor, the Swan Dive nevertheless can be used to highlight this growing ambivalence of local attitudes to the American presence. While its social activities reached out into the community, rowing club members were quite hostile to the takeover of their premises and to extensive structural alterations that were supervised by US Navy engineers and took about two months to complete. They were mollified only by eventual assurances that the much improved facilities would be handed over to them when the Americans left.[78]

Perth's growing disillusionment was seen in microcosm at The University of Western Australia. Originally, the arrangements establishing a significant American presence there had seemed satisfactory to all parties involved. The Americans 'expected that the occupancy of these quarters by forces of the United States Navy can not result otherwise than to our mutual benefit',[79] while the University administration was 'only too happy to co-operate at the moment with any of the Forces'.[80]

As the war went on, members of the Engineering Faculty became less willing to cooperate with the visitors, and lobbied the Vice-Chancellor over many months to encourage them to find alternative lodgings. The Americans had been accommodated without question in early 1942, but 'I feel that we overestimated our ability to carry on satisfactorily at that time', wrote the Dean of Engineering a year later.[81] 'When we were asked to accommodate the US personnel we did so with pleasure under the stress of imminent invasion', wrote the Vice-Chancellor, as he passed on the concerns of his Engineering colleagues to the American authorities.[82] After the departure of the Americans, the Engineering Faculty had to wait over twelve months for damage to their building to be repaired.[83]

Eventually the University and other institutions and individuals whose property had been taken over won a victory of sorts. There was considerable argument about whether owners of requisitioned buildings should pay for improvements carried out by the Americans. Some of the argument turned around the question of whether such improvements were permanent fixtures. The US Navy was successful in its claim that sanitary facilities and hot water supplies were not permanent improvements to the University's Engineering Building but 'fitted up in a temporary steel hut erected on a concrete floor' and therefore removable. But it was also eventually agreed that owners of the Nedlands Park Hotel, University Boat Club building and Old Women's Home 'cannot be forced to contribute towards the cost of the improvements effected on behalf of the US Navy...'. The most that was conceded from the Australian side was that 'should the owners claim for damage done to the premises during the period of occupation, an endeavour would be made to offset the value of the improvements against the claim as far as possible'. But this could only be by mutual agreement. There was no obligation on owners to accept improvements, whether or not they were of use to them after the resumption of the premises.[84]

Perhaps the most significant aspect of this debate was that it was taking place in March 1943. Both the argument itself and the legalistic terms of its settlement were already a far cry from the atmosphere in which the American arrival had been welcomed so warmly. The visitors had quickly made a controversial physical impact on the University environment by building roads, removing trees and digging trenches before asking for permission. As early as September 1942 the Vice-Chancellor was complaining to the American commanding officer that the Navy had built a shed that blocked the road to the Agriculture Building and, in making an alternative road, had torn up reticulation pipes.[85] In October the Americans asked to use part of the University grounds as a softball diamond, promising 'in the event that this permission is granted the area will be kept clean and in shipshape condition at all times'.[86] Exactly a year later University staff were reporting that, as a result of the softball, 'the oval is suffering badly. The surface is badly cut and several holes have been dug'. The Americans had ignored a letter of complaint.[87] University authorities were also complaining that 'we are increasingly pestered by broken bottles left amongst our grounds by US Navy personnel'.[88]

Over the same period the social impact of the Americans on the University had become equally controversial. There were complaints from staff and students about the sentries posted at the entrances to the Engineering Building, who prevented student access to classes and delayed delivery trucks.[89] There was indignation that students' bicycles had been stolen from outside University buildings. After an American officer was seen riding one of them, the Vice-Chancellor asked that students should be allowed to enter Naval areas to look for their bikes. The American response was that a permit for such entry would be granted to 'a policeman armed with necessary descriptions to inspect bicycles located on this base'.[90]

In November 1943 Vice-Chancellor Currie took up the most sensitive social issue of all. Tactfully prefacing his letter to the American authorities with praise for the generally 'exemplary behaviour' of their men, he continued:

> Recently, however, there have been instances of enlisted men of the U.S. Navy in our grounds at night accosting some of our women students and causing them considerable agitation… Enlisted men have been hanging around the main buildings at night, peering into library windows…and into the women's end of the Guild building.[91]

The US authorities responded by declaring the parts of the University grounds not occupied by the Navy out of bounds to their personnel, unless they were on official duty or accompanied by a student or member of staff.[92] But neither this measure nor the deployment of an American shore patrol in the University grounds

*UWA: informality in the grounds*
(Lt. Wiegand, USN, Matilda Bay Catalina Base 1942–43: UWA Archives)

*UWA: even flying personnel needed bikes*
(Lt. Wiegand, USN, Matilda Bay Catalina Base 1942–43: UWA Archives)

solved the problem. Early in 1944 the Vice-Chancellor was complaining that a woman student walking to the tennis courts had been alarmed when an American sailor had emerged from the shrubbery in front of her and started to remove his clothes: 'Nothing else happened —but the incident was to her unsavoury.'[93] A month later there were complaints of two more cases of 'molestation of women students': 'In each case the girl was cycling down through the grounds along a road flanked on one side by the wooden buildings and on the other by small trees. The girl was accosted and pushed from her bicycle and generally rough handled.'[94]

The Americans' quest for female company at their Crawley base involved more than women students. Caretakers were concerned about the activities of Americans meeting girlfriends off the buses that stopped outside the University. 'The couples have not been very particular about their behaviour in front of the public gaze,' wrote the

Vice-Chancellor, 'and this has hurt the caretakers' sensibilities... Perhaps they could make their tryst in a more secluded spot.'[95] Even Bill Barker, an American who was largely oblivious to the University community, recalled that the authorities had become concerned with the way some of his compatriots were sharing sleeping bags with their girlfriends in the quieter parts of the campus.[96]

However offensive such behaviour might have been to some locals, they can hardly have been surprised about it. As the next chapter will show in detail, the Americans' relationship with the female population was by far the most important aspect of their social impact on Western Australia.

# FLEETING ATTRACTION

*Chapter Seven*

## GIRL QUESTIONS

RELATIONS WITH LOCAL WOMEN were at the heart of the American social impact on the Perth metropolitan area, and on Albany in its short, intense period of contact. For many women the newcomers personified the dream world of Hollywood—handsome men in tailored uniforms bearing expensive gifts and bouquets of flowers, and speaking in accents that were simultaneously both exotic and familiar. In the view of other observers, especially men, the Americans displayed a mixture of brashness and vulnerability and manners both courtly and crude. They also carried money printed and minted in ways so mysterious to them that its expenditure seemed as unreal as their futures were uncertain. But the cliche 'over-paid, over-sexed and over here' is as inadequate as it is hackneyed. Sexual liaisons, ranging from the wildly romantic to the coldly commercial, involved ecstasy and exploitation on both sides of the gender divide. And they affected many more people than the couples who clung together for a few impassioned hours or a lifetime.

Accounts of vivid, often traumatic experience are both important and potentially misleading illustrations of the wartime atmosphere. It would be a distortion to omit the distress caused to individual women

*Handsome Americans were not always in tailored uniforms*
*(Currie Hall, UWA)*

and their families by relationships with Americans that turned sour, but it is no less a distortion to see the American impact as an amalgam of sad stories and moralising distaste. The historical record is always more likely to be swollen by complaint and controversy than the gratitude of the contented. And while the sheer variety of individual women's experience defies easy generalisation, the most measurable evidence lies in statistics about illegitimacy, abortion and venereal disease that confound contemporary fears of wholesale social disorder.

When the Australian Chief Publicity Censor, E. G. Bonney, set out guidelines to the press in the hope of minimising tension between American and Australian servicemen, he was also implicitly outlining the most obvious reasons why the Americans were welcomed so warmly by Australian women. He was especially hostile to reports that could cause Australian soldiers to feel 'eclipsed by their American allies, by reason of their affluence, their personal good looks and their ability to drink without getting invariably bellicose'.[1]

The kind of resentment Bonney was predicting was expressed by a 'Returned Soldier (this war)' in a letter to the *Daily News* in March 1942, at a time when the press was still forbidden to refer to Americans by name:

> Returned soldiers have found themselves spurned and passed over in favour of non-Australians. I myself have walked the streets of Perth. I have been snarled at and insulted. I have had non-Australians held up to me as examples of exemplary behaviour… Every show I have been to has been full of non-Australians and their girl friends (local).[2]

At this period, however, as we have seen, most Australian soldiers were overseas and their absence was undoubtedly a further reason for the American appeal to local girls. By the time they returned in numbers in late 1942 and early 1943, the Americans had used all the advantages outlined by censor Bonney to exploit their distinctive sex appeal.

Affluence was a major factor, with rates of pay for American servicemen generally twice the Australian levels. The Australian Government rejected demands that, because of the inflationary pressures, the pay of American servicemen should be held to the equivalent of similar Australian ranks, the balance to be paid on their return to the United States. The Prime Minister declared that 'the manner in which the Government of the United States arranges to pay its own forces is entirely a matter for it'.[3]

The American military equivalent of an Australian private was paid the wage of an Australian captain. The differentials were particularly great in Western Australia because the bulk of American servicemen were submariners and Navy aircrew, both privileged groups receiving 50 per cent higher wages because of their hazardous work. One man who became particularly aware of the discrepancy was Cecil Anderson, the only Australian to serve for some time on an American submarine—and hence the only Australian member of the latterday US Sub. Vets Association. As an Australian Captain, receiving an extra £1 sterling per day for his special service with the Americans, he considered himself financially well off, until he found the African-American mess stewards were better paid than he was.[4]

The Americans' affluence quickly gave them a stranglehold on retail outlets and services most relevant to romance and entertainment. Some shops illegally reserved certain goods for Americans, knowing they would pay more generously for them.[5] Florists, waiters and landlords also frequently overcharged Americans ignorant of Australian prices. But taxi drivers were most notorious of all.

Most regular taxi drivers had been young men who joined the military at the outbreak of hostilities. Sharp-thinking profiteers had bought licences cheaply, and, searching for 'Yankee cream', they gave the visiting servicemen preference over Australians.[6] To many young women, one of the many novelties of associating with Americans was the opportunity to ride in a taxi for the first time. For Pat Catt, on the other hand, marriage to an Australian sailor ruled out any chance of

*Romance did not always begin with flowers and chocolates*
(Mask Productions, Perth)

travel by taxi to her honeymoon hotel, not an entirely disagreeable situation since American monopoly of accommodation meant there were no rooms available north of the river anyway. The main thing another woman feared about pregnancy was going into labour and being unable to find a taxi to reach hospital in time.[7]

The Yanks made the most of their privileged status. As one of the self-confessed highly paid 'Catalina millionaires' recalled, the taxi drivers, especially at first, were quite happy to be paid in cigarettes, which he could obtain for as little as 'a nickel a pack'. For a carton the drivers would take him anywhere and do almost any favour he asked. In 1944, when he began more often paying in money, it was just as easy to buy services. 'A pound didn't mean much to us and, if you gave them a pound they'd go get you a sack of beer or something. I don't know what the beer was but it was really inexpensive... They'd probably pay a few bob for it and come back and keep the change'.[8]

Oblivious to the value of local money, the Americans were probably equally oblivious to the effects they were having on both the local economy and local attitudes. In the last months of the war an American consular report on retail prices in Perth concluded:

> Shortage of taxis and American servicemen competing with one another for cabs, have resulted in the most flagrant abuses in prices charged. Fantastic charges have been reported such as ten pounds for a thirty shilling ride (Fremantle–Perth or vice versa). Frequently *each person* in a five-person party will be called upon for the full fare. Almost invariably, unless dealing with a reputable taxi company, up to 100% excess is charged. This situation is due to the reluctance of passengers to make an issue with police. No meters are installed.

Despite such exploitation, the Americans had established the previously unknown tipping system: although 'one shilling would be ample for any trip in the city', they frequently gave more.[9]

Even outside the metropolitan area taxi drivers showed similar opportunism, although perhaps the Americans were less free with their money to judge from reports from Albany in 1942. On 20 April a number of complaints about overcharging prompted the mayor to decide that a scale of charges would be put at various starting and stopping places: 'Then if people wished to pay more in their anxiety to get to places that would be their own funeral.' Although on this occasion no mention was made of Americans, a week later two US Navy personnel complained that they had been charged £8, or double the normal fare, for a trip along the coast to the town of Denmark. The driver's explanation that he had charged the extra amount because he intended to return to collect the men sounded less than convincing, but eventually charges were dropped after a refund was made.[10]

The American servicemen also enjoyed better working conditions than their Australian counterparts. The United States Navy had generous leave provisions and facilities. Submariners typically had one- or two-week breaks between long tours of duty at sea, and Catalina crews every third day off duty, after flying and attending to maintenance problems on the previous two.[11] Both groups had unlimited access to the city hotels the Americans had rented to the virtual exclusion of all others. According to the same consular report, 'hotels are now extremely reluctant to serve meals to persons not registered as guests, on account of shortage of dining-room staff'.[12] As we have seen, even enlisted Catalina men could afford to pay long-term rentals on rooms in the city closer to bars, night life and the enraptured section of the female population.[13]

As Chief Censor Bonney's instructions had suggested, the majority of Australian servicemen could not compete for the affections of those local girls who were impressed by the fancy presents and expensive entertainment that the Americans could provide. At the same time the air of affluence contributed in other ways to what the Australian Army hierarchy referred to as the 'girl question' in a late 1942 report on violence between its men and Americans.[14]

In many cases the 'personal good looks' that Bonney had seen as a threat to Australian male self-esteem were a matter of clothes rather than physique. Again and again women's reminiscence about the period confirms the frequent contemporary newspaper stress on the stylish, clean cut appearance of the men in American naval uniform. It has been suggested that many women assumed initially that all the Americans were officers, since all wore ties, whereas only Australian Army officers did.[15] In time quite a number of women made distinctions between gentlemanly officers and brasher enlisted men; but only a few encountered former American recruiting officers like John Battle, who could tell them of the many unkempt illiterates he had seen transformed by haircuts, discipline and the magical uniform.[16]

But even if local women were disappointed to discover the reality beneath the outward appearance, they had more reasons than one to undress a Yank. The American uniform was made from superior quality material, tailored and far more attractive than the baggy, rough Australian issue. The cloth of American uniforms was highly sought after by Australian girls, who used it to make themselves suits of much better quality than those that could be bought with clothing coupons.[17]

This was no trivial issue, for the American arrival not only coincided with rationing but was swiftly followed by Government attempts to dictate economical styles of clothing. Nobody was fooled by references to 'smart spring frocks' into thinking that there was anything stylish about 'Fashions for Victory'. The Government had decided to simplify clothing 'in order to secure the utmost economy in the use of available materials so that the maximum amount of wearing apparel can be produced'. It wanted to 'eliminate types of garments, trimmings and useless adornments, which are not essential and which are absorbing labour that is urgently needed for essential war-time tasks'.[18]

With their clothes, their money, their fascinating accents and their general good looks, the Americans clearly had many assets to appeal to young women largely deprived of local male company. It is not hard to understand why the fond recollections of many women long afterwards were sometimes tinged with guilt that they had so much enjoyed the war while their menfolk were absent in dangerous situations.

The two social clubs that came to operate within a short distance of each other near the Barrack Street Jetty represented opposite extremes of

**FASHIONS FOR VICTORY**

These men season's styles conform to the Fashions for Victory announced by the Minister for War Organisation of Industry (Mr. Dedman) on Sunday night. Mr. Dedman announced that simplification of clothing for men, women and children is necessary to conserve available materials so that the maximum amount of essential wearing apparel can be produced. Victory fashions were carefully selected by the National Council of Clothes Styling, a committee of designers, clothing trade representatives and consumers' representatives.

The Minister for War Organisation of Industry (Mr. Dedman) tells his secretary that double-breasted coats are now out. The "Victory" suit worn by Mr. Dedman is a two-piece suit with no buttons on the sleeves, no cuffs on the trousers, and the trouser bottoms limited to 19-inch width. The new Fashions for Victory for men, women and children were announced by Mr. Dedman in a broadcast last Sunday night.

These smart spring frocks, designed to conform to the new Fashions for Victory stylings show that there is plenty of scope for individuality. From left:—(1) Nün-fitting two-piece suit shows that maximum sweep of skirt permits pleating, five buttons being allowed for fastening; (2) forking and shirring are permissible if used for shaping; (3) tailored frock for every-day wear has flared skirt and belt not more than two inches wide.

*(West Australian Newspapers)*

American interaction with Perth's women. The wild party that preceded the establishment of the chief petty officers' club left the ANA sailing premises looking—in the words of the club secretary—'a bit like the back end of a brothel'. While the club's cleaner was disturbed at the sight of 'women's pants everywhere', secretary Harvey's only concern was his argument with the police, which was essentially 'because of the sheilas'.[19]

Once that issue was resolved and the way was cleared for the long-term lease of the premises, the Americans' continuing taste for 'the sheilas' was a source of entertainment for Harvey and his fellow-Australians. They would lean over the balcony in their half of the club to watch for marauding police and to check the passengers emerging from each arriving taxi. While not much could be seen in the gloom, it required little imagination to visualise the broad pattern of Australian–American relations that was unfolding in the bamboo scrub in the middle distance. According to folk memory, only one couple had to be extracted from the gloom, removed by ambulance and unfolded paramedically.[20]

Such outdoor frolics were not to the taste of that redoubtable chief petty officer, Mac, but perhaps partly his fault, since the only double bed he would tolerate on the premises was his own. Installed in the enclosed compartment built for him by Navy carpenters on the American half of the club balcony, the bed could often be heard but was rarely seen, as Mac's privacy was protected by an artfully concealed entrance to his executive office.[21]

According to Syd Harvey, the chief petty officers' club was essentially about women, gambling and drinking. By contrast the Red Cross's Swan Dive advertised a much more complete range of social opportunities in its *Porthole*. The Navy provided food, transport, guns and ammunition for kangaroo hunts; and also organised young lady companions for bike-riding, horse-riding, boating, Saturday afternoon tennis and beach parties. No doubt the rugged expeditions to the bush appealed to some, but there must be a question mark over the number of red-blooded young Americans who leapt at the chance of an excursion sixty miles northeast of Perth 'to see a sheep being sheared'. It is no real insult to sheep to imagine that 'the flashing smile and feminine curves that flit around' the Swan Dive at its nightly dances were more warmly appreciated than the scrawny legs and cropped belly of an upended merino.[22]

Certainly, Jim Purcell, American Red Cross field director, was in no doubt that the main attractions of the Swan Dive for the submariners and other Navy personnel were the hostesses who were always there to provide companionship. He had about sixty girls on his books, although most nights there would only be about thirty or forty of them at the club. Perhaps aware of what might emerge from the nearby bamboo, he screened them carefully to eliminate any hangers-on who might be prostitutes. His claim that there was no shortage of respectable young Perth women eager to meet American servicemen seems to be borne out by the decorous pages of the *Porthole*. In contrast to the high-speed liaisons transacted in and around the ANA club, the Dive featured 'Hostess Balls': every twelve weeks girls who attended twelve consecutive balls 'are honoured and ask the boys to the dance'.[23]

These impressions are both confirmed and qualified by the recollections of one of the young hostesses. Interviewed for the position by Miss Dumas, a local lady of some formality, she was required to wear hat and gloves in accordance with the dictates of polite fashion; but she also had to promise to learn to 'jitterbug'. She managed to do so quite quickly, without ever achieving the extravagant contortions she had seen at the Embassy Ballroom. And if that experience made this American innovation seem risqué, she was left in no doubt that the Swan Dive was not intended to be a rival pick-up place to Perth's most celebrated pleasure palace. Girls were forbidden to leave the premises with any of the men, a restriction that did not overly concern the novice hostess, who was not looking for anything more intense than the dancing she was soon enjoying with no fewer than five regular partners.[24]

Whatever the house rules of this official facility, there was of course nothing to stop more rapid relationships developing between individuals meeting there, or in numerous other locations, ranging from private parties to public dance halls, from Kings Park to the Perth Zoo.

*The Swan Dive: no shortage of respectable young women*
(Pat Tully)

And there was no shortage of places for them to go to become more closely acquainted. At one point in 1943 the Security Service became irate that American officers were entertaining females on board their submarine every night of the week. This, the Service suggested with unintended humour, was because passes to the wharf area were 'being issued promiscuously'. A subsequent signal from the Admiral 'that no Officer was to entertain any civilian on board the submarine more than twice a month' was probably not a big obstacle to burgeoning romances, given the Navy's virtual monopoly of Perth's hotel accommodation through most of the war.[25]

Any romance, however, could mean different things to different people, both the two participants or outsiders who observed it with emotions ranging from enthusiasm through genuine concern to outright envy. These varying tendencies, common in any circumstances, were accentuated by cultural differences. Wherever they went, the Americans displayed a style that made traditional Australian courtship seem casual to the point of crudity.

It may have been youthful rebellion that made Pat White of Subiaco glad to defy her father's injunction never to go out with an American. Certainly it was not infatuation that prompted her to accept a date with the less than charisimatic Ben, who could jive but had no idea about 'proper dancing'. But to be picked up in a taxi and weighed down with a corsage of flowers was treatment unimaginable before the Americans came and unforgettable after they left. Pat's reactions may have been shared by many, but not by the writer Dorothy Hewett: 'I scorn the Yanks, pasty faced boys who seem to think an orchid or a box of chocolates can buy them anything... Nobody can buy me... I prefer Australians, who give neither orchids nor chocolates, who are inarticulate but seem to promise love and even silent understanding.'[26]

Hewett was probably ahead of her time in finding the rituals of American courtship insultingly patronising. Certainly there was no dawning feminist sensibility in the Australian male view expressed by Syd Harvey: 'The Yanks were very popular with the girls—they used to go around with a bunch of flowers in their hand and we used to think that was bloody stupid.'[27]

*Perth Zoo: girls were not the only attractive locals*
(Mask Productions, Perth)

Both Syd and Pat White would agree, however, about one thing. 'They had all the money in the world', said Syd. To Pat, who even fifty years later could remember the prices, to the last halfpenny, of nearly every item in the grocery shop where she worked, the Yanks were remarkable for 'all the money they were throwing around'. They were also throwing around cigarettes, a habit which impressed many, but not non-smoker Pat. Her father would know his veto on dates with Americans had been ignored if she passed on to him the carton of Lucky Strike that accompanied Ben's floral offering.[28]

As a virtual teetotaller, Pat White was amazed but not excited by the whisky and brandy bottles decorating every table in the 'Silver Dollar', one of the new 'cabarets' that the American presence had spawned in central Perth by the end of 1942. She was prepared to 'make a horrible fool' of herself by trying to jive, but not by drinking the whisky pressed on her by her escort. He may have got 'fuller and fuller', as the evening wore on, but he remained far from legless, for the last Pat saw of him he was running alongside her sluggish tram to Subiaco, pleading with her for the date to continue.[29]

Ben's less than suave performance is not the only hint that American affluence and charm were no more than flowery introductions to a familiar masculine agenda. The first tour of duty in 1943 for Catalina pilot Bill Barker was 'strictly bars and going to girls' houses'. It was a routine punctuated, but hardly interrupted, by work and illness: a spell in Geraldton hospital with flu was enlivened by 'a little red-head nurse'. In Perth, girlfriends were dated and discarded with a casualness only once seriously challenged. Awakened in his Quonset hut at the University by an unwilling reject, he was embarrassed by the presence of several interested colleagues in adjacent beds. After his half-hearted response to the young woman's advances he was known for some time as 'Kiss-me-properly' Barker.[30]

In her eagerness to pursue a Yank, that young woman was typical of many. 'My, this is a friendly country!' was the first reaction of Jack Glotzbach, an enlisted radio operator on USS *Pelius*, who could scarcely believe his eyes at the throng of girls awaiting the ship at the Fremantle docks. Within days of the American arrival the *Daily News* was quoting a chief inspector of police that 'some girls are getting out of hand in city streets and it has to be stopped'. Two sisters, eighteen and twenty, had been charged with disorderly conduct after being seen 'arm-in-arm with two visiting servicemen, singing and dancing' and bumping deliberately into passers-by.[31]

Very similar scenes were occurring in Albany at this same period. On 23 March 1942, when the American arrival had still not been officially announced, the *Albany Advertiser* commented: 'Many of the visitors who have been in our streets recently must be fed up with being baled up every few yards by mostly youngsters seeking autographs... What the bigger girls and women do—well that's their business.' A week later, when it was at last permissible to refer to Americans, the paper seemed to think that what women did was perhaps its business after all:

Of course it is for the young women of our town to help extend a welcome to the gallant lads of the USA…but those very things that we are fighting for—the sanctity of our homes and purity and honour of our women folk—in the glamour of the moment and newness of the situation are likely to become sullied by the actions of the fickleheaded.[32]

Phyllis Vaughan, who could only say 'Mmmmm!!' when she first glimpsed her future American husband, had no doubt that 'during wartime sex becomes so much more important than it is ordinarily; it was just amazing to see this happen'. Feeling very lucky that she had found Ralph Gurley and enjoyed instant and prolonged mutual attraction, she was very sorry for the young girls who 'held out' and were quickly 'dropped off' by the insatiable visitors.[33]

There were so many Americans for those few months in Albany that shore leave had to be rationed to one night in three, so that the more adventurous girls 'didn't get entirely worn out'. The arrangement, however, allowed those with stamina to run two and three boyfriends at a time. Especially friendly in this way were many

*Yes, it was a friendly country*
(Mask Productions, Perth)

girls who worked at the local woollen mill. Constantly receiving flowers from the newly established local florist, they were being courted for the first time in their lives by men who made them feel special in a way Australians had never done. When the *Pelius* left Albany many of them followed it to Fremantle. Twice they had to be hauled back by police to keep the mill in business.[34]

Although there was the potential for some women to be offended by unwanted attentions, there is little evidence of this being a major problem in Albany. One mother of teenage children, who played piano at a canteen three nights a week, was initially annoyed one evening to be propositioned outside a hotel by a drunken American. But when he arrived at the canteen some hours later and told her it was his twenty-first birthday, she asked him to tea the next day and baked him a cake. In one of life's freakish coincidences her daughter met this same American by chance on a visit to the United States more than fifty years later.[35]

Albany people on the whole were conscious of the distinction between American officers and enlisted men, not least because the two groups were required to use different facilities for dances held at the same time to keep them apart: the Town Hall for officers and the Oddfellows Hall for the men. But although it was the enlisted men whose libido was rationed to one night in three on the town, and whose absence threatened wartime production of wool, the officers had very similar interests in mind. The few houses they had rented in Albany were stocked with liquor, said Phyllis Gurley, who married one of them, because they were 'after the women'.[36]

On the other hand, Mrs Marjorie Ward was more conscious of different behaviour by officers and enlisted men staying at her Derward Hotel in Murray Street, Perth. Although she had been immensely relieved by the sense of security the American arrival had brought, she became 'quite fed up with the girls flocking around them'. It was hard to know whether to blame the girls, whose boyfriends had all gone, or the Americans themselves. For the most part, the officers were 'very nice' and well behaved. But the enlisted men included 'a lot of small town fellows who'd never been away from

*Far from the front in Albany*
(Mask Productions, Perth)

their home towns before'. These men 'went a bit crazy. They were young and would drink and they wanted the girls.'[37]

Going down to the dining-room of a morning she would often discover that waitresses had disappeared. Sometimes they were discovered upstairs after being out all night with a couple of Yanks, and she would have to drag them under the shower to wake them up. A nursemaid employed to care for her children had suddenly gone off with an American. Reminiscing in 1994 in her Nedlands home, Mrs Ward acknowledged that such behaviour would now seem less remarkable, but 'we were rather moral in those days and had a different attitude to it'.[38]

Certainly conventional morality was cracking under the strain of the American presence, not least in the Nedlands area itself. Bill Barker recalled talk of 'pretty wild' parties, fuelled by beer, organised in a house near the University campus by one known only as 'Grandma' and attended by girls young enough, but far too numerous, to be her granddaughters.[39]

It was not here but in Mount Street, Perth, that the war's most notorious sexual escapade took place. Whether invented or merely reported by the local scandal sheet, the *Mirror*, the story of women's breasts dangled in champagne, and a nipple bitten off by an American, was quickly and widely believed, not only throughout the metropolitan area but, within twenty-four hours, in both Geraldton and Albany, thanks to the miracles of the 'bush telegraph'. According to Syd Harvey, the women who partied with such intensity were not prostitutes, any more than were those the Yanks brought to his club, but the 'pick of the town'.[40] This was an assessment broadly in line with the memories of more sedate women, who watched, with a mixture of disapproval and envy, the sensuous dancing of young girls of 'good family' in the tight confines and loose atmosphere of American-dominated cabarets and ballrooms.[41]

Yet many local girls, and many Americans, were far from wild. For Pat White and Pat Matthews the war years were a time of unprecedented and unrepeated enjoyment, marked by the absence of local boys, the presence of the Yanks and the relaxation of convention. But Pat White settled for an Australian sailor husband after Ben's footsteps faded into the Subiaco blackout. Her continuing involvement with Americans was through the blossoming relationship between her widowed sister, Doreen, and John Battle from the Subiaco torpedo base.[42]

This romance may have been initially opposed by the girls' father, but it was conducted with a sincerity that challenged both his stuffy conventions and others' easy generalisations about the American pursuit of pleasure. By the time romance became marriage John had been fully accepted as a second father by Doreen's young daughter, Lois. Staying with the two adults in Rockingham, Lois provided her own jolt to conventional assumptions by telling fellow hotel guests that she was sharing her Mum and Dad's honeymoon.[43]

For her part, Pat Matthews found that many Americans had much more than sex on their minds, as they enjoyed a taste of the home life they had recently lost by visiting her family, sometimes in groups. The outside deck of the Swan Dive on a warm summer's evening had an atmosphere made for romance. But despite the easy opportunities to pursue it extramurally with one or more of her dancing partners, Pat's fondest memories of the Dive were of the nightly entertainment by professional dancers and the officially organised group excursions. There were river trips to Point Walter, with dancing at the rotunda. And there was the novelty of American-style hay-rides, sometimes in a cart drawn by a Clydesdale horse, sometimes by truck, travelling as far afield as Wanneroo, but always culminating in a barbecue.[44]

Perhaps Pat Matthews was unusually naive in seeing a roll in the hay in such literal terms. It was, she admitted, long after the war that she became aware that she may have shared floor space with prostitutes in places such as the Embassy Ballroom. And she had no idea at the time of what went on in Roe Street.[45] Certainly there were other girls who 'lost their innocence' much more quickly. Confronted with American charm and money, even the most protected of local girls could be led astray. Syd Harvey recalled a 'prim and proper' assistant in a jeweller's shop—a girl he was sure had 'never read a

*The Swan Dive: nightly entertainment*
(Pat Tully)

naughty book'—serving an American who was 'looking for a watch for one of his sheilas'. Within minutes he had bought one for her as well. 'She finished up with a Yank and with a fat tummy—that was the way it worked in those days.'[46]

This young woman was merely one of the inevitable casualties from hurried romances, brief sexual flings and deep attachments to men soon temporarily or permanently absent. Just as inevitably, the hostility of fathers and other family members was often part of the pain endured by those exploited, deserted, jilted or bereaved. There was also criticism of married women 'making themselves available' to Americans while their husbands were overseas; and there were terrible scenes when husbands returned.

One woman considered herself fortunate that she had understanding friends to give her shelter and support from the ire of her husband when he returned unexpectedly from the Middle East and asked searching questions about the 'submarine pin on my left breast'. One such friend was her husband's own sister, who perhaps took her

Excursion to the bush from the Swan Dive
(West Australian Newspapers)

side because she 'had quite an interesting American herself at the time'.[47]

A letter to the American Consulate in May 1942, just two months after the Navy's arrival, from a husband who was not overseas, illustrates the turmoil that could overtake even the most respectable families. Expressing concern for the 'ultimate happiness' of his 'young wife' and two small children, a South-West doctor begged the Consul to inquire 'at once and *ever so discreetly*' whether a certain officer on US Submarine *Swordfish* was married or not. He had been 'loath to write about a personal matter' but this was 'a most urgent matter' and 'there is no level to which I would not stoop to be sure of my own continued sanity'.[48]

Consternation of a different kind affected a Perth family. Mason Turner was approached by the father of a woman wanting to marry a US serviceman. His concern was that she was unaware she had been adopted. After some correspondence with his Sydney superiors, the Consul was able to approve the acceptance of a birth extract rather than the full birth certificate as part of the formalities for approval of her visa application.[49]

Cases such as these illustrate the inevitable complications that could beset American relations with local women. The only trend they represent is the certainty that the American Consul was more likely to hear complaints and problems than expressions of satisfaction. It is impossible to weigh accurately the impression they give of dis-enchantment and distress compared to the obvious pleasure enjoyed by those who found romance, sexual initiation or lifelong partners among the Americans. But at least some perspective can be provided by considering the preoccupations of those most concerned about sexual and associated moral issues in the fractured social environment of the era.

At the time of the American arrival in March 1942, the wartime atmosphere was already giving new urgency to longstanding campaigns by women from middle class and professional back-grounds to combat promiscuity, prostitution and venereal disease. As purveyors of welfare and advocates of reform, they felt a new sense of urgency about their traditional roles as moral guardians. But in these early months of 1942 they rarely blamed the Americans, even as they acknowledged the unsettling effects of their presence.

The Women's Service Guild (WSG) was an organisation that had been unrelenting over the previous three months in its attempts to shore up a crumbling moral order. On 20 March the Guild's state executive had welcomed the success of the campaign to close liquor outlets at 6 p.m.—a measure finally implemented two days before—

but then moved on to discuss the need for voluntary women police to 'help in controlling the young girls in the streets'.[50]

In the following week the Guild's concerns were intensified when a young girl was found dead 'through overintoxication' at the Ritz Coffee Palace. The inquest into the death of fifteen-year-old Lesley Essex was given some prominence in the *Daily News*. A nineteen-year-old girl testified that she and Lesley had met two sailors in St Georges Terrace in the late evening and gone to the Ritz to drink whisky and rum. Aroused by the Town Hall clock striking 4 a.m., the girl found that the sailors had disappeared and Lesley was lying face down across a bed.[51]

The WSG's state secretary wrote to the Perth Town Clerk expressing concern. Were premises such as the Ritz registered as boarding houses and subject to council inspection? The Town Clerk's reply was evasive and far from reassuring. It acknowledged that a fifteen-year-old girl had died 'through suffocation while she was in an intoxicated condition in the company of sailors' but concluded that the room had been let to two sailors and 'the proprietor cannot be held responsible for what goes on…'.[52]

Nothing was said to suggest that the sailors were American, least of all by the WSG state executive. At the same time as it discussed the need for an 'indignation meeting' to protest about 'young girls being taken into hostels and given liquor', it commended American troops' behaviour to the Australian authorities. No doubt recalling the mayhem that Australian troops had caused in the metropolitan area in the first two years of the war, the executive agreed to write to the Minister of the Army suggesting he create a Department of Morale, similar to that in the US Army. It was suggested that this department 'was responsible for the splendid behaviour of the US men stationed in Australia'.[53]

A favourite campaign of the Guild and many other women's groups was for a substantial force of women police.[54] On 8 April the Women Justices Association of WA sent a deputation to the Minister for Police to discuss 'the whole problem' of the 'behaviour and morals in our streets and public places', arguing that more women police were essential.[55] This, however, was an issue of some controversy among women, for a number of groups such as the Modern Women's Club, the Women's Progressive League, Labor Women and even the Mothers' Union agreed that 'extra policewomen are very much needed', but insisted that they should be paid officers rather than volunteers.[56] But at this point, in the early months of 1942, none of the protagonists levelled censure against the newly arrived Americans, as they discussed the need to 'clean up the city streets at night'[57] or 'to consider the economic conditions of women coming under the supervision of the vice squad'.[58] In June 1942 the refined WSG had no qualms about forming a 'Younger Set' of two hundred girls over the age of sixteen to help with the reception of servicemen and act as dance partners.[59]

In combating vice, women were as concerned with physical as moral health. On 15 September, under the headline 'Control of Venereal Disease', the WSG's *Dawn* reported that a special unit of plain-clothes police had been formed in Perth to work in cooperation with other services 'with the object of dealing with certain types of women in Perth streets'. Its purpose was 'to clean up the city streets at night and to combat the spread of disease'. Since its introduction a month earlier forty-three women had been charged under the vagrancy sections of the Police Act. Some cases involved fifteen- and sixteen-year-old children.[60]

Although the *Dawn* still made no reference to Americans, the US Consul had by now become nervous about the potential for scandal. He had also become a touch irritated that it took a week's correspondence to find out what the age of consent was in Western Australia. On 9 September he had written to the WA Solicitor-General asking whether 'statutory rape' existed in the state and if so what was 'the specified age'? Evidently unwilling to give a straight answer that would show he understood this distinctive American terminology, the Solicitor-General replied that rape was a crime under the Criminal Code—which should be consulted for a precise definition. Pressed to say whether a person could be prosecuted 'for seducing a woman under any specific age', the Solicitor-General eventually revealed that 'consent by a girl is no defence in cases of unlawful carnal knowledge or indecent dealing where she is under 16; when she is over 16 proof of consent is a good defence'.[61]

This official advice was received on 15 September, and a memorandum to his Sydney superiors on the same day almost certainly explains why Consul Turner had sought it. Two US seamen, Hupt and Woodman, from the submarine tender *Holland* at Fremantle, had been jailed at Kalgoorlie because they were travelling with two fifteen-year-old girls. It was not this fact alone that made the two men rather inept deserters, for they also drew attention to themselves by attempting to borrow money from an American resident of Kalgoorlie to get them to Melbourne. Put on a train for Perth instead, the four were removed at Coolgardie, the girls for their own protection and the seamen to be jailed pending the arrival of US Navy guards.[62] The case received no publicity, but it was one example of a trend in which Americans were coming to be seen more regularly as a threat to public morality, especially through the effects they were having on young girls.

The trend was seen most clearly in various sections of the Police Department's Annual Report for 1942. In the section dealing with work performed by women constables, Chief Inspector Doyle referred to 'the great number of the members of the War Services in the city and suburbs, who are to be seen about the cabarets, dance-halls and hotels with young girls and young married women'. Many of the girls had been 'accepting money from service men and living with them in rooms'.[63]

Although these comments could have embraced other nationalities, the well-known predominance of Americans in the public facilities named makes it especially a comment on their influence. As the Chief Inspector of Licensed Premises pointed out in his section of the report, cabarets 'have come into existence recently, principally due to an influx of American troops. Eight are known at the present time. Some of the cabarets admit only officers and their friends.'[64]

In the same annual report, the Commissioner of Police complained that 'numbers of young females are parading the streets at all hours of the night'. The introduction of six o'clock closing of hotels in March had not solved problems associated with alcohol, thanks to the opening of 'a number of cabarets and night clubs': 'The evil effects of this uncontrolled drinking has [sic] been very apparent and in numerous instances disastrous to young females.' Among the other factors that the Commissioner noted in explaining the prevalence of drinking were 'the temperament of citizens changing owing to war conditions', the presence of 'hundreds, frequently thousands of troops in the city' and 'Allied forces with money to burn and looking for ways to spend it'.[65]

Not surprisingly, in the face of this large-scale challenge to public morality and safety, there was great concern over the threat of venereal disease (VD). In the eyes of the police, 'the need for a suitable institution where girls and young women could be placed for treatment of venereal disease is extreme'.[66] In October 1942 the WSG organised a conference on 'social diseases'[67] and in November the Women Justices Association sent a deputation to the Minister for Health to discuss the threat of VD.[68] But all this activism was a mixture of understandable fears, impractical suggestions and inaccurate analysis.

Concerns for those drawn into promiscuity and semi-prostitution were given some credence by official health statistics. Despite an overall decline in VD, these reveal a complete reversal in the relative incidence between the sexes. From 675 reported cases of gonorrhoea in 1939, only 134 victims were female. By 1943, there were 308 female victims from a total of 565.[69] On the other hand, the women justices' principled insistence that 'there should be an equal moral standard and equal justice meted out to both sexes' was linked to the suggestion that, if a prostitute was caught with VD and convicted, then the men implicated should also be convicted.[70] Not only was this much more easily recommended than implemented, it betrayed a common but false assumption of strong links between prostitution and disease.

Naturally, under the stimulus of wartime demand, prostitution boomed. Yet overall the sex industry was remarkable for its positive contribution to social order. Prostitution may have been morally repugnant to many—and sometimes associated with unwelcome public behaviour—but American demand did not lead to a VD crisis.

In Australia as a whole a brief surge was under control by August 1942. The rate declined partly because of the movement of troops north away from the larger cities as the year wore on, but partly also because of improved control measures. The American authorities praised the cooperation of their Australian counterparts and attributed some of the success to a new Commonwealth Venereal Disease Act, which improved the methods of dealing with known contacts.[71]

In Western Australia, the Public Health Department returned the international compliment, attributing a reduction in cases of VD to the military presence because the Americans were so strict about the sexual hygiene of their men.[72] Condoms were more readily available to visiting servicemen than to the general public. Prophylactic stations were open twenty-four hours a day in Perth and Fremantle. When Americans returned to their ships after a period of shore leave they were required either to inject themselves with a substance that was meant to rid themselves of venereal disease, or bathe in whisky.[73]

If there was an American factor in the temporary growth of VD in 1942, it is likely that it was the result of large numbers of merchant seamen from American vessels, who were temporarily ashore and leading far more dissolute lives than the men in uniform. In July 1943 Dr F. H. Baker of East Fremantle complained to the United States Consulate-General in Sydney that the Perth Consul was not helping his care of the many hundreds of American merchant seamen he had treated in the previous six months. By giving to them all pay owing to them on discharge from hospital the Consul was enabling them to resume heavy drinking, and several had had to be re-admitted to hospital. As a long three-way correspondence ensued, it became apparent that many of the men had been hospitalised with VD. Perth Consul Mason Turner pointed out that such men in Sydney were treated in the United States Army hospital. Locally, the US Navy was borrowing space in a military hospital and was 'willing to accept merchant seamen into these facilities providing that they can be made subject to Navy control', a proviso that was quickly agreed to.[74]

While Naval education and discipline were major factors, the local authorities also played their part in containing disease. The police held files on men who were known VD carriers, and enforced appropriate medical treatment. They also encouraged madams to allocate each woman a regular room, and then recorded the furnishings and decor of all brothel bedrooms. Authorities could then usually determine where a venereal disease victim was infected by asking him what the prostitute's room looked like.[75]

It is one thing to argue that sexual diseases were well under control, much harder to evaluate the impact on public attitudes to the Americans of their enthusiastic patronage of prostitutes. The existence and whereabouts of brothels were well known by most of the people of Perth and Fremantle, and well advertised on American ships before they reached port. In some cases, military trucks actually drove the men direct from the ships to the brothels.[76] When brothels appeared in Albany in April 1942, many people suspected that they had actually been established by the authorities because of the large numbers of Americans in that relatively small town.[77]

Roe Street of course was a centre of Perth prostitution long tolerated by the police. Now boom conditions made it particularly notorious among the public, especially as the queues of men could clearly be seen from trains as they pulled into the city station. One newcomer from the country claimed years later that he sometimes saw queues of four to five hundred men outside the street's six brothels.[78] Offensive to some, though amusing to others, was the involvement of young Australians as go-betweens. Fifty years later Pat Catt could still recall a teenage boy, with a shock of red hair and a mass of freckles, standing on the Horseshoe Bridge across the railway, waving Yanks in the right direction with one hand and collecting money with the other: 'He had his head on the right way. He had it all worked out. He knew where to send the Yanks; he even knew which were the best places for them to go to.'[79]

More private controversies sometimes took place in the brothels. Free drinks were available at most, but these were often heavily laced and several clients consequently lost their wallets and other valuables.[80] The Roe Street women were well known to regulars at the Embassy Ballroom, where they would go to dance before heading off to work.

Many of them made enough money from their 'war work' to purchase houses, most leaving Perth for the anonymity of the eastern states.[81]

Police in Fremantle also accepted the inevitability of prostitution in such a social climate and ignored the activities of brothels in the early years of the war. But here the absence of regulation caused more problems than in Perth. A brothel known as 'The Palms' in Bannister Street was especially well patronised, and was of particular concern to local businesses. Within a month of the Americans' arrival, in the first of many complaints to the Fremantle City Council, the S. H. Lamb Printing Company reported several windows broken in the brawls that were becoming increasingly commonplace.[82]

Despite frequent discussions by the Fremantle councillors, until June 1944 little action was taken to prevent the brothel from operating.[83] Threatened with prosecution unless the business closed immediately, the madam, Ms Jessie Jones, stood defiant for many months.[84] She finally succumbed to police pressure in February 1945, probably long after she had made her fortune, certainly long after many of her best customers had returned to the United States.[85]

By this time American servicemen were no longer immune from criticism by the women's groups so long concerned about public morality. In June 1944 the WA National Council of Women [NCW] discussed the problem of 'girls being accosted and pestered by Allied servicemen' and resolved to 'write to the Commissioner for Police asking for police patrols of the streets to afford protection for these girls'. In meetings over the next two months the Council's Secretary and President found the Commissioner of Police and an American spokesman both 'very sympathetic': 'They explained the system and the difficulties of controlling all men on shore and requested the Council or any individual member to notify either the civilian police or American Shore Police immediately any such incident occurred.'[86]

With so many Americans 'on shore' for so long, it was scarcely surprising that such incidents occurred. No doubt press censorship helped to suppress reporting of many of them. On the other hand, the consistent sensationalism of the one anti-American journal had made matters sound much worse than they probably were.

It is significant that, in the midst of its negotiations with the Police Commissioner and American authorities, the NCW also resolved to write to the editor of the *Mirror* in protest at the 'objectionable items' it published. Although molehills of fact may often have underlain the mountains of sleaze in this scandal sheet, its staple fare of adultery and divorce, rapes, murders and bashings gave a very distorted impression of social life in Perth. No doubt its attacks on American relations with local women, and especially its glee at the collapse of marriages and other relationships, revealed as much about itself and the prurient tastes of its readers as about reality.

Fifty years after the war it was hard to find anybody, local Australian or visiting American, who had regarded the paper as anything more than an entertaining purveyor of outlandish stories. Yet in the period there was at least one occasion when it drew official, if confidential, protests from Australian and American authorities. In April 1943 Gavin Casey, the State Publicity Censor, dealt with a complaint from Army Security, 'obviously expressing an American point of view', about the *Mirror's* provocative 'habit of gloating over matrimonial troubles of Allied Service men'. Casey evidently rather surprised himself by being 'able to point to recent copies of "The Mirror" in which no such men were named as co-respondents'. But this did not save him from 'a fairly useless sort of conversation in which the Army seem[ed] to have a frustrated longing to shoot the editor of "The Mirror" and burn all copies of the paper'.[87]

Nevertheless it is necessary to use any organ of the press with the greatest caution as evidence of community attitudes. It is not only the grubby pages of the *Mirror* that illustrate the dangers of relying on single newspaper sources.

In direct contrast to the *Mirror* in 1943, the *Fremantle and Districts Sentinel* was an enthusiastic reporter, and even advocate, of international marriages throughout 1942. On 16 April it was

pleased to note that Mrs Evatt, wife of Dr Evatt, Australia's Minister for External Affairs, an American woman, has voiced her opinion in favour of the removal of any legal obstacles being allowed to remain to prevent American men from marrying Australians, or Australian men from marrying Americans.

And the same edition, a mere six weeks after the American arrival, included notice of the engagement of Naval Officer Clarence Roderick Rose, Yeoman 2nd Class, to Violet Allpike of Naval Base Road, Hamilton Hill.[88] Succeeding editions contained news of more engagements,[89] followed on 14 May by the announcement of the marriage of Teresa Murphy to Leon Lewis, USN, of Long Beach, California.[90]

Not surprisingly, the *Sentinel's* approval of such announcements was an extension of the almost manic pro-Americanism it had been expressing long before Pearl Harbour. On 25 June it enthused: 'Several weddings may be expected in the very early future, as our friends the "Yanks" have started to make sensible suggestions to some of our available and pretty Aussie eligibles, and so things are more promising for the future.'[91] After reporting more marriages in July—and conveying the impression that American Independence Day had become a Western Australian festival[92]—in September the *Sentinel* revelled in 'the suggestion of Mrs Roosevelt that Americans who marry Australian women should stay with their wives in Australia: we want them here in millions'.[93]

This torrent of enthusiasm ended abruptly. From the beginning of 1943 both the ideal of friendly domination by the United States and the reality of local unions between American men and Australian women disappeared from the pages of the *Sentinel*. They were as absent as holdings of the paper for the latter years of the war are from Perth's Battye Library. The reason is not that romance had suddenly and completely been supplanted by the sordid relationships reported by the *Mirror*, merely that ownership of the paper had changed.

As the organ of the left-wing Anti-Fascist League, the *Sentinel's* ideals were now international socialism, its heroes the selfless workers of the Soviet Union. Its editor was Edward Beeby, son of a judge but a man whose radical radio broadcasts were constantly irritating the Security Service. As the State Publicity Censor reported on one occasion, 'among phrases eliminated from his scripts were references to Franco as "a vicious little murderous thug" and "a psychopathic monstrosity" which however closely they approximate the truth are hardly suitable, I think, for the air'.[94] Under Beeby, the United States was not totally denigrated by the *Sentinel*, but its flaws, especially in its race relations, were frequently highlighted, while the paper's worship of the Stars and Stripes was displaced by probing critiques of the Aboriginal problem and the exploitation of women. Where there had recently been announcements of American–Australian betrothals and weddings, there were now reports of earnest resolutions from the League's far-flung local branches. Post-1942 holdings of the paper are to be found in the Australian Archives in Melbourne, with reports, resolutions, and especially the names of the League's supporters, underlined in red, no doubt by the authorities that were monitoring its activities.

In 1942, when the *Sentinel* was so brazenly ogling Uncle Sam, its eagerness that the whole nation should lie back with it and enjoy being Americanised was worse than romantic gibberish: it betrayed gross ignorance of the policies of the country it idolised. United States personnel were forbidden to marry without the permission of their commanding officers.[95] Those officers scarcely needed telling that marriages were disruptive to the organisation and morale of their units. And in October 1942 the Consulate in Perth was left in no doubt that Army and Navy commands 'are emphatic in their desire to discourage marriage in this area by every possible means and that neither service is anxious to provide, for the dependents in Australia of personnel already married, facilities which would encourage further marriages'.[96]

Nobody knew better than the Consulate staff how unreal these official expectations were. In the last six months of 1942 they conducted 2410 interviews and received 540 American visitors and 959 other visitors. In his report to the State Department the Consul added that it was 'impossible to get a true picture of the work of this office' from those figures:

> The work during the past few months has been unusual, and though it will be noted that the number of interviews is

comparatively large, the number of actual services recorded appears to be small. This is largely due to the fact that many of the interviews are in connection with marriages contemplated or which have taken place between Australian girls and personnel of the American Armed Forces now in this district.[97]

What was mainly motivating local women was not that desire to be given married quarters feared by the military, but a determination to go to America as soon as possible. Unfortunately for them, as the consular report pointed out, while many interviews were concerned with visa requirements, 'because of the war situation not many people are actually travelling and very few actual visa services have been performed'.[98] Although this situation was frustrating to many, a more important lesson that had already emerged in 1942 was that the marriages the *Fremantle and Districts Sentinel* were so warmly applauding and so breezily encouraging were subject to enormous stress. And what made the paper's hobbyhorse such an unattractive beast was the extreme vulnerability—emotionally, economically and legally—of local women who became entangled with American men.

With no official channel to determine whether or not a visiting serviceman was married in the United States, a woman had to take the word of her man. Submariners in particular were under strict instructions not to reveal their military movements to civilians; no doubt some were not told they were to leave Perth until the very last moment, and many women who felt they had shared some special time with an American found themselves deserted with little or no notice.

Abandoned and aggrieved local females, pregnant or, by the end of 1942, already with illegitimate children, often turned to the American Consul for help. As early as June 1942 one young woman had accrued a comprehensive collection of the problems and dilemmas that, usually separately, were to be the legacy of failed romance. Desperate because she was pregnant, the woman had considered abortion and suicide but rejected them both, as she still hoped to marry the American responsible. The hope was not very strong. Traumatised over the delay in getting a visa to the United

States, she inquired about her status in relation to maintenance—if there was no marriage—and also about the possibility of bringing an action for breach of promise. She was writing in the hope that the Consul would pressure the man into realising the urgency of the situation. Finally, she revealed, she was terrified of telling her parents about her plight.[99]

There was little that Turner could do in such cases except refer women to other agencies. In September 1942 he established that civil liability for the support of illegitimate children was covered by Western Australia's Child Welfare legislation.[100] But in that year, and as late as 1945, he tended to refer complainants to the US Navy Welfare Office in Hay Street, Perth.[101] Without decisive proof of the paternity of their children, such women were unlikely to receive much help from the American authorities.

Equally unfortunate were childless wives and fiancées who were deserted by Americans. In October 1942 Turner was powerless to offer real help to a woman who had been asked to send several sums of money to two American servicemen now in Sydney. One was her son-in-law, the other engaged to her youngest daughter. Obviously not wanting to believe that her daughters had been abandoned and herself exploited, she was nevertheless now suspicious after receiving a third telegram from the men saying that they had not received the money she had sent. Turner received confirmation from the US Army authorities that the two men were deserters.[102]

Whether they were in love with an American, or with the idea of a future in America, women were grabbing at opportunities that might disappear as quickly as they had arrived. But these were not the only reasons for the headlong plunge into wedlock. Ironically, the very measures that were designed to deter marriage actually encouraged it to take place in the most unstable circumstances. Commanding officers were allowed to sanction marriages if the bride-to-be was pregnant. There is ample evidence, from the decline in venereal disease and the absence of any increase in numbers of illegitimate births in the war period, that the Americans knew how to use the freely available condoms when it suited them. But here was an obvious incentive for couples with matrimonial intent to leave them in their wrappers.

Another factor encouraging hasty marriage was United States immigration law. Initially the authorities, civilian and military, American and Australian, were themselves confused about the immigrant status of Australian women marrying American servicemen. Australian authorities had to rescind early advice they issued that such women automatically lost British, and acquired American, nationality on marriage.[103] Different authorities gave varying answers, ranging from one to three years, to the question of how long an immigrant wife would have to wait before being eligible to apply for citizenship.[104] The more crucial issue was that only by already being wives did such women have much chance of being admitted to the United States.

In an era when Australians were allotted only a minuscule one hundred places per annum in the United States' immigrant quotas, the most fundamental initial fears were quickly allayed with the decision that wives of American servicemen would be admitted outside the quota.[105] But fiancées were not so lucky. Eventually, in 1945, when an estimated fifteen thousand fiancées in Australia as a whole were clamouring to enter the United States, some were allowed to do so under visitors' visas. But at the same time a memorandum from a State Department official, Eliot Coulter, summed up the situation succinctly:

> Mr Coulter explained that while an American soldier could file a petition with the Consulate to obtain a non-quota status for his alien wife, a fiancee would be expected to enter USA under standard procedure of the annual quota, which for Australia was 100. Therefore, it would take 150 years to bring in the fiancees alone.[106]

Despite that large figure of fifteen thousand fiancées, many couples either deliberately or accidentally qualified for non-quota status through marriage. But not all of them remained married long enough to proceed with the immigration formalities. As early as 19 August 1942, scarcely six months after the American arrival, the

Consulate was already confronting the fact that some marriages had not only taken place but already broken up. 'Unfortunately,' wrote Vice-Consul Charles O. Thompson to the Western Australian Solicitor-General,

> not all of the marriages recently contracted between Australian women and members of the American armed forces are proving to be of the enduring kind. The question of dissolution of the marital status, therefore, has already risen in a few isolated instances and it is to be expected that the issue will rise on occasion in the future.

Asking for information about the laws of Western Australia, so that the Consulate could deal competently with future cases, he focused particularly on the question of domicile. One local woman had already been told she could not sue for divorce on the grounds of her husband's adultery because she had lost her domicile by marrying him and, as a non-resident, could not prosecute a court action. The replies from the Solicitor-General to this and a follow-up letter from Thompson confirmed that this was so, even if a husband deserted her and moved elsewhere.[107]

Divorce laws, like so many others, varied from state to state and it was a growing sense of the wartime upheavals that eventually led WA's Senator Dorothy Tangney to demand uniform federal legislation 'in an effort to relieve the position of Australian girls deserted by American husbands'.[108] Not all women's groups agreed with the Senator. The WSG's *Dawn*, which publicised her demand, also reported that the Australian branch of the St Joan's Social and Political Alliance had condemned calls for cheaper and easier divorce legislation: 'The result of the proposed legislation would be an enormous increase in such marriages and in the toll of ruined lives, broken homes and fatherless children.'[109]

The mounting evidence of the fragility of marriages and the vulnerability of deserted wives made nonsense of the *Fremantle and Districts Sentinel's* dream that there might be millions of American husbands for Australian women. Yet in one respect the *Sentinel's* fantasy was an improvement on reality. If the aim and the outcome of international marriages had indeed been for American husbands to stay in Australia, some of the worst trauma would have been avoided. For many Western Australian women, in particular, remaining married and trying to reach America proved almost as stressful as losing husbands or fiancés was for others. Although a handful made the move in the earlier years of the war, for most it was an ordeal that awaited them in the latter months and in the immediate post-war period. As such, it is a part of the story that belongs in the final chapter of this book. The intervening chapters are concerned with violence and other frictions which grew partly, but not exclusively, from the American relationship with local women.

# FLEETING ATTRACTION

*Chapter Eight*

## THE RACIAL NEGATIVE

WITH SCANDALOUS STORIES about African-American servicemen, the *Mirror* attempted to exploit a deeply entrenched local racism. Western Australia, in its treatment of Aboriginal people, its enthusiasm for the White Australia Policy and its heavy-handed attitude to fractious Asian seamen, was at least as racially prejudiced as other states. The only reason why race relations remained a minor, mainly uncontroversial, part of the interaction between American servicemen and the Western Australian public was that the numbers of African-American personnel were very small. That negative factor is a most important part of the uniqueness of the state's response to the Americans. Elsewhere in Australia black Americans were the focus of Australian prejudice and yet, at the same time, the cause of animosity between white Americans and Australian troops, who sometimes fraternised with them in a way the Americans found offensive. Had numbers of black personnel been larger, the efforts of the *Mirror* to stir the racist cauldron might well have been more disruptive.

Even in the extreme anxiety of January 1942, a major preoccupation of the Australian Government was that none of the American troops it was so anxiously awaiting should be black. The United States was well aware of Australian sensitivities. Proposing to send principally anti-aircraft units as its first ground troops, it was 'anxious to know what would be your reaction to the proposal that a proportion of United States troops to be despatched to Australia should be coloured'. The Australian authorities were 'not prepared to agree',[1] even when the proposal was quickly re-phrased in a manner befitting negotiations between two equally racist governments. The 'negro units' were really labourers: 'The intention is to use them at Darwin for the heavy labour in connection with installation of aircraft defences and aerodromes, for which they are peculiarly fitted.'[2] This did not reassure Roland Wilson, Secretary of the Department of Labour and National Service, who was convinced that 'any suggestion of importing coloured gangs from the United States would have the most disastrous consequences'.[3]

Yet even as ministers were agreeing that 'any such proposal is most dangerous'[4] and 'instructing' the local United States command that 'coloured troops are on no account to be stationed in Australia',[5] the Americans were simply preparing to do what they wanted. On 19 January the War Cabinet reiterated that 'no coloured troops will be stationed in Australia'.[6] But two days later it had to accept the inevitable. Its reaction to such troops 'would not be favourable' but 'the composition of the forces that the USA Government might decide to despatch to Australia is a matter for that Government to determine... It is not the desire of the Commonwealth Government to make any stipulations which might destroy the nature of the organisation of the Army formation.'[7]

By late March 1942, a secret memorandum circulating among official agencies was acknowledging that 'coloured American troops have arrived in Queensland and are at present working here on guard and in labour corps'.[8] Still hoping to keep the news as quiet as possible, the Australian Chief Publicity Censor on 9 April decreed that 'no letterpress or photographs of coloured troops with the US Forces may be published'.[9] His New South Wales underling immediately applied this policy to the Sydney papers, but expressed his fears that 'these troops…will before long present a pretty problem to the Federal Government. Already, according to a submission by the "Daily Telegraph", which was killed, they have been placed out of bounds by certain city hotels and dance halls.'[10]

As segregated facilities were established, not only in Surry Hills, Sydney,[11] but also in Brisbane, the problem emerged very quickly in far from pretty form. On 16 April an Australian military policeman, after patrolling South Brisbane with an American counterpart, reported that Australian soldiers 'have been seen drinking with the (colored) troops, and the (colored) troops are getting on a higher plane than is good for the city's safety. I think some action should be taken to curtail the relationship to a certain extent and keep the (colored) troops in their place.'[12] And on the following day the Queensland State Publicity Censor was suppressing news of 'a fracas between American white troops and negroes in a suburban area, in which two white men were injured and two negroes shot in the rear by USA provost men'.[13]

For a short time Australian and American authorities were united in their attitudes to the 'colour question'. Australian censors gladly vetoed a story 'about the making of a record of nigger minstrel singing' and another about 'American Negroes playing baseball in Sydney'. And Chief Censor Bonney, after wrestling with 'a difficult one' about the colour of Filipinos, was 'inclined to agree with the US conception that "coloured troops" refers only to the Negro Labour Corps'. At the same time, he was only too happy to accede to a request from the US Army press liaison office 'that you issue instructions prohibiting the use of a soldier's colour in any stories which may appear'. The Americans were concerned about brawls between white and black soldiers in Australia, 'and it is felt that use of the term negro or black or coloured is detrimental'.[14]

Within two months, however, American and Australian authorities suddenly had quite different attitudes to publicity of racial issues. While only too willing to accept on 28 June the 'total deletion' of reports of 'a riot in William Street, Sydney involving coloured troops',[15] the Americans no longer wished to hide the fact that such troops were serving in combat roles rather than merely as labourers.[16] A secret Australian memorandum on 15 July recognised that Washington was 'under pressure to recognise "the negro war effort"'.[17]

The memorandum did not spell out the nature of that pressure. Civil rights leaders were dissatisfied with the gestures made by the Roosevelt administration in response to a threatened mass march on Washington the previous year. Feeling that the march had been too quickly cancelled, following cosmetic promises of fair employment practices in some areas of federal government, they were now openly linking black support for the war to the demand for racial justice. The 'Double-V' slogan—victory over fascism abroad and racism at home—has been seen by some as an attempt to energise the downtrodden black masses by presenting war service as a route to equality. Others have regarded it as a device for damping down a near-revolutionary black hostility to supporting white America in its war against the coloured Japanese. In either case the real and threatened militancy made it tactically unwise for the United States Government to hide black participation, even though it had no intention of desegregating its armed forces.[18]

While there is no evidence that Australians were at this stage sensitive to these nuances of American policy, they had no option but to accept the outcome, albeit in as limited and grudging a way as possible. With the backing of the Prime Minister the censors decided that the embargo on news about 'coloured' troops 'should continue to apply to publication in Australia, but that correspondents should be allowed to send suitable messages back to America'.[19]

Despite the occasional evidence of fraternisation between Australian troops and African-Americans,[20] this censorship was not a bizarre quirk of official minds but a reflection of the racism that was widespread in the Australian community. After an African-American was refused a drink, the Minister for the Army, Frank Forde, acknowledged that the US Army had issued no instructions to prohibit the sale of liquor to 'coloured' soldiers. 'It may be', Forde suggested, 'that the barman concerned was confusing American negroes with Australian aboriginals.'[21]

By this time, in August 1942, there were 7258 African-American troops in the country. Representing nearly 8 per cent of total US forces,[22] they were a problem not only standing in bars but flying on planes. In September, officials of Qantas complained to the Director-General of Civil Aviation that they were asked 'from time to time to carry American coloured Troops':[23]

> There is no doubt that this is a difficult and embarrassing problem. It is embarrassing for the Company and for white passengers in the small confines of an aeroplane, and there is certainly a real difficulty in so far as hotel accommodation is concerned when the hotels flatly refuse to accommodate them. On the other hand most of the passengers carried today are service personnel, including Americans, with whom we believe the colour ban is far more accentuated than it is with us.[24]

'A tactful sounding of the American Authorities'[25] did not confirm this latter assumption. The Chief of Air Section, United States Army Services of Supply, South West Pacific Area, thought it was a matter 'which should be decided entirely by the Australian authorities according to their usual good judgment and interest in furthering the war effort'. But his personal opinion was 'that the only sound basis of approach is recognition of the fact that all soldiers wearing the American uniform are members of the American Army'.[26]

The judgment of the Australian authorities was that any person or group to extend the hand of friendship to 'coloured' Americans was subversive. There were some grounds for its assumption that it was the Australian left that provided the most outspoken opponents of racism.[27] As early as May 1942, the Commonwealth Investigation Branch made much of an official Communist Party circular sent to all of the organisation's Districts a short time previously: 'Re Negro Soldiers and White Chauvinism'.[28] Yet this document was much more an indictment of racism than evidence of sedition. As it called upon the party to 'strive to create the friendliest feelings between the civil population and the Negro soldiers and sailors, and especially between the Aussie armed forces and the Negroes', it acknowledged that 'it may be injudicious to attack the "White Australia" policy, but the campaign can be developed along the lines that the coloured soldiers are here to help defend us'. And it concluded by acknowledging that racial prejudice was rife within the party: 'Members often use the terms "coon", "nigger", "chows", "dagoes", "pommies", calling the Japs "yellow" etc.'[29]

For a short time the official mind was as suspicious of right-wing extremists as it was of communists. By October 1942 there was considerable interracial friction involving African-American troops in Queensland, culminating in a violent incident in Ingham, when about fifty tried to gain entrance to a dance and two drew guns when confronted by the military police. A report from the Security Service in that state also focused on discontent among 'coloured' troops in Townsville and led to a circular to all states from Security head-quarters, headed 'Unrest among US Negro Soldiers', which asked 'whether you are aware of any information to suggest that Axis agents or sympathisers may be concerned in stirring up this trouble?'. The replies, however, tended to dismiss this suggestion and reaffirm the suspicion of the left. In New South Wales the Security officials had consulted a USAFIA intelligence officer, who 'expressed the opinion that the unrest is not caused by Axis agents, but is due to the activities of a communistic element, who advocate equality between the white and coloured servicemen'.[30]

This same circular asked for a return of numbers of 'Negro troops' in each state. The reply from Perth on 20 October 1942 was that 'up to date there have been NO negro soldiers in WESTERN AUSTRALIA'.[31] There were of course, then and throughout the remainder of the war, some black naval personnel in the state. But even though submarine crews could have up to a dozen in low status, low-paid mess steward positions, the proportion of black servicemen was always very small compared to the situation in most eastern states centres. There the American presence was predominantly Army, a branch of the services which had far more African-Americans than the Navy. It was not only the larger numbers of black Army personnel that caused problems but their organisation in segregated units, which made them more provocative to Australians and white American soldiers alike.

The relatively small number of African-Americans has to be regarded as a major factor influencing the unique relationship that developed between American forces and the Western Australian community. Even though Aboriginal people were to serve in the armed forces, in some cases with great distinction, the war had no immediate impact on prejudice against the indigenous black population. A circular issued by the Security Branch of the Australian Army in Perth recounted the concern of authorities in Queensland about the doubtful loyalties of the indigenous population in the event of a Japanese invasion:

> These half-educated half-castes and aboriginals have been largely influenced by Communist and Anti-Capitalist propaganda for many years, and can almost invariably be swayed by the agitator. They are extremely class-conscious and consider that they have had a raw deal from the white man. These sentiments are NOT displayed to the white man's face, but are most evident when the coloured people are together in groups. There is little doubt that the JAPS would find many of them willing helpers.

The document may have originated in Queensland, but it was deemed worthy of circulation in Western Australia 'in view of the fact that similar opinions are held regarding the natives in this State'.[32]

Even if such opinions had not translated completely into prejudice against black Americans, it is hard to believe that the attitudes recalled by most people interviewed long after the war would have been so tolerant had the numbers of black sailors been very large. However much local people might have been inclined to see American blacks as exciting exotics, a more racially mixed American contingent would have brought with it the same kind of ugly internal frictions that had been apparent in other parts of Australia.

Despite their small numbers, the presence of American 'Negroes' gave the *Mirror* especial scope for scurrilous stories, and it duly made the most of any incident associating African-American men with local women. When Josie Baraffi was found sleeping with 'a Negro sailor' in the grounds of the University she was sharing 'a blanket filled with lice'. Despite her claims that the man had been supporting her financially for some time, she was sent to gaol for four months. The *Mirror* not only approved of this but was also pleased to be able to demonstrate her poor character by revealing that she had previously 'lived with a Chinaman'.[33] Prominence was also given to the conviction of another woman for being 'idle and disorderly' when she was found asleep with a 'Negro' near a 'beach lavatory' at Crawley Bay.[34]

Of course the *Mirror* was pandering to a racism that could be a real problem for African-Americans and for the women attracted to them. As people recalled the period many years later, men and women alike had no doubt that blacks were attractive to many local women. But their reminiscences hint at the underlying tensions. Insisting that local white girls liked them, and denying that there was any segregation, Syd Harvey had to qualify his first memory that they sometimes entered the chief petty officers' club near the Barrack Street Jetty. His eventual conclusion that they probably did not seems highly likely, given the exclusive nature of its clientele and the fact that in the US Navy of that era no African-American could have achieved the necessary rank.[35]

Equally suggestive are the conflicting recollections of the racial policies of the nearby Swan Dive, a club open to all ranks in the Navy. The insistence of its founder, Jim Purcell, that African-Americans would not have been excluded, but that none ever came there, is at odds with both pictorial and anecdotal evidence of their presence in small numbers at the club and their participation in its excursions. Such activities and other reminiscences clearly illustrate a situation far different from that prevailing in Sydney and Brisbane, with their segregated social areas. Yet the instructions to hostesses at the Dive betrayed a certain uneasiness about racial issues: some danced with blacks but all were told that they could refuse if they wished, as long as they did so pleasantly.[36]

*African-Americans were admitted to the Swan Dive*
(West Australian Newspapers)

African-Americans were also seen and admired as dancers in public ballrooms, but again there is a hint of the challenge to decorum they represented in the way this was described. Told of the racial prejudice of the era within American ranks, Pat Catt argued that 'we never saw a great deal of it and I must admit that I've even seen our girls *dancing* with them'. The ones that she could especially recall doing so were the town's elite jitterbuggers, girls famous for their loose limbs and looser morals, including one whose name, suggested Pat Tully, 'was always in the *Mirror*'.[37]

A young woman who frequently took groups of servicemen back to her home and family was scolded severely by her mother for including an African-American on one occasion, and was told never to bring any home again.[38] Another woman recalled the family consternation when a female relative became romantically entangled with a black serviceman. It is a measure of the trauma of the time that even fifty years after the event the woman directly involved was unwilling to talk about the relationship.[39]

Such circumstances were relatively unusual. What is surprising about the first incident is not the mother's abysmal failure to guess who was coming to dinner, but the evident acceptance of a black by a group of white servicemen. In the racist American forces such fraternisation was distinctly unusual, and official segregation was rarely challenged from either side of the colour line. Although E. V. Taylor recalled seeing black and white Americans mixing at Steve's hotel in Nedlands,[40] most other reminiscence from the period, both Australian and American, told a different story. Even though it was seen formally most clearly in the eastern states, the mistreatment of black Americans by their white compatriots did not go completely unnoticed in the West.

George May, who had grown up with Aboriginal people and had always been opposed to racism, was disgusted by the way the handful of black cooks were 'treated like dirt' by white Americans in Geraldton. This was the main blemish on an enjoyable and beneficial relationship with the Yanks. He recalled only one 'Negro' sharing a drinking session with his fellow-Americans—'and he was pretty white'. George was well aware that it was not only American but also Western Australian racism that made sexual relationships the most sensitive potential issue between black and white. This was an era when he was not allowed to talk to Aboriginal women, and when a white-looking Aboriginal acquaintance had been mistakenly arrested in Perth for conversing in public with his black sister.[41]

The kind of activist middle class women most vocal about the threat of men in uniform to moral and physical health were not racist. Indeed from their ranks had come open hostility to the Mirror's slurs and, over a long period, some of the most consistent and outspoken sympathy for the plight of Aboriginal people. But it certainly would not have occurred to them in the atmosphere of the period to be advocates of any kind of liaison between white women and black Americans.

In response to these realities African-American servicemen adopted defensive postures. According to American submariner Jack Hanks, some told Australian girls they were American Indians to avoid the stigma of being 'black' in an era when the Indians of the movies were at least 'braves' before they bit the dust. Most tended to stick to themselves, not going to nightclubs and avoiding trouble as well as they could. It was only white American sailors, recalled Michael Papadoulis, who were involved in the frequent fighting that occurred around hotel closing time in the inner city area of Perth: black and white Americans never mixed. The 'Negroes' in Geraldton, said George May, kept a very low profile and always seemed very nervous. They never caused any trouble: 'They weren't game to.'[42]

Carl Uphoff was an American who thought highly of the handful of black sailors serving on his submarine. They were hard workers and loyal and protective towards their friends. But, because it was 'taboo for them to go with white women', Carl thought it was 'fine' that they sought out Aboriginal girls, despite being warned against this by American authorities. George May recalled that the downtrodden Geraldton African-Americans 'did have a couple of native girls, but nobody worried about that'.[43] Once again, the reticence of individuals makes it hard to give substance to anecdotal evidence of Aboriginal children fathered by black Americans.[44] In August 1944 the *West Australian* claimed that a racket had been organised to solicit girls away from Moore River and other Aboriginal settlements to live with African-American servicemen in the city.[45] If the claim was vague, the attitudes of Commissioner Bray of the Western Australian Department of Native Affairs were in harmony with the official American disapproval, since such relationships threatened an unwelcome growth in the coloured population.[46]

Although the sensationalism of the *Mirror* was unique, there were enough hints in the regular press of how different things might have been with a larger black American presence. In March 1943, for instance, the *Daily News* reported that three Negroes had been injured in a brawl at a house in Farley Street, West Perth. One had a fractured skull, another a broken jaw and the third 'his nose nearly bitten off'.[47] While this report carried no commentary, in April 1944 two incidents were evidently newsworthy only because of the racial dimension to otherwise quite banal circumstances. The arrest of a fifteen-year-old unemployed girl from Norseman for sleeping on a Perth beach was headlined 'Girl with Coloured Sailor'.[48] A few weeks later 'Smooged with Negro Sailors' was the heading for a comment by 'Detective Jones' that 'he had seen white women smooging and drinking with Negro men in a house in Raglan Road, North Perth'.[49]

As a later chapter will show, there were no racial ingredients in the affray south of Fremantle that led State Censor Casey to report Australian military and American Navy hostility to the *Mirror* in April 1943. But it is not hard to imagine how much more serious such incidents might have been had there been large numbers of black personnel in the state, and especially how much more damage might have been done both by the *Mirror's* scurrilous sensationalism and even by the more understated racism of the *Daily News*. Generally harmonious though the American relationship may have been with the people of Western Australia, especially in its early stages, some violence was inevitable in the wartime atmosphere. The following two chapters deal with this coarser side of the American presence, first in the social playground of central Perth, then in the much more threatening atmosphere of the Fremantle dockside and adjacent areas.

# FLEETING ATTRACTION

## Chapter Nine

## PETTY VIOLENCE

THERE WAS PROBABLY MORE VIOLENCE involving Americans in wartime Western Australia than most locals realised. Strict media censorship virtually obliterated from the contemporary public record all evidence of the fights, street brawls, stabbings and rapes that are the almost inevitable underside of any large-scale military presence in civilian areas. Yet, if the resultant blandness of the newspapers is a distortion, so potentially is the alternative record. Police files may reveal a great deal about the one major riot involving American servicemen, but much less about the incidence of smaller scale affrays. Rather than overemphasise the most extreme incidents, it is more fruitful to place this ugliest side of the relationship in national perspective and local context.

In the first place, what was distinctive about the Western Australian interaction with American servicemen was the low level of violence compared with the almost legendary bloodlettings that occurred in Brisbane, Sydney and elsewhere in Australia. Secondly, there were very great differences within Western Australia between Fremantle on the one hand and Perth, Albany and Geraldton on the other. This chapter deals with the essentially petty violence in those three places, especially central Perth, where the Americans were part of a new unruliness but where much of the brawling was within their own ranks. The much more threatening atmosphere of Fremantle is discussed in the next chapter.

A national perspective demands, first of all, acknowledgment that, long before the American arrival in Australia, wartime unrest was widespread. The troops who had caused havoc in the Perth metropolitan area had counterparts throughout Australia, and the violence that had erupted on the Fremantle wharf with the shooting of Chinese seamen in January 1942 was merely one example of nationwide disturbances in strategic industries. The censorship files bulge with telegrams, letters and memoranda to the press and ABC, forbidding mention of strikes and go-slows in munitions industries, as well as on the waterside, and riots and brawls among troops as far from the ocean as Alice Springs. From July 1940, when there was a ban on news of a fight between garrison and AIF troops, to September 1941, when reports and pictures of major riot damage and looting were suppressed, Darwin was a running sore of military discontent, with occasional minor eruptions of labour unrest. So too was Brisbane from October 1940, when the media were asked not to 'unduly emphasise soldiers' participation [in an] incident', to January 1942, when AIF rioters 'smashed up' the Central Railway Cafe.[1]

Against such a background, it could hardly be expected that the American arrival a month later would turn Australian troops into choirboys. On 8 December 1942 the Australian Army's Major-General F. H. Berryman sent a circular to numerous military units:

> When Australia was in immediate danger of invasion some 9 months ago, U.S. Air Corps and Army Troops began to arrive here in large numbers. Since then the friendly relations based on comradeship and common service against the enemy, which have existed between the two forces in Australia, have been marred by a long series of street brawls, stabbings, and actual fights between small groups. The incidents have been widespread, but have occurred principally in TOWNSVILLE, BRISBANE and MELBOURNE.[2]

The immediate stimulus for these comments was no doubt the notorious 'Battle of Brisbane' on 26 November, in which widespread and drawn-out rioting resulted in numerous casualties although only one death, that of an Australian soldier. This came soon after the 'Battle of the Trains', in which troops from the two nations had fought bloodily at a railway siding in Queensland, and was in turn followed by a major brawl in Melbourne, watched by a thousand bystanders. The effects of all these incidents were probably made worse by censorship. Suppression of publication allowed the rumour mills to inflate grossly quite modest numbers of casualties.[3]

It is not difficult to see why Western Australia was not mentioned in this report. As we have seen, by the later months of 1942 the numbers of 'US Army Troops' in the state had dwindled to a handful, while Air Corps were mainly dispersed to remote locations. At the same time as the American presence was less provocative, Western Australia's intense sense of isolation made it especially welcome. These factors, however, only minimised rather than ruled out violence, for the state experienced many of the problems that accompanied the Americans elsewhere in Australia.

Foremost among these was the syndrome of frictions referred to as the 'girl question' in that Australian Army memorandum of December 1942. These included Australian outrage at the 'loose behaviour' of married women, the cheap regard Americans had for Australian girls, 'the way Americans "paw" them and embrace them in public' and the rejection of Australian men by girls in favour of Americans.[4] In most people's memories, however, the associated violence was unremarkable. The first response of nearly every person interviewed forty-five to fifty years later was to play down the incidence of violence. Even though further recollection often qualified that generalisation, there was no sense that violence was a serious blemish on otherwise good relations between Americans and the host community.

In response to the standard question 'Did you see or hear of much violence?' one woman replied 'Not a great deal.' But she immediately continued:

> Our boys were insanely jealous. And I can understand them being
> jealous—they were losing their girlfriends, even their wives in lots
> of instances, because the Yanks had the money…and these girls
> were playing up with them and our boys were left for dead. So they
> would go into town to the hotels etc. and get into fights—great
> fights in there.

The Yanks would take their girls to hotels such as the Wentworth,
where 'old Ma Thomas was robbing them every way but getting away
with it—they didn't care'. They would spend the night there 'and then
of course our boys would wait for the Yanks and belt them up'.[5]

Kath Pouleris was one of the many Perth girls who felt that the
Americans treated them better than did Australian men, and she
eventually married an American submariner. But, in agreeing that the
main cause of fights was Australian jealousy, she also had some
criticisms of the Yanks:

> The Americans had a pretty bad habit of saying, 'We've stolen your
> girls' or 'We've come to get your country back'—which was not
> really the way to go, particularly if it was to an Australian service-
> man who had come back from the Middle East. He couldn't be in
> both places at once.[6]

Mrs Marjorie Ward, whose seventy-one rooms in the much more
genteel residential Derward Hotel were virtually monopolised by
Americans, had to be 'continually on the go' watching them because
they would drink too much and do wild things. One smashed through
the glass front door one night and another fell out of a window upstairs. But these incidents were irritating rather than serious, and she
had no recollections of violence between Australians and Americans
on her premises.[7]

As Mrs Ward's recollection suggests, sometimes connected with
the 'girl question' but very often a quite independent cause of tension
was alcohol. This was not a problem exclusively associated with the
Americans, but it could scarcely have been a random coincidence that

supplies of alcohol were being restricted at the very moment when they first arrived.

On 2 March 1942, ten days after the first US Army units arrived and one day before the inauguration of the Fremantle submarine base, the *Daily News* reported an acute shortage of bottled beer: 'We don't know the reason, but I think a lot of bottled beer must have gone into the canteens for the troops recently.' One factor not mentioned by the *News* was the official desire to use civilian manpower to the best advantage: the Swan Brewery had been ordered by manpower regulations to cut production by a third and release the superfluous labour to work in war industry.[8] But almost certainly connected with that decision was the desire to contain the violence associated with excessive drinking, for this was the period during which the campaign for six o'clock closing of hotels achieved its goal. This was something the *Daily News* did know the reason for: 'Recent scenes in the streets of Perth made imperative the tightening up of controls of the retail liquor trade. The spectacle of hundreds of drunken soldiers, many accompanied by young girls, was shocking.'[9] This was by no means an attack exclusively on Americans. As we have seen, the behaviour of Australian troops in transit had stimulated the demand for restrictions in the previous year.

A couple of months later the restrictions were made even more severe for local troops, when Western Command banned the sale of bottled beer to Australian men in uniform. Although police reported that troops often overcame this ban by paying civilians to purchase alcohol for them,[10] this was far from a complete solution because civilians, too, were chasing a scarce commodity.

The rationing of supplies to hotels forced many bars to open for only a few hours during the daytime. The pressures that hoteliers were feeling were shown in January 1943, when Cornelius Henry Gordon of the Carlton Hotel was charged with refusing to sell liquor contrary to Section 118 of the Licensing Act. A customer had asked for a schooner and two bottles, but was told no bottles were for sale and had been served only with the schooner. Pointing out that there were four crates of bottles there, he was told they would be served between

5 and 6 p.m. Gordon managed to have the case dismissed when he told the magistrate that his allocation of twenty dozen bottles daily would disappear in a flash if he did not restrict hours of sale:

> If I sold a bottle of beer before 5 p.m. I would have all the women in the district asking for it and men arriving in taxis to take bottles away. Therefore I find it necessary to cease supplying bottled beer during the day in order to provide for the needs of workers between 5 and 6 p.m.[11]

While Australians chafed under such restrictions, American servicemen could obtain signed vouchers from their officers to purchase beer direct from the Swan Brewery.[12] The officers themselves did particularly well. The owner of the Kalgoorlie Brewery, Alice Cummins, had a house on Crawley Bay called 'The Bend of the Road' (dubbed 'The Bend of the Elbow' by enlisted men), where she often entertained officers.[13] Cec Anderson, the Australian Army officer who served with American submariners, arrived on leave with them at a Perth hotel to find one dozen bottles of beer, a couple of bottles of Scotch and other rationed goods under his bed. This, he felt, was standard treatment for most American officers.[14]

Enlisted Americans, however, never went thirsty. American canteens were always well supplied with Australian 'wet-stock', although many Australians were unsure of the methods the Americans used to obtain this.[15] Spirits, wine and beer were frequently imported from the United States under the guise of goods for official use, leading to an ongoing dispute between the Australian Department of Trade and Customs and the Americans, who had accrued a bill of more than £70,000 in unpaid customs duty by early 1945.[16] No doubt these processes partly explain the abundance of liquor so often noticed by Australian patrons of the new Perth cabarets, by visitors to American clubs and guests at their parties.

Even the Americans were affected by 6 o'clock closing, not least by the fact that this was not always completely enforced by authorities.[17] It became a nightly 'game' for servicemen to find out

*No shortage of liquor*
(West Australian Newspapers)

which bars were open.[18] When a bar selling beer was discovered, it would attract such a crowd that supplies would often last only ten minutes, and the publican would be unlikely to receive another keg that day. A member of the United States Navy recalled: 'We never could fathom the mysterious operating hours. We solved the problem by storing cases...under our bunks.'[19] Another serviceman made friends with the green-keeper at the local lawn bowls club and could exchange tobacco for a bottle or two of the amber fluid.[20] Failing all else, there were always the taxi drivers who, for some Catalina men at least, became 'virtually our barmen'.[21]

Naturally, alcohol was not only symbolic of often resented American affluence but also a fuel for violence. The Australian Department of Information distributed a brochure to United States troops soon after they arrived warning them of the dangers of Australian alcohol: 'Australians drink considerable beer—watch your step with it—it is a whole lot heavier and more alcoholic than most United States beers. Australian wines also have to be watched. The cheapest grades have a kick like T.N.T.'[22] It might have added that so did Australian troops when filled with either wine or beer. As well as having heavy, ugly uniforms, they had boots with similar qualities. Though the Americans could not match the kicking power of Australians, they were often found with heavy finger rings capable of inflicting major damage.[23] And there was also, as a national survey indicated, 'the tendency of some Americans to draw their knives or guns too freely'.[24]

The inevitable fights were not confined to the metropolitan area. In June 1942 the *Albany Advertiser* gave a full page to a report of an assault case under the headline 'A Hard Headed Sailor Man'. An Australian soldier, Ernie Marsh, was charged with assaulting American sailor Walter Nath. Two sailors had gone outside from the Strand Cafe to settle a row. Nath had followed with others to watch, and had two bottles smashed over his head.[25]

Reminiscences suggest a similar pattern of bar-room brawling in Geraldton. According to George May, Americans were told to keep out of trouble and largely did so, a sensible course of action as they were outnumbered by Australian and New Zealand troops in proportions of forty thousand to twenty or thirty individuals. The Yanks had 'a few stoushes', but these were often amongst themselves. During one brawl at the Freemasons Hotel, a passing friend was stunned by a pot flying through the door.[26]

American Bill Barker recalled that most fights were with Australians, but 'all in good fun': there seemed to be no hatred of Americans and violence was 'entirely due to the beer'. Geraldton was a wonderful place with a friendly small-town atmosphere. Cosy bars, much smaller than those in Perth, were run by lively barmaids who knew how to entertain the men and keep them at arm's length at the same time. This was approximately the distance at which Barker interacted with some of the diggers, who were 'great guys' when it came to a fight. On one occasion he was lured by a malicious fellow-American into offending Australian custom by turning his beer glass upside down. He found himself instantly hit from three directions, but was eventually able to explain his mistake to his digger assailants, who then made the practical joker the centrepiece of the brawl.[27]

Widely recalled in all locations was the decisive firmness of American policing. Marjorie Ward, who found so irksome the drinking, petty violence and vandalism in and around the Derward Hotel, concluded that there were 'constant military police around, so it wasn't difficult to get help'. If this was an important factor in containing violence, it was also remarkable in that, strictly speaking, the Americans did not have a 'military police', but 'shore patrols' made up of ordinary personnel. When a drunken Tex emerged abusively from a Geraldton bar, he was given one warning and then knocked cold by a truncheon blow behind the ear. Expressing his surprise at the ferocity of this discipline, George May was told by the truncheon-wielder not to worry: Tex would soon be having his turn at shore patrol and would probably get his own back.[28]

In Albany the young David Bird, who thought highly of the Americans in general, regarded the shore patrols as 'vicious'. In Perth, Jack Sue, an Australian who served with Americans on secret missions

*American personnel took turns at 'shore patrol'*
(Currie Hall, UWA)

and retained an abiding regard for them and their country, remembered the shore patrols as being 'very strict'. They thought nothing of using their batons first 'and asking questions later', but they never touched an Australian service-man. Syd Harvey, who saw extraordinary events at the ANA club, did not associate the Americans with undue violence. He used to drink at the Australia Hotel in Murray Street, next to Boans: 'A few times there would be a bit of trouble; half a dozen [shore patrol] would come in with a bloody great stick and wouldn't

*197*

hesitate to use it; and if things got worse they'd pull the gun out—but I never saw it used.'[29]

For some children, the almost routine violence became entertainment. Michael Papadoulis had vivid memories of his wartime childhood in Perth's Lake Street, between Newcastle and Brisbane Streets, a working-class area north of the railway line. He and his friends would wait eagerly for the fights, or 'yikes', between Americans, Australians and New Zealanders, which occurred about eight o'clock almost every night outside the Royal Standard Hotel, dubbed 'The Bloodhouse'.[30]

Yet while most violence might have been petty and even enjoyable—and kept in check by rugged methods—the possibility of more serious physical damage was always present. It was also from Lake Street, towards the end of the war, that the American Consul received the following remarkable letter from a Mrs Ashton:

> I'm writing to obtain information regarding one of your lads who was sentenced in August 1944 for killing my son the previous June. My son Arthur Reginald Flores who was a member of the R.A. Navy died on June 12th 44 as a result of being attacked by William Penzenik, a U.S. Naval rating.
>
> At first I was very bitter towards him for taking my boy away from me, and although the loss is still great I feel as though I should forgive this boy for what he did, as I know he wasn't in his right frame of mind when it happened. So do you think it possible for that boy to be released, as I feel sure he has learned his lesson by now. He also must have a Mother who loves him dearly and is anxious to have him free. I know how I'd feel if I were in her position, and it's mostly this thought that brings me to writing this letter. I feel too that my son would want me to forgive this boy, so I'd be very greatful [sic] if you could get him released. If he must finish his sentence would it be possible for me to write to him. If so would you be kind enough to forward me his address. I could then tell him he has been forgiven. Could I possibly have his mother's address too.[31]

The Consul was unable to meet any of Mrs Ashton's requests, for Penzenik had been transferred to prison in the United States and was thus as absent from the local scene as his offence was from the public record in Perth.[32] But even if the killing had been widely known, it would be as misleading to draw general conclusions from it as from Mrs Ashton's extraordinary willingness to forgive.

Another Perth woman, who eventually became an American war bride, saw two Australian soldiers accost an American serviceman one afternoon as he waited for his girlfriend at London Court in central Perth. When he said he had neither money nor cigarettes, they began to fight him, and the soldier died as a result of kicks to his head. She recalled the horror she felt, realising that men fighting a common enemy could also feel such emotion toward each other.[33]

Indelibly imprinted into the memory of the witness, that incident was nevertheless completely at odds with the recollections of Bill Barker, who spent several months in Perth in 1943 and returned for a similar period in 1944. With Australians in uniform scarcely ever to be seen in the hotels and nightclubs he frequented, his memories of casual violence within an essentially pleasurable era were almost entirely of brawls between different groups of Americans.[34]

A typical off-duty outing for the Catalina men would begin with a few beers at the mess hall in the University Boat Club, followed by a taxi ride into Perth. More intensive drinking would follow at the Savoy Hotel in Hay Street, where the 'six o'clock swill' produced occasional scuffles, as new arrivals elbowed their way through the crowds to the bar. But such incidents were minor among a largely familiar and entirely male crowd. Women were optional inclusions in the next stage—a meal at a nearby snack bar—and vital to the major proceedings at one of several small nightclubs above shops, also in Hay Street.[35]

The favourite club opened at 7 or 8 p.m., offering dancing space for twenty-five to thirty couples. Officially alcohol was prohibited, but this was no deterrent to resourceful Yanks, who perfected a system of hauling bottles by rope from an alley below through the men's room window. The only violence Barker could recall in this setting was a fight between his first and second girlfriends, a situation which he easily resolved by leaving the premises in search of a third.[36]

According to Barker, violence among the men would have been likely only if an American submariner had entered the club, for this section of town, centred on the Savoy but stretching south to include the bars of the Palace Hotel on the corner of William Street and St Georges Terrace, was Catalina territory. On the other hand, the 'Airdales', as the Catalina men were known, would not normally think of breasting the bar at the Wentworth Hotel, on the corner of William and Murray Streets, which was the focal point of 'Black Shoe'—or submariner—social life, stretching through the north-west section.[37]

Mutual suspicion meant that the two naval groups avoided each other more often than they fought. The Airdales were particularly wary because they were outnumbered, as virtually complete crews of submariners would arrive in town, forty or fifty strong, at the end of a long tour of duty. But Bill Barker recalled a major altercation, involving servicemen of several nationalities, in which submariners hurled huge plant pots from the upstairs balcony of the Wentworth Hotel onto opponents in the street below.[38]

Barker acquired a different perspective when assigned for a time to shore patrol. It was a novelty to be summoned to deal with a drunken friend from the Crawley Base, who had been seen 'making love to a horse in St Georges Terrace'. It was a revelation to deal with the many others who were nestling in the arms of the Western Australian authorities. While the police were generally reasonable in their attitudes to those who had lurched from the straight and narrow, the squalor of the lock-ups was a shock and the urgent priority was to rescue Americans as soon as possible from local custody. Since he was partnered on patrol by a submariner, these efforts might suggest a sense of American solidarity lurking beneath the mutual hostility of the two elite groups. But Barker did not immediately feel the warm glow of patriotism, as his patrol forced him to venture into Black Shoe territory wearing his provocatively distinctive uniform. Thrown bodily into the street from the first bar he entered, he was saved from further rough treatment by his partner's eloquence and improbably huge bulk for a submariner—at least six feet six inches and two hundred and fifty pounds.[39]

The recollections of this individual are vivid, detailed and at least partly corroborated by others. Yet, while they give a valuable American perspective to the situation in central Perth, it is notable that in two periods, each of several months, the informant never once visited Fremantle, where the always volatile cocktail of sailors, women and alcohol was being shaken in a traditionally rough waterfront area made even coarser by wartime circumstances. Although much of the violence here was of exactly the same nature as in central Perth, Fremantle was also a totally different milieu, and it needs to be considered separately.

# FLEETING ATTRACTION

## Chapter Ten

## VIOLENT FREMANTLE

VIRTUALLY EVERYBODY, Australian or American, who recalled the wartime metropolitan area from the vantage point of the late twentieth century regarded Fremantle as an altogether rougher environment than Perth, notwithstanding the many brawls around that city's entertainment facilities.

Jim Purcell, an American Red Cross official, avoided the port as much as he could, finding its waterside atmosphere quite threatening.[1] Many women who recalled the war as the high point of their social lives never went there at any time. This was not primarily because they were forbidden to do so by anxious parents, for similar vetoes on dating Americans had little effect.[2] It was more that the Americans they were dating also turned their backs on the port city. As we have seen, submariners, whose long and dangerous tours of duty began and ended there, used their welcome shore leave to live and play in central Perth. The virtual monopoly they and their equally well paid Catalina rivals exercised over taxis meant that it tended to be the less well paid or the transient who made Fremantle the focal point of their shore leave. In that environment it was inevitable that some Americans would be involved in violence, but the American presence was not its major cause.

Once again there is a problem in verifying specific incidents recorded only in the memories of individuals. According to Beryl Hackner's biography, Rosa Townsend's policeman husband was 'badly bashed on one occasion and on another he saw a stabbed American bleed to death on the pavement before anything could be done to help him'.[3] Censorship of the era makes it impossible to identify this particular incident. Equally irretrievable is the identity of an American submariner pursued by Australian soldiers but assisted by an Australian sailor. That sailor's memoir in a 1992 newspaper article has a dual poignancy: he never asked the name of the man he defended and he heard soon afterwards that his submarine had been lost on its next voyage.[4] Despite their vagueness, such memoirs have real value in evoking the atmosphere of the era, for there is much other evidence to support Rosa Townsend's conviction that 'it was unsafe for women to walk in the streets of Fremantle after 4 p.m.'.[5] There is a great deal to confirm that blood sometimes ran down those streets.

Censorship and security surveillance may have suppressed many specific incidents, but the records of those official agencies reveal others that have not figured in the recollections of contemporaries. More importantly, they make it clear how much the habitual roughness of the waterside was made even more threatening by frantic port activity and ruthless official security. And finally they reveal that the worst violence of all involving Americans had nothing to do with the US Navy based in Fremantle, but was a clash between transient American soldiers and New Zealanders.

It was not the Americans, but the war situation in general, that perpetuated the dangerous atmosphere that had prevailed when troops had been in transit to the Middle East in 1941. The blackout conditions introduced in early 1942 accentuated the always threatening night-time atmosphere of the port. In January of that year, more than a month before the arrival of any American forces, the Mayor of Fremantle warned that 'the streets are not safe for unattended females and are not desirable even with a male escort'.[6]

In March 1942, soon after the Americans arrived, the *Sunday*

*Times* advocated shorter drinking hours, the closure of bars when troopships were in port and restrictions on the sale of bottled beer: 'At any time civilians and soldiers may be called upon to resist a Japanese invasion... We cannot afford to be suffering a hangover when that time comes.'[7] Soon it was not only the always active women's groups that went further and campaigned for a blanket ban on the wartime sale and consumption of alcohol. One of the most vocal organisations was the Ministers' Fraternal, which lobbied the Fremantle City Council consistently throughout the war years. A deputation was received sympathetically by the Council, but the national censor would not allow any debate in the local media, apparently to prevent the enemy from discovering that Fremantle was a port![8]

It was also in March 1942 that there was growing nervousness about the violence that was beginning to occur in the vicinity of 'The Palms', the brothel in Bannister Street. A local businessman complained to the Town Clerk: 'Under the blackout conditions existing in Fremantle at the present time, with Australian, American, Dutch and Coloured Races well represented in the Port it will not be long before a serious riot takes place.'[9]

Local sensitivities were intensified in August 1942 when fifty Australian soldiers were arrested for drunkenness, disorderly behaviour, fighting and using obscene language when the ship *Rajoola* was in Fremantle. As Colonel O. V. Hoad eventually reported from Swan Barracks to Allied Headquarters in Melbourne, the ship was one of a convoy that called at Fremantle. 'During the time the convoy was in port a large number of troops were on leave from the ships... The behaviour of overseas troops passing through Fremantle has been the subject of considerable complaint and the Provost personnel have a difficult task to maintain order.'[10]

Troopships would continue to provide problems and eventually, in 1944, the ingredients for the metropolitan area's biggest riot, in which Americans—albeit Army rather than Navy personnel—were undeniably prominent. But too much emphasis on American servicemen, or indeed those of other nationalities, can distort the picture of port activity in wartime Fremantle. As vital to the war effort as the facilities for submarines and other naval vessels was Fremantle's role in the flow of merchant shipping. A great deal of the ugliness of the waterfront was connected with the unruliness of merchant seamen and the often draconian violence with which authority attempted to control them. Even though an increasing proportion of the shipping was American, the most violent incidents had nothing to do with Americans.

The shooting of Chinese seamen on 28 January 1942 was followed by a very similar incident a month after the US Navy arrived. The Chinese crew of the Dutch tanker *Saroena* had been in dispute with the master over pay for a long period. When the master rejected their demands to be discharged in Fremantle, the crew refused to work. In the words of the Security Service, the situation became 'ugly' on 31 March, and the master called for help from the Dutch minesweeper *Abram Crynssen*, which was lying nearby. An armed party boarded the *Saroena* and, when the crew still refused to be ejected, 'bayonets were used and one Chinese was run through. He subsequently died.'[11]

The rest of the Chinese then 'panicked' and ran for the side of the ship with the intention of escaping to the wharf over the decks of another Dutch ship, the *Ena*, lying alongside the *Saroena*. In the melee the guard fired on the Chinese, killing one outright and wounding four others. The quartermaster of the *Ena* was wounded, apparently by a ricocheting bullet, and six Chinese were taken into military detention.[12]

An Australia-wide censorship cable on the following day insisted: 'There must be no news references to Fremantle riot involving mutiny crew of Dutch tanker. Believed one sailor only killed.' And the same authority suppressed reporting of the inquest at Fremantle on 7 April 1942, which recorded an open verdict on the two sailors actually killed.[13] Behind the scenes, however, there was consternation. Anxious correspondence passed between the Western Australian Premier and the Prime Minister, and the state's Solicitor-General admitted that there was 'unquestionably' a prima facie case for a charge of murder against the Dutch captain and two ratings.[14]

Although these suppressed mutinies in 1942 had the most disastrous outcomes of all the violence associated with merchant seamen, in other ways waterside conditions were even more unstable in the following year. By then, the Security Service was employing an ethnic Chinese, Sergeant Fan, who 'visits all ships carrying Asiatic crews and, in addition, makes general inquiries around the wharves, particularly mixing with Asiatic seamen'.[15] Yet before long there was another confrontation, involving soldiers with fixed bayonets and some hundreds of Chinese seamen from several ships, armed with 'stones, clubs and meat-axes'.[16] Fortunately this incident ended without any further deaths.

Racial tensions were also evident in a threatening incident involving American merchant seamen. When the SS *Katrina Luckenbach* arrived at Fremantle on 14 January 1943, the US Navy moved in quickly to remove the boatswain and prevent violence spilling over onto the wharf. According to a 'Finding of Facts' signed by Victor Sadd, Lieutenant Commander, USNR, a US Navy Board of Inquiry, held in Perth on 22 January 1943, concluded that the dangerous situation on board the ship was

> primarily the result of the hate and fear of the Boatswain, Felipe Garcia, by practically all members of the deck force. Due to the fact that Garcia has threatened to do bodily harm and kill many members of the crew individually and members of the armed guard collectively. His reputation and temperament is such [sic] that in the minds of the crew he is liable to carry out his threats.[17]

Consul Turner, however, in a letter to the ship's owners in New York, reported that an earlier Naval Board of Inquiry, held on the ship, had identified a broader problem than the menacing instability of the boatswain. It had found

> that a situation existed on board which might cause loss of life and endanger the vessel. It was also found that the condition existing was principally the result of the attitude taken towards the

boatswain by practically all members of the deck force as a result, primarily, of his being a colored man.[18]

It was probably fortunate that on this occasion the tensions were contained on board ship, since, coincidentally, this was the start of a period in which social turbulence increased as the port became even busier with merchant as well as naval shipping. In February 1943 a visiting US consular official noted the irony that, immediately after Mason Turner's Vice-Consul, Charles O. Thompson, was transferred to Sydney at the end of December, 'American vessels commenced to arrive at this port with startling frequency'.[19] By the middle of the year Security was reporting a continuing growth in port activity. An average of fifteen ships a week were calling at Fremantle. 'These, however, are beginning to increase mostly because of the greater number of liberty ships calling at the port for orders after conveying materials to the East. During the three months ended 21st July, 146 ships called at the port, including 111 from overseas.'[20]

These trends prompted the US War Shipping Administration in Sydney to send its Marine Superintendent, Harold P. Petersen, to investigate. He discovered port congestion that threatened the war effort:

The port is very crowded and it is an absolute necessity that repairs be held down to a minimum and that all repairs that can be accomplished while ships are at anchor outside the harbor be completed there. The only time a vessel should be allowed to remain alongside the dock is the length of time it takes to give her water and fuel, no facilities being available to fuel and water vessels while at anchor.

Recommending the appointment of a permanent American official to oversee merchant shipping, he argued that it was essential that the appointee should have a car because 'vessels are being docked at both sides of the harbor, wherever berths are available, sometimes as far as five or six miles away from the central port of Fremantle'.[21]

This huge concentration of shipping obviously contributed to a social instability most clearly documented by those charged with keeping the vital flow of goods moving. The biggest problem facing American War Shipping official Samuel Richter, appointed in response to Petersen's recommendation, was that the absenteeism that invariably plagues merchant navies had more serious consequences in wartime. In September 1943 he received a letter from a representative of the shipping agents R. G. Lynn, complaining about the drunken condition of the crew on the SS *Edward W. Scripps*:

> I would suggest that, in view of the number of unfortunate occurrences of this nature we have had with American vessels during the past few months, every endeavour be made to sail these vessels at 7.30 in the morning and not in the afternoon as on practically every occasion there is trouble on board with drunkenness and in most cases the vessel incurs additional expense through her inability to sail at the time laid down...[22]

This was a problem both confirmed and tackled by the Australian Security Service in the following months:

> Until recently, considerable trouble was being experienced with men missing from their ships at the time it [sic] was due to sail. This applied particularly to American vessels. This was largely due to the fact that the sailing time was usually round about 4 p.m. when the men were scattered all over the town, mostly in hotels. A recent alteration in the sailing time to late at night has considerably overcome these difficulties.[23]

One man was employed 'doing nothing else but looking for and picking up ships' deserters'. If a deserter was found, he was immediately detained and held, probably for two or three days, until he could be placed on another ship that was due to sail. Although in this way the authorities were able to keep most ships fully crewed,[24] both the activities of the seamen, enjoying very brief shore leave, and the rigour of authority were significant components in the restless atmosphere of the Fremantle waterfront.

The authorities were worried not only by the problems introduced by seamen, but by the threat to wharf security posed by the local population. Soon after the American arrival, concern that petrol drums on the inshore side of Fremantle harbour were being 'pillaged' by civilians led to their removal and to generally tighter security arrangements.[25] Entry to the wharves was restricted to those holding passes. The Security Service issued them for military personnel, the Navigation authority for civilians and the Australian Navy for naval personnel.[26]

By far the largest number of passes were issued by Navigation, mainly because the pick-up shed for fifteen hundred permanent and five hundred casual waterside workers was inside the wharf enclosure. As the Security Service noted in 1943, this was considered to be a drawback, 'but with the present lay-out of the wharves, it would be difficult to overcome'. The wharves were guarded by Commonwealth Peace Officers, 'who appear to be doing a fairly good job. Security Service, Perth, are satisfied with the set-up.'[27]

Almost certainly dissatisfied were the relatives of Walter Temby, of 75 Hay Street, East Perth, who had been shot dead on 1 November 1942 by one of those Peace Officers. It was not of central importance to Temby's death that an American serviceman was involved in the preceding sequence of events. But his account of a night's carousing that became unusual only with the shooting of Temby illustrates the potential for violence in the dislocated wartime social atmosphere.

Edward Eugene Shook, fireman first class from USS *Pelius*, told police that he had become so drunk at a party on the evening of 31 October that he was 'not very clear as to what actually occurred in detail during the night'. He then went on to recall enough details to make the night seem interminable, with enough uncertainty to make his drunkenness incontestable:

> I do remember that after the party I went with my girl, another
> sailor and his girl to a Hotel or restaurant. (I do not recollect exactly

what type of place it was.) At this place we met another American sailor and his girl. A man named 'Walter'…came in with them and I take it for granted that Walter had been driving them around during the night. I would say the time was about 12 midnight. Soon after we all came down to Fremantle to enable my sailor friend to go on board his boat as his 'liberty' expired at 1 am. I cannot remember where we left him and I do not know if we went through the Wharf gates or not. We took this sailor's girl home. That left the sailor and his girl who came in with the driver 'Walter' and my girl and myself. We all then went to a place called 'Bernies' still being driven by Walter. At this place we had a meal and had some more beer. I would say the time was about 2.30 or 3 am by now. From 'Bernies' we all went to my girl's place and Walter, the other sailor and his girl drove off. I asked the driver to call back for me, which he did but I do not really know the time but it was daylight.[28]

Walter then drove him back to his boat. During the night he 'had quite a lot of beer and was fairly drunk'. Although he had sobered up slightly by the time he arrived at the wharf, he was still sufficiently under the influence of alcohol to alarm the American, who was 'fairly sober by this time': 'He was driving very fast and reckless and the car swayed a lot at times.' The officer guarding the first gate on North Wharf stood up, but did not try to stop the car. At the second gate the officer held up his hand or a small flag, causing Walter to slow down from about fifty to forty miles per hour. As the officer stepped back a little, Walter sped up through the gateway.[29]

The American said: 'Christ, you should have stopped!'. Walter replied, 'Oh, I'll stop when I'm going back. They probably want to question me because I'm a private car and have you in it.'[30]

When they came to the entrance to the Wharf proper, Shook 'hurried away without much further conversation'. There had been no agreement that Walter should be paid, 'and he did not ask for money for driving me about but when leaving his car I pulled out a one pound note and about 8 or 9 shillings and put it in his hand. He had no time to refuse or even thank me.'[31]

That was the last the American saw of his companion and almost the last Walter saw of the world. Other witnesses reported that his car stopped on its way back through the security gates, but then, as the guard's attention was momentarily distracted, it drove off. Three shots were fired. Walter was found with 'a bullet wound behind the right ear'.[32]

The American claimed that he had bought about twelve bottles of beer during the night from a hotel: 'I think it was somewhere between Perth and Fremantle. What we did not drink was left in the car because I was not allowed to take liquor on board the ship.' The investigating police officer reported: 'In the back of the car were 41 full bottles of beer, 3 empty bottles, and a broken bottle.'[33]

At the subsequent inquest the magistrate was more concerned to give a lecture about security than offer sympathy to those affected by the tragedy:

> The deceased came by his death at North Wharf Fremantle on the first day of November 1942 from injuries caused by a revolver shot fired by Vincent Yovich in the course of his duty as a Commonwealth Peace Officer. No blame is attachable to the said Vincent Yovich, as he had no intention of injuring the man. This will be a warning to people who go on the wharf that they must obey instructions of sentries and guards in time of war.[34]

The shooting may well have had the effect desired by the magistrate, for there were no comparable later incidents. Neither was a somewhat increased incidence of violence involving American servicemen in 1943 a result of the endemic racial prejudice. As we have seen, the handful of black Navy personnel now present were too few to be the cause of significant hostility either from the host community or from within American ranks. Rather, it was a question of the initial euphoria that had greeted the Americans fading away and the streets, hotel bars and larrikin atmosphere of the Fremantle area providing a battleground.

Security personnel, who had made their own contribution to the uneasy atmosphere of Fremantle, were curiously unable to accept that some violence was inevitable in the port. In one of its weekly confidential circulars in 1943, the Security branch of the Australian Army in Western Australia alerted senior officers to the potential for friction with American servicemen by quoting from a letter written by a member of the AIF:

> When we were coming out of [the] Harbour we passed a little naval launch with six Yanks in it, they were waving and yelling out 'Good on you boys—we'll take care of the girls for you'. It's useless for me to describe the 'nice' answers our boys yelled back... One of our chaps let go with an empty beer bottle but to our sorrow missed by a couple of inches... It does make you wild to hear them talk about what they've done...[35]

Wildness was likely to escalate into violence when servicemen taunted each other in crowded streets or bars, rather than hurling insults and bottles between rapidly diverging boats. Yet Army Security's recommendation was hardly realistic:

> Incidents such as these suggest the absence of a sense of humour and troops should be urged to think up suitable 'come backs' for such an occasion. A lot of these wise-cracks, although in bad taste, are not intended to be taken seriously and in any case, surely the 'girls' have something to say in the matter.[36]

By this time the 'girls' had already said a great deal. Not even a team of comedy script-writers could have equipped diggers with repartee to obliterate the scores of marriages, hundreds of engagements and thousands of relationships between local women and American men.

Indeed the same authorities were simultaneously acknowledging that Australian men were not using slick one-liners to counter American wisecracks:

A very serious view is taken of a brawl which occurred at the Naval
Base Hotel on 28 March between AMERICAN sailors and
AUSTRALIAN soldiers and civilians. Unfortunately ill-feeling
against our AMERICAN Allies still exists among the more foolish
and irresponsible elements of our forces, although it should be
obvious even to such limited mentalities, that if the AMERICANS
were not here the JAPS possibly would be. Occasionally, no doubt,
there exists real as well as fancied provocation on one side or the
other, but soldiers who are willing to sacrifice their lives to achieve
victory should have no difficulty in making the smaller sacrifice
of some slight damage to their feelings or dignity, rather than
jeopardise our common cause.[37]

A thorough investigation, in cooperation with US Navy authorities,
had already established that the disturbance 'was definitely an affray
and NOT a riot, and that the chief offenders were three AUSTRALIAN
soldiers and a number of civilians'.[38] The Army found this civilian
involvement particularly 'unpleasant' and even sinister:

It does not bode well for our resistance to 'Fifth Column' tactics if
troops can so easily be incited by outsiders into actions which they
are well aware are contrary to both policy and discipline. All ranks
should guard against being made the pawns of unpatriotic
individuals who, for their own purposes, seek to create dissension
among or between the Services.[39]

There were no press reports of the 'strong disciplinary action'
taken against the military personnel or the heavy fines imposed on the
civilians concerned on 19 May 1943.[40] It was in reporting to Canberra
the measures he had taken to suppress news of the brawl that Gavin
Casey, the State Publicity Censor, suggested that Army Security and
the American authorities seemed 'to be looking for someone's blood',
preferably that of the editor of the Mirror. In Casey's view 'the ultra-
sensitiveness on the part of the American authorities here at present'
was a result of the Mirror's slurs against American sexual peccadilloes

and recent broadcasts by the suspect local left-winger, Edward Beeby, which had criticised 'certain "reactionary" elements in the USA'.[41]

It is quite probable that by this time the *Mirror's* attacks were finding greater acceptance among a local population less inclined than in early 1942 to regard Americans as glamorous saviours. Yet, however provocative these fringe elements of the media may have been, it seems fanciful to look beyond the obvious factors of drink, sexual jealousy and general masculine unruliness for explanations of usually small-scale street violence involving American servicemen in Fremantle, as in Perth.

In September 1944 a Merchant Marine Detail of the United States Coast Guard reported an almost farcical incident in Mouat Street, Fremantle, at the entrance to the US Naval Base Headquarters. The master of an American tanker was attacked by 'an intoxicated and bloody Australian soldier' while 'in the arms of two local policemen'. The soldier ran 'about twenty feet, at the end of which he struck subject, whose arms were pinioned by the two policemen'. One of two watching US Navy sailors then struck the Australian soldier and one of the policemen knocked the soldier down. The soldier was arrested but the master was also taken off to the police lock-up, where he 'raised hell'. He was accused of being drunk, but the American consular authorities concluded that his behaviour was the result of an understandable sense of outrage at the treatment he had received.[42]

Annoying though it was to its victims, this incident was trivial in a wartime port where 'howling' mobs of Chinese had been quelled by bullets and bayonets, and where the shooting of a civilian motorist could simultaneously be deemed unintentional and a useful public warning about wharf security.

Tensions between Americans and Australians seem even more petty in comparison with the rampages of transit troops in the early years of the war and especially the fearsome reputation earned by visiting New Zealanders. The Mouat Street affray was a tiny knock-about scuffle compared to a huge riot which had gripped Fremantle and spread into Perth earlier that year. Yet that occasion was itself typical only of the almost mindless violence of servicemen passing through Fremantle: it was virtually irrelevant to any assessment of relations between Americans and the host community.

Over a long period local people had come to expect violence from New Zealand troops in transit. American and Australian servicemen were sometimes confined to base when a New Zealand ship was in port, and men from different countries allowed into the city only on alternate nights.[43] Married American soldiers were permitted to venture out, but even these caught taxis wherever they had to go.[44] Young women who had been allowed to mingle freely with Americans were confined to their homes by anxious parents.[45] In the eyes of local police, 'there has not yet been one convoy of New Zealand troops that have behaved themselves decently whilst here, fights, disturbances and damage being more frequent during their short stay'.[46]

While Kiwi crudity was displayed on a broad canvas, there was a widespread belief that the New Zealanders were particularly

*Censorship maintained the appearance of peace in Fremantle*
(Mask Productions, Perth; inset: Battye Library Newspapers)

antagonistic toward Yanks. Americans such as Bill Barker, Homer White, Irving Sizik and Carl Uphoff felt the hostility but were unable to explain it. In the view of Mrs Nicholls, who had such happy memories of the 'wonderful crowd' of Americans at Kalamunda, the reason was New Zealanders' jealousy of American affluence. Michael Papadoulis, on the other hand, was convinced that the two nationalities were like 'a red rag to a bull' to each other because of American hostility to the way Maoris and white New Zealanders mixed together.[47]

The perception that Maoris regarded the Americans as racist was certainly reinforced in Western Australia's most serious wartime riot, which occurred in April 1944. Minor players were British ratings on leave from HMS *Suffolk*, but the major conflict was between Americans and New Zealanders, almost entirely Maoris. The Americans were not submariners based in Fremantle, nor any of the other Navy men who enjoyed extended shore leave there from time to time, but Army personnel in transit overseas on a French transport. The Kiwis were on shore leave from the troopship *Ruys* en route to the Middle East, and had all but taken over the Palace Hotel in Perth and the National Hotel in Fremantle.[48]

It was in the latter location, on the corner of Market and High Streets, that some of the worst violence was to take place. The police were especially surprised at this because, considering the 'huge patronage' of this hotel at the city's main intersection, there was normally little serious trouble. Even now, although this and other hotels were open, there was nothing seriously amiss, apart from the usual 'hilarity' and some minor brawls, until the Americans appeared on a route march through the streets of Fremantle.[49]

New Zealand soldiers filed out of pubs and lined the streets 'catcalling and jeering' the Yanks as they went by. Civilian onlookers were apparently urging the men to fight.[50] Maori soldiers 'in particular were in a riotous mood' and the police were having great difficulty restraining them from attacking the US personnel. The Maoris' opportunity eventually came because some of the Americans peeled off from the march without leave, 'dodging down side streets until the column had passed and then going into the hotels, particularly the National Hotel'.[51]

Witnesses gave different versions of what occurred, but three key Americans—Hicks, Brekka and Arford—admitted to being intoxicated after drinking some eight to ten beers each. Because they had arrived at the crowded National Hotel direct from duty, they still had knives on their belts, in defiance of regulations. The barman testified at the resulting Magisterial Inquiry: 'Immediately, as if it was a pre-arranged thing, some New Zealanders said "Yanks" and then some went behind the partition as if to prevent them from leaving and some approached them from the front.'[52] According to the American Hicks, the fighting began in response to an offensive remark by a New Zealander.[53] A New Zealander claimed that British sailors were also involved in the brawl that broke out, but the casualties were all Maoris and Americans.[54]

Two Maoris, Ned Rako Kelly and Stanley Hooper, died as a result of knife wounds inflicted by the Americans. Soon the violence involved between five and six hundred people, spreading into a series of smaller brawls all along the main street of Fremantle. No Americans died, even though one was under severe threat at one stage in High Street near the Commonwealth Bank: 'He was observed with his pistol belt with waterbottle and other attachments swinging the gear about him in an attempt to keep the Maori soldiers at bay.'[55]

Hicks, Brekka and Arford were just a few of the many casualties of both nationalities who were taken on a truck and in two ambulances to several hospitals. As they were leaving Fremantle Hospital for Hollywood Military Hospital, ambulance driver Edward Armfield asked one of the wounded Maoris if he was willing to travel with Americans. He replied: 'Yes, I've got nothing against the Americans—we started it and we got it!'[56]

Trouble also spread into Perth, where Americans were singled out in hotels and other public places and hauled from buses and trams to be beaten up by New Zealanders. Along with other Americans, off-duty Catalina crewman Bill Barker was urged to get off the streets. Taking his girlfriend into a movie theatre for several hours, he emerged to find the streets very much quieter. He even spent some time in a bar drinking alongside New Zealanders before returning to base to hear general reports of a day of mayhem but nothing of the deaths in Fremantle.[57]

At the Magisterial Inquiry, the Americans pleaded self-defence and, with the help of extensive legal advocacy, were cleared of all charges.[58]

The understandable soul-searching provoked by the riot focused particularly on alcohol. The Ministers' Fraternal began its campaign anew, blaming all the brawls and violence between servicemen on their access to liquor. Wanting men 'to see the beauties of our country instead of spending their leave in hotels', the Fraternal's spokesman, a Reverend Mr Hunt, lobbied for the wholesale closing of bars while troopships were in port.[59] The Fremantle City Council was in full support of such measures, declaring them to be 'in the interests of our war effort'.[60] The Fremantle police also had firm opinions on the subject of alcohol. Sergeant Sholl reported to his inspector after the killing of the New Zealanders: 'I am strongly of the opinion that it is imperative that all licensed hotels in the metropolitan area should either be closed altogether, placed out of bounds, or at least be strongly picketed whilst bodies of troops are on leave.' Sholl believed Allied military authorities should take more responsibility for the supervision and control of their men, especially in hotels.[61]

Although the action that was being demanded was not forthcoming, these warnings were timely, for the latter stages of the war were to see troop movements on a scale that threatened renewed violence. As the next chapter will show, the manner in which various authorities responded to those threats, with recollections of the past and commentary on the future, provides a context for assessing an American presence that faded away almost unnoticed in the last months of the war.

# FLEETING ATTRACTION

*Chapter Eleven*

## RETURN TO NORMALCY

THE 'RETURN TO NORMALCY' was a phrase—and 'normalcy' itself, a word—invented by the United States President, Warren Harding, at the end of the First World War. It promised a return to normal peacetime pleasures, but it also marked the end of his country's brief excursion onto the international stage after more than a century of isolationism. That was a policy of choice for a country with the population and economic and industrial power to be a major force in international affairs. Very different from isolationism were the attitudes of Western Australians. Isolation had left them with ambivalent feelings about the rest of Australia but no doubt that they needed the reassurance of contact with the outside world. For them, 'normalcy' in 1945, had the word been used, would have meant not only the end of war, but return to a situation in which it was once again Britain, rather than the United States, that provided the most important of those contacts.

In Britain's war-shattered state there was no possibility that it could provide the reassurance of physical protection. But in a situation without immediate threat it was at least possible that Britain could resume its traditional role as a significant cultural reference point, for such a process would take place mainly in the hearts and minds of the people.

There were some signs that this role had never been entirely lost, even in the midst of the war and at the height of the American influx. The most public of popular entertainments, the cinema, was dominated by American films throughout the war, but this was a continuation of trends long established, not a consequence of the American presence. While people found escapism in the cinema—and a smattering of information in the rousing stories of its newsreels—it was to the radio that they turned for a regular diet of home entertainment. And the radio was not, in any significant sense, Americanised in these years.

The programmes of every commercial station, not just the ABC, were punctuated throughout the day by BBC news bulletins. Station 6PR had 'Highlights of the Hit Parade', but was also as likely to include Thomas Beecham and the London Philharmonic Orchestra as Xavier Cugat and the Waldorf Astoria Orchestra. 6PM began a typical Sunday's broadcast with 'The Fred Allen Show', presented by the US War Department. Later in the day its listeners could hear Bing Crosby singing 'White Christmas', Deanna Durbin's 'When the Roses Bloom Again' and Fred Astaire's 'I Can't Lie to You'. But if they were dedicated enough or unlucky enough to leave their radios on in anticipation of such delights, they could hardly miss the Royal Air Force Band, HM Royal Horse Guards Band, Victor Silvester and Joe Loss and their respective English dance orchestras and Elgar's 'Land of Hope and Glory'. And if they wanted the spoken word, they could wait up for Edward Beeby's 'The People's Session' at 9 p.m., presented by the Anti-Fascist (and frequently anti-American) League of WA, followed at 9.15 p.m. by the 'Church of England Fireside Talks'.[1]

While wartime radio programmes hint at the survival of traditional ties with Britain, trends in the last year of the war were undoubtedly reinforcing them as the Americans faded from the scene. The American presence was diminishing at a time when the transit of large numbers of British and New Zealand personnel through the metropolitan area was reviving enthusiasm for Imperial links. The

Americans were leaving Western Australia largely as they had arrived: without fanfare. The reason, however, now had little to do with the dictates of security. Partly it was because there was no grand, full-scale departure but a gradual dwindling away from mid-1944 to mid-1945. But the unceremonial exit of the Yanks reflected something much more significant. As they took with them most of the resources commanded by their affluence, they were unconsciously emphasising the essentially fleeting nature of their involvement: they had enjoyed the Western Australian scene without ever becoming integrated into it.

There were of course many individuals—and many families— who missed them sorely, just as there were many who had mourned the loss of submariners and other naval personnel who failed to return from dangerous missions. But there were also those with unhappy memories. Illegitimate children were left largely unacknowledged and most of the legitimate ones followed with the small army of war brides and fiancées. This exodus meant that those who had most completely succumbed to Americans' charm were following them away from Western Australia.

The large-scale movement of troops, which had pitted Americans against New Zealand Maoris in the streets of Fremantle in April 1944, was part of an increasingly successful Allied war effort. Although the United States had been drawn into the war by the Japanese attack on Pearl Harbour, the priority of Allied strategy ever since had been victory in Europe. Now progress in the European theatre at last allowed the Americans to concentrate on the war in the Pacific. Long before the European war ended, on 8 May 1945, this new focus was diminishing the American presence in Western Australia, as the Japanese were pushed further back.

An important stage came in July 1944, when the Catalina squadron left Crawley Bay and their advanced Geraldton base for New Guinea. There was probably more relief than sadness at The University of Western Australia, where initial enthusiasm had long since turned into irritation, as educational routine was disrupted and facilities suffered minor damage. Although it had been agreed a year earlier that owners of requisitioned property would not have to pay for permanent improvements made by the Americans, the accompanying decision was less welcome to the University: sanitary facilities and hot water supplies were not permanent improvements to the Engineering Building but 'fitted up in a temporary steel hut erected on a concrete floor' and therefore removable. When the Americans duly removed them it took more than twelve months for the building to be restored to normal.[2] In Geraldton, on the other hand, it was evidently too much trouble for the Americans to take with them perhaps the most valuable commodity they had brought: large quantities of aviation fuel were simply left in their bulk storage tanks.[3]

It could be argued that the common denominator underlying these contrasting actions was American arrogance, or at least indifference to the local scene. They had come to do a job and were leaving without a backward glance. But of course on the level of individual relationships much more complex attitudes were involved. The mixture of emotions that accompanied their departure can be illustrated by individual cases but defies any overall measurement.

The dashing 23-year-old Catalina pilot, Bill Barker, departed with his leg encased in plaster. He was something less than a wounded hero. Dancing the hokey-pokey at a Geraldton party, and annoyed by the news that the beer had run out, he had kicked the keg and broken his leg. The contrast can seem stark between his masculine exuberance and the romantic notions of his nineteen-year-old girlfriend, Pat. His determination to reject convalescent leave and 'get back into the war' was more successful than Pat's determination to follow him to the United States and marry him. Yet however neatly this broken romance may seem to symbolise the discordant priorities of American servicemen and local girls, these were two people who would remain in touch, each through two failed marriages to other people, for the next fifty years.[4]

As the Catalina men such as Barker left, the submariners remained, but their eventual departure was inevitable from October 1944, when General MacArthur fulfilled his famous pledge to return to the Philippines by launching an invasion with forces comparable in

Bill Barker: not quite a wounded hero
(Currie Hall, UWA)

size to those deployed in the more celebrated Normandy landings five months earlier. Just as D-Day had marked the beginning of the climactic stage in the European theatre, the recapture of the Philippines was the launching pad for the final attack on Japan. Although the Fremantle submarine base would remain into the following year, in a sense the climax came in December 1944, when a children's party organised by the US Navy was effectively a lavish farewell and thankyou to the people of Perth.

This was very far from the first such gesture. Early in 1944 the captain of an American ship had thrown a party for school children which had greatly impressed the Fremantle Mayor with its generosity.[5] But that had been, at best, a mere rehearsal for the huge Christmas party. Fifteen thousand invitations were sent to school children, but on the day many more considered themselves invited. As the *West Australian* put it, 'Every main road, bus, train and tram route during the morning seemed to lead to Gloucester Park, a magnet which drew the youngsters from the city streets'. US Navy trucks, cars and buses ferried children to and from orphanages. A huge crowd of boys and

*Gloucester Park 1945: The fond farewell*
(Mask Productions, Perth)

girls gathered outside the famous local trotting track, persuading the organisers to open the gates an hour early. Next day the *West Australian* estimated that fifty thousand had 'joined in the happy function... Soon after 2 p.m. Gloucester Park had the appearance of the Royal Show on Children's Day.'[6]

One hundred and fifty officers and three hundred and fifty enlisted men helped to supervise merry-go-rounds, pony rides, movies, magnet cars, sideshows and sports. Father Christmas made an appearance and the Americans had doctors and ambulance services standing by in case of emergencies. This was a wise precaution, for the excitement could easily have got out of control. As the *West Australian* reported:

> Surging masses of children rushed the various centres of entertainment and refreshment, and an unenviable task faced the stallholders. The guests stood five and ten deep around all the centres

*Gloucester Park 1945: refreshments galore*
(West Australian Newspapers)

of attraction and by degrees retired satisfied or decided not to wait a turn in the turmoil. Every centre was packed to capacity and for hours on end the servicemen scarcely had time for a breather.[7]

Two and a half thousand pounds had been allocated to the event, most of which was spent on supplying hot dogs, chewing gum and Coca-Cola to the children. 'Imagine', reminisced one participant many years later, 'when we saw this huge navy truck coming in with crates of Coca-Cola. Never before had we tasted this delightful dark brown drink, let alone seen these marvellous "bobby bottles"… Heaven was ours.'[8]

Not surprisingly, a party on this scale remained vivid in the memories of many of the participants fifty years later. For those who were younger children at the time it may well be their only recollection of the American presence. It might even be one tiny factor in the enduring Western Australian enthusiasm for every American fleet to arrive in Fremantle throughout the Cold War and beyond. Yet the warmth of the mutual goodwill displayed at Christmas 1944 was the beginning of the end of a unique but brief era, not the start of the closer identification with the United States that might be imagined by observers of the Americanised culture of the late twentieth century.

In 1945 there were signs in the newspapers that the petty wartime violence associated with servicemen lingered on in Perth. In early May the *West Australian* reported a brawl among sailors at Cottesloe, which had led to two injuries and four charges. It also reported that a woman had been charged with stealing a bottle of whisky, a part bottle of gin, a revolver and a hunting knife after drinking all day with an American sailor. She claimed she had taken the gun and knife because the American was waving them around, but 'she did not know why she took the liquor'.[9]

More relevant to the spirit of the times, however, were other items in the paper at this period. In the same edition the West Australian National Football League announced the official re-opening of the local football competition. And the following day the newspaper reported that 445 war brides and 140 children of Australian servicemen overseas had reached Australia by the end of April. Another 421 wives were awaiting passages, 284 of these being from the United Kingdom. Underlying these disparate pieces of news was the imminent end of the war in Europe. Hitler's demise had been reported by the *West* the day before the brawl at Cottesloe and the international altercation over liquor and side arms. Now the paper's main preoccupation was with the appropriate way to celebrate the partial victory which was about to be achieved, while there still remained much to be done in the Pacific war. Announcing that there was to be no public holiday, the *West* decided that 'most members of the public will lean towards a natural inner rejoicing and public manifestations of thanksgiving, rather than unbridled celebrations'.[10]

It was a moment for the newspaper itself to reflect on the recent past. Its 'Vignettes of Life in Perth Through the War Years' told of the strange atmosphere of the early months of 'phoney war', the 'khaki flood' of troops in transit, and the way in which 'one fine day, when the city's spirits were at a low ebb, a convoy steamed into harbour and the word spread like wildfire—"The Yanks are here"'. It went on to suggest that, while many had been annoyed in the subsequent years, as the roar of Catalina engines woke them in the early hours, 'it brought during those troublous days a comforting sense of security and it was always with relief that Perth welcomed them again each afternoon as they returned from their long vigil'.[11]

Even as it did justice to the Americans, however, the *West* was also looking to Europe. Standing apart in its 'Vignettes of Life in Perth' was a highlighted box headed 'HITLER WAS RIGHT' and celebrating 'the spirit of the British nation'. Hitler had written in *Mein Kampf* that this spirit

> enables it to carry through to victory any struggle…no matter how long such struggle may last or however great the sacrifices that may be necessary, or whatever the means that have to be employed; and all this though the actual equipment to hand may be utterly inadequate when compared with that of other nations.[12]

And alongside, in a separate article, the paper carried a story about the arrangements being made for Australians released from European prisoner-of-war camps to spend a 'restful, enjoyable and beneficial' period in Britain awaiting their repatriation. The British Red Cross was organising their care in staging camps in Europe, their passage to Britain and their welcome at 'two of England's grand old homes' in Eastbourne. While formal arrangements were being made to accommodate them in 'comfortable, home-like billets near the sea… numerous offers of hospitality have been received at Australia House and it will be possible to send an Australian soldier to any part of the British Isles he wishes to see'.[13]

Three months later, on 15 August 1945, the Japanese surrender brought what was variously known as VJ Day and VP Day. It was a moment for the *West Australian* 'to pull aside the veil of secrecy' which had 'shrouded the operations' of the US submarine base at Fremantle. From the most significant base in the Pacific war American submarines had accounted for '2,000,000 tons of enemy shipping and warships sunk and another 3,500,000 tons damaged'. At the same time, the newspaper gave generous and detailed attention to the contributions Americans had made to the local scene. If it hinted at friction, it also showed understanding:

> It was sometimes necessary to remind critical Australians that these men—irresponsible and inconsiderate though they sometimes appeared—were not ordinary joy-riders. They were men whose anxieties and service duties were particularly nerve-shaking and, if their exuberance was at times a little too enthusiastic for the mild-mannered civilian, there were very good reasons for it. There was sometimes a tendency to criticise unduly and even harshly, but few today will wish to suggest that the vast majority of our American visitors were other than worthy representatives of their country— generally gracious and considerate, much more courteous than local standards demanded and wholehearted in their desire to repay any kindness and the wealth of hospitality that was showered upon them.[14]

Yet the *West's* report of the VP Day celebrations also revealed other emotional ties. The assemblage of a hundred thousand people was probably 'the greatest crowd ever assembled in Perth'. It was a pointer to future realities that in the victory parade of nearly seven thousand servicemen and women and ex-servicemen 'the men of the United States Navy, headed by Old Glory, reflected the inspiring vigour of a nation feeling the immensity, and responsibility, of its power'. Yet the report gave just as much attention to 'the small unit of the Nether-lands Navy which followed' the Americans, 'a reminder of greatness in small nations, and stout hearts in the face of shattering adversity'. And it noted 'a special warmth and resounding cheers for the the men of the AMF, some in jungle green, some prematurely aged, some smiling and some grimly indifferent to the enthusiasm of the crowd'. It was a sign that an extraordinary interlude was coming to an end that the women's auxiliary, marching proudly 'in their khaki trim', were 'mostly smiling as if conscious that their job was nearly done, and well done'. It was a sign that traditional ties remained strong that 'the cheers of memory' the newspaper chose to highlight were for 'a small contingent of Royal Air Force personnel who followed the RAAF. They symbolised the few to whom the world owed so much.'[15]

The Victory Parade and Thanksgiving Service on the Esplanade was a solemn 'emotional and spiritual outlet for thanksgiving', backed by a massed choir and the Salvation Army Band. But VP Day was also an occasion for adults to come out to play with great abandon. No doubt some Americans joined in the impromptu street parties that marked VP Day. But by this time their reduced numbers meant they played no special part in the *West Australian's* report of the 'carnival atmosphere' as an estimated thirty thousand people frolicked in the streets of Perth;[16] and no part much later in the memories even of those who recognised forever the contribution they had made to the winning of the war.

Pat Catt, sister of a war bride and proud aunt of a Perth-born American niece, had a stock response to Australian grandchildren who complained about 'the bloody Yanks reckoning they won the war':

> Look, what you kids should learn…is this—if it hadn't been for the Americans we *wouldn't* have won the bloody war… When the Americans came in and helped us, we needed the help and they gave it to us. There's too many Australians forget that now.[17]

Yet on VP Day the Americans were as irrelevant to Pat as to the thousands of fellow Sandgropers who welcomed the return to normalcy with behaviour as abnormal as any that had occurred throughout the war. 'All the whistles started blowing early in the morning…and the horns were blowing and the cars were tearing around everywhere', and all Pat could think of was going into town. Her husband refused to desert his shore post in the Australian Navy: 'So, I thought, bugger you, mate, I'm going to town!' Leaving her small baby in her mother's arms, she went.[18]

*VP Day: William Street, Perth*
*(West Australian Newspapers)*

In the old Metropole Hotel her friend Betty Atkinson was standing on a table singing, free beers were coming from all directions and the doors were locked to prevent a catastrophic crush. Once outside again, there was no choice but to 'go with the mob' as it surged through the inner city streets. A baby was snatched playfully

*VP Day: rushing into town*
(West Australian Newspapers)

from a pram, hoisted aloft on friendly shoulders and carried down the street, its mother in anxious pursuit. Australian soldiers removed a policeman on point duty on the corner of Barrack and Hay Streets. Some sat on him in the shadow of the Town Hall, while one took over to direct a flow of entirely pedestrian traffic. In Forrest Place more servicemen removed the driver of a small car and heaved it to the top of the Post Office steps. Others dumped the driver of a number six tram on the footpath and rode it, with many passengers and little control, from the city, past the Children's Hospital in Thomas Street and down the hill until gravity halted it outside the Subiaco Hotel in Rokeby Road.[19]

The wildness of VP Day was of course exceptional, but not so the virtual irrelevance of the Americans. On the following day another

*VP Day: going with the mob*
(West Australian Newspapers)

public children's party was held, this time organised by the WA Trotting Association and held at the WA Cricket Association's Ground, across the road from Gloucester Park, where the Americans had entertained so lavishly eight months earlier. The US Navy supplied chewing gum.[20]

The Americans had been vital to the defence of an isolated state, exciting to many in a lonely female population and crucial to the outcome of the war. But over the preceding months of 1945 it was not only newspaper reports that had made it clear that the social impact of American servicemen in Western Australia would be less sustained than might have been expected four years earlier.

As the American presence was winding down in 1945, things were still very far from normal in Perth. But the final spasms of social upheaval were helping to highlight both the uniqueness and the impermanence of the American interlude. As attention focused on the war with Japan, servicemen of many Allied nationalities passed through Perth and Fremantle in tens of thousands, evoking memories of the upheavals of the first two years of the war before American entry. The crucial effect was not that the American presence was obliterated by this new wave of uniforms but that its unique self-sufficiency was highlighted.

The affluence and self-confidence that had made the Americans so attractive to a threatened populace four years earlier now made them largely irrelevant to those dealing with immediate problems and preparing for the post-war world. These trends were especially apparent in debates about the proposed closure of Perth's largest social and welfare facility for visiting servicemen.

The Phyllis Dean Service Club and Hostel, on the corner of Murray and Irwin Streets, provided meals and beds for hundreds of servicemen each day and night. Throughout 1945 its supporters and voluntary workers, led by Mrs Dean herself, fought a protracted battle to convince Australian Army authorities in particular that the financial benefits of closure were likely to be far outweighed by the social costs.

At first the main concern was to provide for Australians. Although the women were pleased that the war had taken such a favourable turn, 'we feel the need still exists for service men who are on home leave and perhaps from country districts'.[21] Very soon, however, both Phyllis Dean herself and federal MP Dorothy Tangney were writing to the Acting Minister for the Army about the need to cater for a new, large-scale international influx of servicemen. Over the previous three months catering services had provided for more than 20,000 British seamen. On VE day alone, over 6000 servicemen and women had attended a luncheon, while each night more than 830 were provided with beds.[22]

As a debate began with Army authorities who resented paying rent for the building,[23] the women volunteers rejected suggestions that they were moved by anything other than altruism. Mary McKinlay, president of the Women's Auxiliary of the RSL State Executive, told

Senator Fraser: 'The many protests you receive are coming from the voluntary workers themselves. The closure of the Club would mean lighter duties for them but they are not thinking of themselves but of those who are doing so much for us.'[24]

Genuine though such gratitude was, it is also true that supporters of the club included people anxious to avoid recurrence of the violence that had occurred in 1941 before its foundation. Prominent among these was the Federal Member for Perth, Tom Burke, who thought it would be 'extremely undesirable that visiting servicemen, either of our own forces or of allied services, should be denied the provision of accommodation'.[25] Closely associated with both Burke and the Young Australia League, whose premises had been taken over for the hostel, was *Sunday Times* editor J. J. Simons. Writing to the Minister for the Army, Frank Forde, Simons pointed out that 30,000 New Zealand troops were due to come through Perth in the following three months. He also noted that Mrs Dean had been asked to provide Christmas dinner and entertainment for 2000 servicemen, mostly RAAF, due to arrive on Xmas Eve on the *Athlone Castle*: 'If it had not been for your decision to keep the place open, New Zealanders, and the troops on the Athlone Castle, would have been left to roam the City.' Explicitly recalling the violence of 1941—and almost certainly remembering the Maori–American bloodshed of April 1944—Simons thought it was 'obvious' what would happen if the hostel was closed, even though the war was over.[26]

As Simons developed a conspiracy theory, which saw rampaging troops as a means of discrediting the federal Labor government, prolonged debate, principally conducted in confidential correspondence between Perth and Canberra, involved many more detailed arguments than are relevant to the story of the American presence in Western Australia. Indeed, it is the total irrelevance to the Americans of the Phyllis Dean Hostel and the question of its closure that is most important to this story. As we have seen, they had found little use for this and nearby clubs, hostels and canteens as they revelled in the abundance of their own messes and private clubs. Now, as the arguments raged among Australians about the fate of the locally organised club and hostel 'for servicemen of all nationalities', the Americans were making their own independent decisions about the facilities they had set up for themselves.

Far less conspicuous than the massive party that lavished hospitality on the children of Perth, but equally revealing of the nature of the American relationship with Western Australia, was the departure of the submarine chief petty officers from their private club on the Esplanade foreshore. They had demonstrated their carefree affluence by renting the premises for a sum that had rescued their landlords from the threat of insolvency. Now, after alternately amusing and amazing their local neighbours with their indifference to bureaucratic niceties and their access to exotic luxuries, they left the place almost as they had found it, stripped of expensive curtains, air-conditioners and sundry fittings otherwise either unobtainable or unknown. If their biggest innovation was as immovable as the fuel tanks abandoned in Geraldton, the contents of the huge septic tank were distinctly less useful.[27]

In this last year of the war there were many individual regrets, on the Australian side, that the Americans were leaving, as well as some official acknowledgment of the vital role they had played in a time of desperate vulnerability. But in the background was a renewed sense of the importance of British and Imperial ties.

No public figure had been more enthusiastic in welcoming the Americans in 1942, with warm words and hospitable gestures, than Lord Mayor Meagher. Yet three years later, in April 1945, Dr Meagher was presiding over a very British occasion. The visit of the newly appointed Governor-General, the Duke of Gloucester, was a particularly strong symbol of traditional links that would see Australians calling themselves British for another decade and more. Whatever they may have thought about the collapse of Singapore, and about British culpability for the desperate circumstances that had led their Prime Minister to turn to the United States, the Lord Mayor and Perth City councillors were only too pleased to welcome a Duke who was not only British but the brother of King George VI. And however grateful they were for the American presence in the previous few years, 'mayors and road board chairmen from all over the state, with their wives, sons and daughters' revelled in the opportunity to attend a reception for the Duke and his Duchess in a Town Hall 'transformed into a floral bower', where 'tall bamboos flanked the stairway leading up to the main hall, while in the hall itself a red carpet led to the dais between veritable gardens of maidenhair ferns, coleus and begonias'.[28]

Any thought that this lavish occasion was a hollow gesture, empty of real sentiment, must have been dispelled in the following month, May 1945, when Dr Meagher joined the chorus of protest over the threat to the Phyllis Dean Hostel:

> As Lord Mayor of this City I consider it of paramount importance that provision should be made for the entertainment of visiting personnel of the Royal Navy and the services of our Allies. This is a definite way in which the citizens of Western Australia can show

*Return to normalcy: the Duke and Duchess of York at Perth Town Hall, April 1945*
(West Australian Newspapers)

their appreciation of our kinsfolk in Great Britain for the many sacrifices they have made on our behalf.[29]

On the following day, Mary McKinlay of the RSL contended that all service amenities should be retained in the city, especially for the sake of 'the lads of the RN':

> Not only do the British Navy boys appreciate the provision of meals and beds but the fact that the Service Club is run by women voluntary workers means much to them. We remind them of their womenfolk at home. After long service on the Coast of India they tell us how wonderful it is to be able to speak to us—sometimes even in their very own local dialect.

To close the hostel now would mean 'we are closing the door of hospitality to those who with the AIF are going to see the job through in the Pacific'. She pointed out that many of these sailors had not only enjoyed the hostel's amenities in Perth but, through its agency, had been billeted in Australian homes. This was 'a contact which may have far reaching effects'.[30]

The effects hoped for had been spelled out by Phyllis Dean herself two months earlier, as she wrote to Army Minister Forde about the 'blot on Western Australia should we have to close down for want of support'. She was writing 'with the knowledge that these men from overseas may be the prospective migrants of the future and their welfare is most important'. Her eventual gratitude for Forde's intervention made it clear which part of 'overseas' she was thinking of:

> On many days the majority receiving meals and beds and other accommodation are from the R.N. These men need comforts more than their American cousins, who have greater spending power and can therefore secure comforts which are out of reach of the British lads.[31]

There is, of course, always some doubt about how representative the special pleas of individuals may be, especially those of politicians. Tom Burke may have thought it tactically essential to stress that he was not in collusion with Mrs Dean but responding to the representations of 'other citizens...expressing the fear that, if this club should be closed, servicemen would be unable to obtain the facilities which it provides'.[32] Far more convincing evidence about public opinion is to be found in the conspiracy theories developed by Burke, J. J. Simons and others. In their confidential correspondence with Canberra they argued that moves to close such facilities, when they were sorely needed by British personnel, were intended to make the Labor government seem anti-British. As Simons told Frank Forde,

> There is definitely a political 'pull' in the move to close down the work. During your absence in England all sorts of strings were pulled to close clubs of this kind. As you know we have our scouts out for news from the staffs of our papers, and we are in an unique position to get first-hand knowledge. We know definitely that there was an Australia-wide effort on the part of certain interests to create a position in which, while personnel of the British Navy were here in force, they would be without the amenities which were kept going when the Australian forces were in greater numbers.

He cited evidence from Sydney 'that an effort was made to create a situation from which the charge could be made that the Labour [sic] Government was purposely withdrawing amenities for members of the British Navy'. And even at the end of January 1946 he reiterated that in the previous June 'a movement was on foot to stop amenities for British seamen—that was when our men were receiving wonderful hospitality in England'.[33]

While Imperial sentiments may have been particularly strong in the West, national migration policies were also reaffirming traditional links in this last year of the war. In October a parliamentary questioner noted that the government's offer of free passage facilities to British servicemen and their dependants as immigrants 'had been received exceptionally well in the UK' and asked for the same privileges for former US servicemen. The Minister for Immigration, Arthur Calwell, replied that this was not possible because the British Government was paying the passages of its emigrants and the Australian Government paying for their settlement. He believed completely in the desirability of American ex-service immigrants, but 'their situation is not analogous with that of British ex-Servicemen, whose migration to Australia will be in the mutual interest of the United Kingdom and Commonwealth'.[34]

There was little to suggest that the policies were thwarting potential large-scale American immigration. True, the US authorities had agreed as early as March 1944 that their servicemen could be discharged overseas; and the Australian Government was willing to give 'favourable consideration' to such men to remain in Australia as long as they were 'of *European race or descent...*'.[35] But quite apart from the emotional pull back to the United States, there were strong economic deterrents to settlement in Australia, perhaps particularly in the West. At the end of October 1945, the US Consulate in Perth prepared 'Basic Information for American Ex-Servicemen Contemplating Residence in Western Australia', pointing out the probability of keen competition for post-war jobs with Australian ex-servicemen: 'While America enjoys at the present time a considerable popularity in Western Australia, increasing economic pressure may well operate to deny any alien advantages which might be at the expense of the Australian.'[36]

The Consulate's response to the specific inquiries that came its way was to draw attention to the pessimistic message of this pamphlet. Two inquirers were American Navy radio operators. Miss M. O'Neill of Carlisle was well prepared for bad news when she approached the Consulate on behalf of her 21-year-old fiancé, who planned to return the following year to study advanced radio engineering. She was concerned about his likely job prospects, especially as 'there will be many Australian servicemen to be placed in Radio jobs'.[37] Less realistic was E. V. Tate, who had spent six months in Fremantle, become engaged to a Cottesloe WAAAF and now sought a post as radio operator at the Consulate.[38] Not only was there no such position but, the Consulate told a would-be immigrant shipfitter and welder, there was no ship-building industry in Western Australia either.[39]

Even more significant than the lukewarm response to such inquiries is that there were so few of them. As Perth consular official Courtland Christiani wrote in late October 1945:

> Of the American servicemen entertaining the desire to return to this State for settlement, evidence of interest known to this office is limited to perhaps a score of inquiries, plus the expressed intention on the part of several husbands to return here in the event that their wives, for one reason or another, are unable to join them later in the United States.[40]

This comment highlights the overwhelming trend of the era: in the same document Christiani summed up what the Consulate in Perth regarded as an essentially happy American relationship with the people of Western Australia. More than four thousand Naval personnel in Perth and Fremantle had been 'in the main, well received by the local inhabitants and they, themselves, reacted favourably to their surroundings'. But while those favourable impressions had produced only this 'limited' interest in permanent residence, the locals most impressed by the Americans were desperate to leave:

> Marriages and engagements reached four figures, the result being that, with the departure of practically all the American personnel, there is a residue of several hundred Australian wives, a great many children and a considerable number of fiancees, all of whom besiege this consulate for visas and aid in procuring transportation.[41]

Although a tiny handful of Americans, such as Homer White and Bob Kane in Albany, and Charles Farkas, Bill Pouleris, Andy Andersen, Irving Sizik, John Glotzbach, Carl Uphoff, Jack Hanks and Dewey Balcombe in the Perth metropolitan area, remained in Western

Australia with their local wives, or returned sooner or later to take up residence, they were a tiny proportion of the thousand or more who had married local women.

On 16 August 1943 the *West Australian* had reprinted a warning from a highly placed United States Army official that many Australian women marrying American servicemen were likely to be disillusioned about the mode of living in America: 'The girls' ideas have been coloured by what they see in the films but not every working family's home in America has beautiful enamel sinks and plenty of electric labour-saving devices.'[42] The warning had little effect. Australian brides, in the remaining years of the war and in the immediate post-war era, went to America in their thousands. For very many of them there was a difficult waiting period before they tested the reality of

*Hal and Edna Lee: married at Baptist Church in Perth, 10 February 1945*
(Edna Lee)

America against the Hollywood ideal. For those from Western Australia it required especial patience and resilience, whether their American ambitions were fired by movie-induced fantasy or the electricity of true love.

The ordeal began close to home. Unless they were pregnant, most had to wait officially for six months for permission to marry. Although the *West Australian* reported that 'investigation was made only when enlisted men were concerned or officers in special circumstances',[43] Australian clergy were expected to obtain written permission from the Commanding Officer of an American serviceman before performing nuptials. The intended brides of enlisted men had to undergo an investigation by the American Red Cross, partly to ascertain that they had no 'coloured' blood. Whether they were married or simply engaged, applicants for visas had to await police clearances. Consular records for 1944 revealed a number of cases where visas were refused because of convictions for petty theft and, in one case, being 'idle and disorderly', which was interpreted as being a prostitute.[44]

The same records contain much correspondence between the Perth and Sydney Consulates, and some letters from Thomas Cook Ltd in Perth, about the difficulties of wives and fiancées of American servicemen obtaining passages to the United States.[45] It required special perseverance, some status and a certain naive self-confidence combined with good luck for Johnson Head and his new wife, Triss, the nurse he met in Geraldton and married at Crawley, to overcome these obstacles in 1944.

Speedy marriage had been an affirmation of commitment, not a device for overcoming the immigration delays affecting fiancées. Even fifty years later, the couple were unaware of how much more difficult it would have been to pursue Triss's original plan of following after the war for a wedding in the United States. The unofficial arrangements that Johnson was able to make for his new wife to fly to the eastern states were unusual, even for fellow officers. Even so, it was some time before his persistent badgering of every United States Navy office in the east paid off, with the securing at short notice of a passage to the United States from Melbourne.[46]

More cautious spirits might then have baulked at the prospect of an unescorted voyage across the Pacific and later been terrified by an abrupt evasive action to avoid Japanese submarines. But if the couple could so easily have been unlucky, they were well aware of their almost unique good fortune in being able to travel together on a ship carrying some three hundred war brides but only two other American grooms.[47]

Unknown to them, their good fortune was implicitly being spelled out in the weeks between their marriage on 17 March and their departure in late April 1944. On 5 April, when Perth Consul Mason Turner reported that there were currently 146 wives and 127 fiancées 'listed at this office as visa applicants', it was also reported that many were going to the eastern states to get visas, as there was no transport directly out of Fremantle. The US Navy was doing nothing to help its personnel transport their women, many of whom were being stranded, often without adequate financial support.[48]

While it was true that most bride-ships left from the eastern states and only one from Fremantle throughout the war, it proved to be an unwise decision to go east before acquiring a visa. As the numbers of brides and fiancées far outstripped transport capacity in the last two years of the war and beyond, berths were allotted in accordance with the dates visas had been issued.[49] Long before they became aware of this pitfall, however, virtually all such women, except Triss Head, had experienced the unique Western Australian hardship of transport to the eastern states. Widespread adverse publicity made this always cramped, and often hot and harrowing, train trip across the Nullarbor an even sterner test of true love than the military and bureaucratic minefield that had to be negotiated to achieve permission to marry and the documents to travel.

The journey across the Nullarbor on the 'The Perth Perambulator' took five days to Melbourne, where Western Australian women met up with hundreds more war brides before heading on to Brisbane or Sydney.[50] Fresh water was rationed carefully, and even those with babies were supplied with a special soap that allowed them to wash in salt water.[51] Always taxing, the journey was occasionally horrific. In September 1945, there was an outcry in the press, and much correspondence between American Consulates in Melbourne, Perth and Sydney, about the atrocious travelling conditions—'even prisoners-of-war would never be given such treatment'—suffered by thirty-four war brides and their nineteen children on the trans-continental train. With as many as eight women and four babies crowded into some compartments, the worst part of the journey was from Perth to Kalgoorlie, as voluntary helpers were organised at Adelaide to provide relief for their physical and emotional distress.[52]

By the time these women reached the east coast the problems associated with the shipping shortages were already well publicised. On 6 December 1944, under the headline 'Long Wait for Ships: Desperate Financial Plight', the Sydney *Daily Telegraph* reported that a large number of war brides in Sydney had been told they might have to wait twelve months for a ship. To illustrate its theme that 'many of them are without relatives or friends in Sydney, and their financial resources are rapidly dwindling', the *Telegraph* focused especially on the plight of brides staying at the Traveller's Aid hostel.[53]

All but one of the women at the hostel came from Perth, and had no relatives in Sydney. Interviews with seven of the Perth women were reported in detail. Already waiting in Sydney for three months, and unable to rent flats because landlords refused to take children, they were forced to live in the hostel, which did not provide meals. Claiming that their children were constantly sick from eating nothing but cafe meals, they also complained about the cost of living, which averaged about £10 a week for each of them.[54]

After several anecdotes of their difficulties with sick children and frustrations with the search for accommodation, the article ended: 'Girls from Perth are warned by Thomas Cook and Son they must take the risk of remaining in Sydney for an indefinite period—possibly many months—before they can secure passage to America.'[55]

If anything the shortage of shipping, and the low priority placed on the movement of servicemen's dependants, grew worse in 1945, as the European war ended and naval resources were concentrated on the Pacific. And even the following year, with the war well and truly over, the problems did not disappear, especially for fiancées. On 14

June 1946 a Miss Saxon and a Miss Townsend wrote to 'the Governor of Australia, Sir James Mitchell' (who was actually the Lieutenant-Governor of Western Australia), 'appealing for help for transportation of Australian girls engaged to US Servicemen':

> As we are British subjects with no claim on the U.S. Government, we feel its up to Australia to help us… Fiancees from Australia are prepared to pay their own fare for transportation. In holding up transportation for fiancees it is breaking up marriages that are most likely to last. Most fiancees have been waiting to join their fiances in the States, up to three & four years. How can we possibly hold are [sic] men, if transportation difficulties stand in our way?[56]

While so many young women were desperate to leave, there must have been as many families sad to see them go. Because of the overland preliminaries for Western Australian brides, most departures were not marked by the concentrated collective emotion of the dockside farewells from eastern ports. The exception was the departure from Fremantle, at Easter 1946, of the *Fred Ainsworth,* carrying large numbers of local women, very many of them with children, to join the husbands who had departed long before.

The agony for all concerned was prolonged because the scheduled sailing time on Good Friday could not be met for reasons which suggest how little change the Americans had made to local custom. After standing on the dockside for hours, unable to talk to their departing loved ones, relatives were told that provisioning of the ship was incomplete because the shops were closed for the holidays. A woman farewelling her sister recalled the eventual departure as 'one of the saddest things that I've ever experienced':

> There were girls all along the deck and they were crying, sobbing, trying to say goodbye to their parents, not able to get close enough to them. There were some very pathetic cases there: there was one young girl who cried for the whole time and she was holding up a *black* baby.[57]

What lay in store for that mother and child can only be guessed. The post-war lives of these and other war brides in the years to come belong to other books than this one. Many facets of their experience have already been revealed, not least in *War Brides*, a book by Lois Battle, adopted daughter of an American serviceman who was herself a child passenger on the *Fred Ainsworth*.[58]

Most women who left kept in touch with Western Australian relatives. In some cases they returned to them for brief visits, or even permanently, over the half century ahead. It is impossible to make any measured judgment about the effect of that diffuse, but long-term, after-shock of the Americans' wartime impact. All that can be achieved with some individual illustrations of the sheer variety of the experience—from the sublime to the awful—is further illustration of the unique wartime atmosphere in which lifetime decisions had been made in the most frenetic circumstances.

Another passenger on the *Fred Ainsworth* was a Subiaco girl who had married an American at the age of sixteen. Now with a child, she was on her way to rejoin him, looking forward to seeing all the wonderful places he had promised to take her and convinced that she was going to a mansion. Instead she found a husband who was basically decent and hard-working but who lived in the most primitive rural poverty without decent sleeping accommodation or running water. Eventually this couple survived to modest prosperity and the woman remained in America even after her husband died.[59] Another Perth woman had a much shorter stay—after she was met at dockside in America by her fiancé, accompanied by his wife and children.[60]

Even those brides and fiancées who did not experience such severe disillusionment faced awkward adjustment, not merely to unexpected living conditions but, after long periods of separation, even to renewed acquaintance with the men they had fallen in love with. Struggling to recognise their particular men among the crowds greeting their ships, many women quickly faced the reality that the glamour that had engulfed them in wartime Perth was no more. 'Gosh, don't they look different in civvies!' was a cry that said a great deal about past romance and future uncertainty.[61]

And yet the wartime marriage of Johnson and Triss Head, which survived for more than half a century, showed that the fragmented courtships and often hasty decisions to marry that were so characteristic of the war era were not all doomed to disillusionment. Even more than the Heads, the marriage of Avis and Vernon Koenig had all the ingredients of impulsive romance doomed to failure. After meeting on a blind date in Geraldton, they began a courtship in Perth months later that was always subject to the rarely interlocking schedules of Vernon's Catalina operations and Avis's shift work as a radar operator.[62]

Eventually a separation of months was ended with a telegram from Cairns proposing marriage a few days later in Sydney. At least Vernon's connections enabled Avis to fly to the eastern states rather than endure the transcontinental train marathon that was the lot of most war brides. And the courtesy of a fellow passenger, who made available his baggage allowance, enabled Avis to take all the possessions she had thrown together literally overnight. But a hastily arranged wedding, attended only by bride, groom and hastily recruited best man and matron-of-honour, was typical of wartime opportunism. And so were the preliminaries to the post-nuptial celebration at the Australia Hotel in Martin Place, Sydney. Waiting on the pavement for the groom and best man to pay the taxi driver, the bride and her attendant had to fend off two American servicemen asking for a date.[63]

This brief wedding was followed by a honeymoon of only three days. It was another eighteen months before Avis was reunited with her husband in the United States. Yet this was also to be a marriage that survived almost fifty years, until Vernon's death in retirement in Armadale on the southern outskirts of Perth.[64]

For Avis, the wartime opportunities to move beyond the dull life of the public service had led to a marriage that had exposed her to places and people totally outside her pre-war expectations. Vernon had worked in the post-war years firstly for the formidable, redoubtable and famously eccentric Howard Hughes and then in the American space programme for NASA in the United States, Spain and eventually Canberra. Equally unforeseeable was the eventual comfortable life in Atlanta of Triss Head, raised on a sheep station, educated in a convent boarding school, and trained as a nurse at Woorooloo, Geraldton and then Kalgoorlie.[65]

While such success stories are no more representative than the tales of those who struggled, fought or separated, most marriages—good or bad—shared the common factor of emotional separation from loved ones in Western Australia. Avis Koenig left a mother and other relatives temporarily 'devastated' by the suddenness of her overnight decision to leave for her marriage in the eastern states. And even fifty years later a small shadow tinges the Heads' pride in the mutual commitment that was so much at odds with the image of casual wartime dalliance. Unpredictable travel plans made conventional goodbyes impossible. It would be years before Triss could make good the omission with a return visit, leaving the sadness of her parents as a reminder that even the most successful international romances could carry an emotional burden.[66]

For many Western Australian families, sadness, perhaps less acute but nonetheless real, had also focused on Americans who were transferred out of their lives, or who failed to return from hazardous submarine missions. In September 1945 Mrs Roy Murnane inquired anxiously about the safety of submariners she and her husband had entertained in their home. They had 'become fond of them' and corresponded regularly after the men had left. But now a three-month silence meant 'we have become anxious about them'.[67]

In December, letters from the O'Neills of Carlisle showed how the friendships of many young women must have drawn servicemen into warm relations with whole families. Mrs O'Neill wrote to the Consul on 2 December 1945 querying whether the US Submarine *Bream 243* had been lost, as a sailor had told her. She knew several of the crew, who came to her house all the time as friends of her daughter.[68] A week later Miss J. O'Neill was inquiring about the whereabouts of US Submarine *Rock*. She was anxious to know if a friend aboard had arrived home safely. She knew several girls who had not heard from it, and somebody had said that it had been sunk. 'I hope that this is just another rumour.'[69]

All Mason Turner could do was refer such inquirers to the US Navy Department in Washington DC. 'As you may possibly realise,' he told Mrs Murnane, 'practically all submariners have now departed from Western Australia, and as the service record of each man goes with him on his departure, it is very doubtful if anyone in this area will now be in a position to provide you with information.'[70] This did not mean that the consular staff were unsympathetic. In September 1945 Mrs Mary Teague of Peppermint Grove wrote to Mason Turner with less anxiety than some, but equal affection. She was expressing appreciation for the kindness of the Consul and his staff after visiting them that morning: 'The boys of the USN are an exact replica of what you were today gentlemen. While in our home they made it as such and brought a great deal of happiness with them. We shall miss them awfully much.'[71]

# FLEETING ATTRACTION

## CONCLUSION

IN 1948 AN AMERICAN SHIP, the *LST 711*, carried members of the American War Graves Registration Service Expedition on a thirty-thousand-mile search of the Pacific 'looking for, and recovering where possible, the last of the U.S. war dead for burial in U.S. war cemeteries'. Interviewed as the ship docked in Melbourne on 30 September, the leader of the expedition said he wanted 'to leave Australia reasonably certain that all U.S. war dead had been cleared from the country'. As three officers and sixteen men embarked on an overland trek from Melbourne to Townsville, the *LST* began a voyage clockwise around Australia to 'cover the coast from Fremantle to Townsville by way of Darwin', picking up the overland party six weeks later.[1]

The dead were going home with a good deal more ceremony than had accompanied their living compatriots, as they had moved on from Western Australia in 1944 and 1945: 'The ship carries a crew of more than 100. A 24-hour guard of honor is kept on the temporary caskets in the ship's hold.'[2] But the repatriation of the handful of Americans buried in Perth's Karrakatta cemetery closed completely an extraordinary interlude in the history of Western Australia. Whether

250

it was more than an interlude—whether it pointed the way to new horizons by sweeping away 'encrusted encumbrances of the colonial past', as the American journalist Joseph Harsch had predicted in March 1942—is far less certain.

When he revealed his 'sense of momentous impending changes' Harsch was writing of Australia as a whole. Western Australia shared many effects of the American presence with the rest of the country. The Perth metropolitan community was merely one of several population centres in the nation that had to come to terms with some extremely selective economic benefits. Taxi drivers, shops, hotels and brothels flourished in the wartime climate of 'Yankee' affluence, often to the detriment and annoyance of the local public. These, however, were largely short-term changes, scarcely important, in Harsch's words, 'to the long view of history'.

Conceivably of longer term importance was the entering wedge of post-war consumerism, especially in food and drink products. A competition to decide who really sold the first hamburgers in Australia would probably be inconclusive, but it certainly would have many entrants, including several from the West. Hamburgers, steak sandwiches, Coca-Cola, new varieties of canned food, new brands of cigarettes, stuffed olives and other delicacies all feature in the memories of an Australia-wide generation as wartime American innovations. Collectively they may have provided basic ingredients of a later—and now very familiar—fast food and supermarket life-style. But, given its eventual world-wide penetration, it seems fanciful to put too much emphasis on the wartime introduction of such consumerism.

And there lies much of the problem in assessing the American impact as a whole. The Australia that the Americans left was on the verge of a dramatic metamorphosis: from a cultural, geographical and economic backwater, a modern, Western industrialised society was emerging. Certainly the Americans had paved the way by winning the war. But the European immigrants who poured into Australia after the Second World War were a major factor in this transformation. Their presence interacted with improvements in communications to diminish isolation and modify parochialism in Australia as a whole. Air travel became increasingly affordable and accessible. Television, introduced a decade after the war, made a huge cultural impact, exposing almost the entire population to the pictorial realities of world events as well as to documentaries, movies and popular entertainment from countries around the globe.

Focus on one of the most significant changes in post-war social attitudes can only confirm the complexity of wartime influences. The Second World War allowed many women to demonstrate capacities that challenged stereotypes of domestic subservience. But if this was a stage on the long road to equality, it was one that was not widely recognised at the time, even by significant numbers of women let alone society as a whole. In the post-war period women made the slowest of advances towards equal pay and the more significant equality that eliminates the concept of 'women's work'. The adoption of a coherent feminist agenda owed more to influences from that wider post-war world than to the war itself. And if wartime circumstances played any part in the raising of consciousness, it had little to do with Americans, whose main contribution was a 'romantic' style of courtship, which may have been preferred to Australian crudity, but which was intensely patronising.

There can be little doubt that the post-war economic and social transformation of Australia would have occurred regardless of the wartime experience. The most that can be said in a general sense is that the stimulus and challenge of the American presence may have contributed to a readier acceptance of change by a significantly less innocent society.

It was a presence that encouraged a re-evaluation, but not necessarily immediate rejection, of British traditions blindly perpetuated in Australia. Puritanical alcohol and entertainment laws were reviewed, but 'the six o'clock swill' and less severe licensing restrictions continued long after the war. The Americans had been repelled by the austerity of Sunday observance and Australians were quicker than the British to accept professional sport on Sundays in the post-war years. But it was still cricket, not baseball, that they watched. Even in the

1960s they were still standing to the strains of 'God Save the Queen' at the start of cinema programmes. And while the presence of African-American servicemen may have prepared the way for more tolerant racial attitudes, there is little evidence of an immediate post-war effect, either in improved treatment of Aboriginal people or abandonment of the White Australia Policy.

Although much of the Western Australian interaction with Americans was similar to that of eastern states centres, there were also significant differences, just as there were in the post-war, and especially post-1960s, economic transformation of the state. Those differences need to be emphasised, for they have entirely escaped the notice of other writers.

Western Australia was unique and the Americans unique interlopers. To people living in the most isolated capital city in the world, 'protected' from diversity by the White Australia Policy, distance and prohibitive travel costs, the Americans were products of a society frequently glimpsed, but never seen clearly, through the medium of the movies. Their immediate impact would have been great in any circumstances. In the crisis of early 1942 it was colossal. Local fears of invasion by the Japanese meant acceptance and even admiration of self-assured American behaviour verging on arrogance. For many months even the community's moral guardians singled out the Americans only to praise them and absolve them from blame for the perceived escalation of drunkenness, prostitution and threats to the morals of young girls. As novelty faded and the war situation improved, the welcome wore thin, without ever fraying into ugliness and violence on the scale that soiled relations in eastern cities.

It is significant that the worst violence occurred in the port of Fremantle, which would have been violent whether the Americans were there or not. There was violence inflicted by the authorities themselves on Asian seamen whose industrial action affected the war effort, violence against breaches of wharf security and violence involving troops in transit. The fatal clashes between Americans and New Zealand Maoris were far more typical of the disturbances that both preceded and followed the American presence than of relations between either submariners or Catalina crews and the local population.

The very small number of American dead eventually exhumed and taken home in 1948—and the fact that all of them were killed in accidents or died from illness—shows how different the outcome had been from the expectation in March 1942, when 1256 burial plots had been taken and a further three thousand reserved for possible use. The worst fears of desperate defensive battles had subsided within a few months, allowing the US Army to move on and making the American presence in the main centres of population exclusively a matter of Navy and Marine personnel.

The Navy brought with it some African-Americans and at times treated them in ways offensive to some locals. But the numbers were too few to trouble the many Western Australians who were potentially as racist as white Americans, and too few to require the creation of segregated recreation areas of a kind that had brought controversy in Sydney, Brisbane and other eastern centres. And they were too few for interracial violence within the American forces to become an issue in Western Australia, as it had elsewhere.

Contrary to the belief of John Hammond Moore, this exclusively naval presence did not mean that these Americans 'had much less contact with Australia and its citizens than American soldiers [because of] the very nature of their work'. Unless Western Australia is not really Australia and Western Australians are not Australian citizens, that remark displays manifold ignorance. There is ignorance of the operational routines of submariners, whose long tours at sea were punctuated by substantial periods of leave; ignorance of the presence in metropolitan Perth of hundreds of US Navy air and support crew, with approximately one third of their time available for contact with local citizens; ignorance of the extent to which both of these groups were much more highly paid than the overpaid GIs of his book; and ignorance of the more than one thousand Western Australian women who became American war brides.

It is true that much of the 'work' of Navy personnel was done off shore. Among Catalina crews, flying far into the Indian Ocean from Crawley and Geraldton, casualties were remarkably low. Among submariners and personnel from conventional American ships they were much higher.[3] In all cases they happened out of sight, but not out of mind, of local people who had welcomed, befriended and in many cases planned permanent futures with those who were lost at sea.

The lurking possibility of such tragedy intensified rather than dampened social excitement in a metropolitan area that was rest and recreation centre as well as operational base. Inevitably it was local young women who shared most of the excitement. But concerned letters from middle-aged couples and suburban families to the American Consulate showed that many Americans had looked for and found more than sex and romance among the people of the Perth metropolitan area. The warmth they had given and received as they were welcomed into local families meant that some people were mourning the loss of surrogate sons.

Although its immediate impact was great, and its influence on some individuals profound, the American presence did not have a lasting general effect. Announcement of research for a book of this kind inevitably brings response from those most affected by the subject matter. The lives of some who came forward with enthusiasm had been transformed by their encounters with Americans. These include not only the several now elderly women who still correspond with men they met half a century earlier, but also the Gingin farmer Ian Edgar.

The presence of an American radar facility on his property for six months in 1942 produced lifelong friendships, maintained through correspondence and reunions in the United States. Interviewed in April 1994, only weeks before his death at the age of 92, Mr Edgar had memorabilia and written records of a proud family history rooted in Scotland and flowering in Western Australia since the mid nineteenth century. But the dominating feature of his retirement unit was a huge Stars and Stripes draped across his bedroom wall. Yet probably more typical of the broader relationship of the era than Mr Edgar's sustained interest is the way the Americans had arrived on his property without notice, lived in comfort and harmony with the locals and departed as suddenly as they came.

George May, who had been closer to the Americans than most Geraldton people, had no post-war contacts at all: 'To me, they went as quietly as they came.' Neither, except for a brief chance encounter years later with two Americans returned on vacation, did Syd Harvey. 'What grated' with Syd was that 'when the war ended the Yanks took every damned thing, even the curtains! We thought they'd leave the stuff around the joint, but no way!' The only thing they didn't take was the septic tank.

As they removed all other traces of their presence from the luxurious facility they had created on Perth's riverfront, the American chief petty officers left behind strong memories with Syd, the local who had known them best. But essentially they were memories of a unique, almost unreal, period. Asked what permanent changes the visitors had introduced, Harvey—along with many others of his generation—could think only of Coca-Cola and steak sandwiches, and conclude: 'Things sort of settled back to how they'd been before when the Yanks left.'

Publicly that process was beginning in the last year of the war, as local dignitaries greeted a royal Governor-General with lavish deference, and as women volunteers organised hospitality for British and New Zealand servicemen passing through Perth in large numbers. The stage was being set, in some instances quite consciously, for the post-war immigration which in this state would always be more British than anything else. The renewal of those ties, combined with the Americans' removal of most physical traces of their presence, does much to explain distinctive contemporary Western Australian attitudes of respect for British tradition and excitement at the periodic arrival of the US Navy.

It has been said that the American arrival in Australia in 1942 represented 'the moment when image and reality met'. In the unique circumstances of Western Australia this meeting was, in no serious sense, a collision. It was only those who followed their heroes to the United States who had to confront the reality behind the shining image. For many other women who had been courted and entertained by Americans, the experience had been an unreal, unforgettable, almost unmentionable interlude: 'It's an awful thing to say,' said one anonymous woman, reflecting the sentiments of many others, 'but we had a wonderful, wonderful time when the Americans were here!' It was an experience without long-term effects, but one re-lived for a few days by generations of their children and grandchildren over the next half century. As US aircraft carriers and other vessels lay anchor in Gage Roads, thousands of American sailors—black and white, male and female—pouring into the streets of Fremantle and Perth have continued to be a major, but essentially fleeting, attraction.

# ABBREVIATIONS IN THE NOTES

AA-ACT   Australian Archives, Australian Capital Territory

AA-NSW   Australian Archives, New South Wales

AA-VIC   Australian Archives, Victoria

AA-WA   Australian Archives, Western Australia

AWM   Australian War Memorial, Canberra

Battye   Battye Library, Perth

CF   Confidential Files of the Perth Consular District, 1937–1949: RG 84, Records of the Foreign Service Posts of the Department of State, United States National Archives and Records Service, Suitland Annexe, Maryland

GR   General Records of the Perth Consular District, 1937–1949: RG 84, Records of the Foreign Service Posts of the Department of State, United States National Archives and Records Service, Suitland Annexe, Maryland

USNA   United States National Archives and Records Service, Washington, DC (and Annexe, Suitland, Maryland)

UWA   University of Western Australia Archives

# NOTES

## INTRODUCTION

1   *Christian Science Monitor,* 24 March 1942.

2   Philip Bell and Roger Bell, *Implicated: The United States in Australia* (Melbourne, 1993) p. 90.

3   J. Hammond Moore, *Over-Sexed, Over-Paid and Over Here: Americans in Australia 1941–1945* (St Lucia, Queensland, 1981); E. Daniel Potts and Annette Potts, *Yanks Down Under 1941–45: The American Impact on Australia* (Melbourne, 1985).

4   Personal communication from Ms Robin Surridge, United States Information Service, Perth, December 1994.

5   Figures supplied by United States Consulate, Perth, December 1994.

6   Potts and Potts, *Yanks Down Under 1941–45,* p. 406.

7   Rosemary Campbell, *Heroes and Lovers: A Question of National Identity* (Sydney, 1989). The mutual attraction betwen Americans and local women is referred to in virtually all works of the period, and especially in Annette Potts and Lucinda Strauss, *For the Love of a Soldier: Australian War Brides and their GIs* (Crow's Nest, NSW, 1987).

8   Moore, *Over-Sexed, Over-Paid and Over Here,* p. 282.

9   ibid., p. 98.

10  Potts and Potts, *Yanks Down Under 1941–45,* p. 303.

11  The error about Mason Turner is perpetuated in the most recent work on the American presence in Australia: Bell and Bell, *Implicated: The United States in Australia,* p. 100. Although this is a book that surveys a much longer period—devoting only one of six chapters to the Second World War—and although it deals with much more than the 'home front', it is typical of so many others in virtually ignoring Western Australia.

12  Potts and Potts, *Yanks Down Under 1941–45,* p. 404.

13  ibid., p. 403.

14  Interview: George May.

15  John P. Squibb's unpublished honours dissertation, 'Fremantle Solidarity: The Response of a Port City to World War Two', The University of Western Australia, 1984, devotes one chapter to the social impact of the American troops on Fremantle, as part of his major concern with their maritime and technological influence.

16  David Creed, *Operations of the Fremantle Submarine Base, 1942–45* (Sydney, 1979); Lynne Cairns, *Submarines in the Harbour: The World War Two Allied Submarine Base at Fremantle* (Fremantle, 1994).

17  Lois Battle, *War Brides* (London, 1982); Dymphna Cusack and Florence James, *Come In Spinner,* (London, 1951); Henrietta Drake-Brockman, *The Fatal Days* (Sydney, 1947); Xavier Herbert, *Soldiers' Women* (London, 1962); Robin Sheiner, *Smile, the War is Over* (South Melbourne, 1983); Randolph Stow, *The Merry-Go-Round in the Sea* (London, 1965).

*Chapter One*—ANXIOUS ISOLATION

1   C. T. Stannage, *The People of Perth: A Social History of Western Australia's Capital City* (Perth, 1979), p. 339.
2   *The Secession Referendum Act, 1932, and the Secession Referendum Act, 1934... The Case of the People of Western Australia in Support of Their Desire to Withdraw from the Commonwealth of the Australian Constitutional Act (Imperial)* (Perth, 1934), p. 84.
3   ibid., pp. 84–85.
4   *Current Notes on International Affairs*, January 1942, p. 1.
5   *The Broadcaster*, 7 July 1943, pp. 20–21.
6   Interview: David Bird.
7   'Note on Population', GR 1942, vol. 5.
8   Interviews: Marjorie Ward, Syd Harvey.
9   Interviews: Joy Anderson, Pat Tully, Pat Catt, Marjorie Ward. *City and Suburban Plans and Street Index*, 1947.
10  F. K. Crowley, *Westralian Suburb: A History of South Perth* (Perth, 1962), pp. 90–91. Correspondence with E. Dwyer, New Hampshire, U.S.A. Interviews: Marjorie Ward, Pat Catt.
11  Crowley, *Westralian Suburb*, p. 90.
12  Interviews: Joy Anderson, Pat Tully.
13  Interview: Syd Harvey.
14  Interview: Avis Koenig.
15  Terry Craig, 'Radical and Conservative Theatre in Perth in the 1930s', in Jenny Gregory, *Western Australia Between the Wars, 1919–1939* (Perth, 1990), pp. 107, 112.
16  Interview: Syd Harvey.
17  Minutes of State Executive of the Women's Service Guild 1938–1953. A2530 MN 585, vol. 44. Evidence Submitted by the Women's Service Guilds of WA Inc. before the Royal Commission to Inquire into the Administration of Health and Building Bylaws of the City of Perth, June 1938, in ibid., vol. 55. Battye.
18  Women's Service Guilds of Western Australia: Aboriginal Affairs, 1934–47. AA-ACT, A431, 1947/2492.
19  Fremantle Municipal Tramways and Electric Lighting Board Minutes 1939–1943. Battye: Acc. 1331, AN 306, Item 13, 1939–43, 3 November 1939, 2 May 1941.

20 Michal Bosworth, 'Fremantle Interned: the Italian Experience', in Richard Bosworth and Romano Ugolini, eds. *War, Internment and Mass Migration: The Italo-Australian Experience* (Rome, 1992), pp. 75–88.

21 *The Western Cricketer: Western Australian Cricket Association (Inc.) 1993–94 Year Book*, 'Table of Interstate and International Matches', pp. 142–145.

22 Interviews: Pat Tully, Pat Catt.

23 Michael McKernan, *All In! Australia During the Second World War* (Melbourne, 1983), p. 185.

24 A. D. Spaull, 'The American Presence in Australian Schools, 1939–46', *Journal of the Australian and New Zealand History of Education Society*, p. 17. Correspondence from the Fremantle Town Clerk to Associate Professor F. Alexander, 31 March 1941, City Of Fremantle General Correspondence, 1940–42. The first full-year course in United States history at UWA was introduced in 1983.

25 GR 1942, vol. 2, 26 May 1942.

26 ibid., vol. 5, 14 November 1942.

27 GR 1940, vol. 2, 1 January 1940; GR 1941, vol. 2, 1 January 1941; GR 1942, vol. 3, 1 January 1942.

28 Francesco Violi to Consul, Laverton 2/9/40: inquiries from a relative, Geno Bertolaccini in Somerville, Massachusetts, revealed that two more Italian-Americans, Ferdinando Grassi and Esmaele Tolaini, were interned at Harvey. GR 1940, vol. 2.

29 Captain V. H. Walker, Wirth Bros Circus, to Consul, 10 August 1940, in ibid.

30 *Sunday Times*, 30 March 1941. GR 1942, vols. 2, 3. Joseph P. Ragland, American Consul, Brisbane, to Colonel Alexander Johnson, US Army HQ, Brisbane. RG 407 (The Adjutant General's Office) 98-USF37-2.18 USAFIA G-2, Memoranda and Miscellaneous Papers, n.d.

31 *Fremantle and Districts Sentinel*, 16 January 1941.

32 ibid., 23 January 1941.

33 ibid., 20 February 1941.

34 ibid., 14 March 1941.

35 ibid., 27 March 1941.

36 ibid., 8, 21 August 1941.

37 ibid., 16 January 1941.

38 ibid., 20 March 1941.

39 GR 1941, vol. 3.

40 Correspondence from the Fremantle Town Clerk to Associate Professor F. Alexander, 31 March 1941. City of Fremantle General Correspondence, 1940–42.

41 J. H. Prowse, MP, to PM Curtin, 29 October 1941. AA-VIC, MP150/1, 449/201/886, 1941.

42 *Fremantle and Districts Sentinel*, 4 December 1941.

43  Information and copy of letter of reminiscence from Mason Turner to US Consulate-General in Perth supplied by William H. Itoh, US Consul-General in Perth, 1986–90.

44  GR 1940, vol. 2; 1941, vol. 1; 1942, vol. 2.


*Chapter Two*—UNWITTING PREPARATION

1  W. D. Jamieson, *A History of the Army in Western Australia in World War II* (Perth, 1978), p. 2.

2  Report on Organisation and Activities of Security Service—Perth Branch, 22 September 1943. AA-ACT, A373/1, 7431.

3  ibid.

4  ibid., 'Annexure D—Investigations'.

5  Acting Chief Publicity Censor to Senator H. S. Foll, Sydney, 10 January 1941, Publicity Censorship, Perth. AA-VIC, SP109/3/1, 337/24A.

6  Note to Bonney signed DKR, 16 February 1942, in ibid.

7  27 January 1941, in ibid.

8  Note to Bonney signed DKR, 16 February 1942, in ibid.

9  Walter James, State Publicity Censor, Perth, to E. G. Bonney, Chief Publicity Censor, Canberra, 10 October 1942. AA-VIC, SP109/3, 389/02.

10  Publicity censorship, Perth, 1941–45. AA-VIC, SP109/3/1, 337/24A.

11  *Fremantle and Districts Sentinel*, 18 December 1941.

12  Jamieson, *History of the Army in Western Australia*, p. 2.

13  Breaches of Censorship—File of Correspondence, 8 February 1941. AWM 54, 175/7/1.

14  ibid., 18 March 1941.

15  ibid., 3 May 1941.

16  ibid., 18 March 1941.

17  ibid., 3 June 1941.

18  'Preliminary Voyage Report, Fremantle to Colombo'—HMT Y3, 15 May 1940. AWM 963/13/19.

19  Breaches of Censorship—File of Correspondence, 26 August 1941. AWM 54, 175/7/1.

20  'Voyage Report—HMAT S1, Fremantle to Suez, 1940.' AWM 54, 963/13/18.

21  Minutes of the General Council, WA National Council of Women, June 30, 1941. Battye: 1389A MN 187, vol. 8, 1933–45.

22  Fremantle Council Records and Minute Books, 1941–1945. Battye: AN 217/6. For examples see: Correspondence from the Town Clerk to the President of the Conference of Methodist Churches in Western Australia, 25 February 1942; correspondence from the Town Clerk to Colonel McWhale, Officer in Charge of Western Command, 3 February 1942.

23    Correspondence from Town Clerk to the Honourable Premier of Western Australia, J. C. Willcock, 20 March 1942.

24    Notes furnished to Mr Harding by Mr George Nelson, Chairman, Citizens' Reception Council, Perth, n.d. AA-VIC, MP/742/1, 259/87/197.

25    Interview: Pat Catt.

26    Interview: Marjorie Ward.

27    Notes furnished to Mr Harding by Mr George Nelson, Chairman, Citizens' Reception Council, Perth, n.d. AA-VIC, MP/742/1, 259/87/197. Major J. H. O. Hargrave, Asst. Director of Hirings, Swan Barracks, Francis Street, Perth, to Director of Hirings, Melbourne, in ibid., 11 August 1942.

28    *The Dawn,* 21 January 1942, p. 2.

29    Interview: Avis Koenig.

30    ibid.

31    *The Dawn,* 21 January 1942, p. 2.

32    ibid., 18 March 1942.

33    D. M. Tangney, M.P., to Senator Fraser, Acting Minister for the Army, 22 May 1945. AA-VIC, MP/742/1, 259/87/197.


*Chapter Three*—OUT OF THE BLUE

1    [Owen Stanley's Reports] Documents and Notes used in Writing Volume 5 (Army) South West Pacific Area First Year [Official History]. AWM 54, 577/7/32.

2    Report of Organisation and Activities—United States Army Forces in Australia, 7 December 1941 – 30 June 1942, with Inclosures 1 to 30 and Appendices 1 to 23. USNA: RG 407 (The Adjutant General's Office), 98-USF37-0.2 USAIFA.

3    [Owen Stanley's Reports]. AWM 54, 577/7/32.

4    Annual Report for the Northern District, Western Australian Police Department Annual Report 1942. Battye: Acc. No. 430, AN 5/3, Item 3246, 1942.

5    E. K. White, President of Australian–American Co-Operation Movement, to Curtin, PM, 5 January 1942; similar letter from Sydney Secretary of Australian Comforts Fund to his National Secretary in Melbourne, 20 January 1942. AA-VIC, MP508/1, 95/701/93.

6    ABC Inter-Office memoranda, signed M. F. Dixon, 7, 12 January 1942, AA-NSW, SP314, A1.

7    [Owen Stanley's Reports]. AWM 54, 577/7/32.

8    ibid.

9    'Report of Organisation and Activities—United States Army Forces in Australia.' USNA: RG 407, 98-USF37-0.2, USAFIA.

10   'Extracts from War Historians' Diaries', Melbourne 22 May 1943 [Owen Stanley's Reports]. AWM 54, 577/7/32, D1/33.

11  Fremantle Defence Committee — Reports and Minutes of Meetings, 1940–43, 18 December 1941. AA-VIC: MP1185/8, 1855/10/1.

12  ibid., 26 December 1941.

13  ibid., 2 January 1942.

14  *Daily News*, 13 January 1942, p. 5.

15  ibid., 15 January 1942, p. 6.

16  Fremantle Defence Committee—Reports and Minutes of Meetings, 1940–43, 23 January 1942.

17  ibid., 17, 19, 27 February 1942.

18  'History (Incomplete) 1941–1944.' USNA: 98-SS3-0.1 USASOS,SWPA. 'Shooting of Chinese Seamen by Australian Guards at Fremantle 28/1/1942'. AA-ACT: A981, CHIN 7.

19  ibid.

20  ibid.

21  ibid.

22  ibid.

23  Cutting from Sydney *Daily Telegraph*, 21 February 1942, in ibid.

24  'Telephone Conversation with Canberra, Mr Bonney calling Mr Rorke', 29 January 1942. AA-NSW: SP106, PC17 PART 1. Secret Memorandum: J. J. Barry, Queensland A/Collector of Customs to Secretary, Department of Interior, 27 March 1942. AA-ACT, A433, 45/2/6281. E. G. Bonney, Chief Publicity Censor to Lieutenant Colonel Lloyd Lehrbas, Press Relations Officer, Headquarters, USA Army Forces in Australia, Melbourne, 9 April 1942. AA-ACT: SP109/3, 308/17. H. H. Mansell, State Publicity Censor, NSW, to E. G. Bonney, Chief Publicity Censor, Canberra, 11 April 1942. AA-ACT: SP109/3, 308/17.

25  Jan Ryan, 'Geraldton 1942: A Year to Remember', p. 1. Battye: Q994.12 Ger.

26  Release of News and Photographs, re American Troops in Australia. AA-ACT: SP/112/1, 352/1/72.

27  ibid.

28  ibid.

29  *Daily News*, 19 February 1942.

30  *Daily News*, 20 February 1942.

31  ibid.

32  ibid.

33  ibid., 26 February 1942, p. 8.

34  'Bickley Battery, Rottnest Island.' Battye: PR 11032.

35  'Geraldton District: Possibility of Enemy Action: Plans for Protection of Civilians', 1942. AWM 54, 831/3/60.

36  'Resume of Meeting Held at the Office of Elder, Smith & Co. Limited on Thursday 12 February 1942.' AWM 54, 183/5/13.

37  Interview: George May. Ryan, 'Geraldton 1942: A Year to Remember', pp. 5–7.

38    Interview: George May.

39    USNA: 98-B1G-0.1 Base 6 (Perth) History—draft.

40    AA-ACT: A433, 44/2/1864.

41    Turner to Palmer, 24 February 1942, GR 1942, vol. 2.

42    State Department to Thompson (telegram), 25 February 1942. GR 1942, vol. 1.

43    Turner to Palmer, 30 March 1942, Enclosure 1: 'List of American citizens departing from Perth consular district since January 1.' GR 1942, vol. 3.

44    Turner to Secretary of WA Railways, 6 March 1942. GR 1942, vol. 3.

45    Most had gone to Sydney or Melbourne in transit to the United States, but nineteen on the *Island Mail* sailed direct from Fremantle to the west coast of the United States: Turner to Secretary of State (telegram), 8 April 1942. GR 1942, vol. 3.

46    Turner to Palmer (Sydney Consul-General), 12 February 1942. GR 1942, vol. 2.

47    Palmer to Turner, 18 February 1942. GR 1942, vol. 2.

48    Turner to Palmer, 24 February 1942. GR 1942, vol. 2.

49    'Bickley Battery, Rottnest Island.' Battye: PR 11032.

50    Correspondence with Wood, 1991.

51    GR 1942, vol. 5.

52    David Creed, *Operations of the Fremantle Submarine Base 1942–45* (Sydney, 1979), pp. 2–4.

53    'History (Incomplete) 1941–1944'. USNA: 98-SS3-0.1 USASOS, SWPA; 98-SS3-0.2 USASOS, SWPA. 'History of the Efforts Made by the Original United States Army Agencies in Australia Early in 1942 to Relieve as Much as was Possible the Beleaguered Troops in the Philippines During the Closing Phases of the Campaign Against the Japanese in that Area', 4 August 1944. USNA: 98-SS3-0.2 USASOS, SWPA.

54    'Notes on Exmouth Gulf Advanced Base—World War II Operation "Potshot".' AA-VIC, MP1587/1, 186W.

55    Interview: Lindsay Peet.

56    'Notes on Exmouth Gulf Advanced Base—World War II Operation "Potshot".' AA-VIC, MP1587/1, 186W.

57    Avis M. Koenig, *Catalinas on the Swan River—Perth* (Perth, 1994), p. 3.

*Chapter Four*—'THANK YOU, PRESIDENT ROOSEVELT!'

1    'Extracts from War Historians' Diaries', 1 March 1942 [Owen Stanley's Reports]. AWM 54: 577/7/32.

2    ibid.

3    Interviews: Michael Papadoulis, Joy Anderson.

4 *West Australian,* 3 March 1942.
5 Mary Bain, *Full Fathom Five* (Perth, 1982), p. 330. Annual Report for the Northern District 1942, WA Police Department Annual Report 1942. Battye: Acc. No. 430, AN 5/3, Item 3246, 1942.
6 *West Australian,* 4 March 1942.
7 *Daily News,* 4 March 1942.
8 *West Australian,* 3 March 1942.
9 *Daily News,* February–March 1942, *passim.*
10 ibid., 12 March 1942.
11 WA Police Department Annual Report 1942. Battye: Acc. No. 430, AN 5/3, Item 3246, 1942.
12 Fremantle Defence Committee—Reports and Minutes, 27 March 1942.
13 *Daily News,* 24 March 1942.
14 Interview: Marjorie Ward.
15 City of Fremantle, General Correspondence. Battye: AN 1596, Acc. 217/6, Box 5, 1940–42.
16 Police Department File. Battye: Acc. No. 430, AN 5/3, Item 997, 1942.
17 *Daily News,* 16 March 1942.
18 ibid., 20 March 1942.
19 ibid., 9 March 1942.
20 Interview: Syd Harvey.
21 ibid.
22 Interview: Marjorie Ward.
23 Interview: Joy Anderson.
24 Interview: Pat Catt.
25 Interview: George May.
26 ibid.
27 *Albany Advertiser,* 26 June 1942.
28 Interview: David Bird.
29 ibid.
30 ibid.
31 Interview: Phyllis Gurley.
32 Lighting restrictions for vehicle headlights had been announced on 2 March, but it was 20 April before a total blackout was introduced: *Albany Advertiser.*
33 Interview: Phyllis Gurley.
34 Statement by the Prime Minister, 'Aid From the United States', 1942, in 'US Forces In Australia: Cable and Press Statements by Prime Minister'. AA, Shedden Collection A5954/1 569/5.
35 *Commonwealth of Australia Parliamentary Debates,* vol. 170, p. 364.
36 *Daily News,* 5 March 1942.
37 *Geraldton Guardian,* 7 March 1942.
38 *Albany Advertiser,* 19 March 1942.

39   ibid., 26 March 1942.

40   *Fremantle and Districts Sentinel*, 5 March 1942.

41   ibid., 12 March 1942.

42   ibid., 26 March 1942.

43   ibid., 18 June 1942.

44   R. Wooding to Consul, 18 March 1942. GR 1942, vol. 5.

45   Victor Daniel Hague to Consul, 8 April 1942, in ibid.

46   June Birt to Consul, 28 March 1942, in ibid.

47   ibid.

48   Mason Turner, 'General Information Regarding Perth'. GR 1942, vol. 2.

49   WA Police Department Annual Report, 1942. Battye: Acc. no. 430, AN 5/3, Item 3246, 1942.

50   Vice-Chancellor Currie to President, Guild of Undergraduates, 6 July 1942. UWA.

51   Fremantle City Council Minute Books. Battye: Acc. 1377, AN 217/2, vol. 42, 16 August 1943.

52   *Daily News*, 14 March 1942.

53   ibid., 13 March 1942, p. 12.

54   ibid., 21 March 1942.

55   *Albany Advertiser*, 30 March 1942

56   Turner to Palmer, 24 April 1942. GR 1942, vol. 4.

57   *Albany Advertiser*, 30 April 1942.

58   Moore, *Over-Sexed, Over-Paid and Over Here*, p. 100.

59   ibid., p. 99.

60   *Christian Science Monitor*, 1942–1944, *passim*.

61   Potts and Potts, *Yanks Down Under*, p. 314.

62   *Australian Women's Weekly*, 2 May 1942.

63   Irene V. Duff to Consul, 20 March 1942. GR 1942, vol. 2.

64   M. Davis to Consul, 10 April 1942, GR 1942, vol. 5.

65   Edison C. Churchward to Consul, 8 April 1942. ibid.

66   Mrs P. E. Coombs to Consul, 1 May 1942. ibid.

67   *Albany Advertiser*, 19 March 1942.

68   ibid., 23 March 1942.

69   ibid., 2 April 1942.

70   *Geraldton Guardian*, 25 April 1942.

71   W. R. Orr, Secretary, WANFL, to Turner, 9 April 1942. GR 1942, vol. 2.

72   *Daily News*, 26 February 1942.

73   Minutes of Sports Panel of the Australian–American Co-operation Movement, 28 August 1942, GR 1942, vol. 2.

74   Interview: Syd Harvey.

75   Interview: Jim Purcell. Lord Mayor to Consul, 28 April 1942. GR 1942, vol. 5.

76   Bernard Morey to Consul, 22, 29 May 1942. GR 1942, vol. 5.

77    Mollie Fraser to Consul, 17 May 1942, in ibid.
78    Notes furnished to Mr Harding by Mr George Nelson, Chairman, Citizens' Reception Council, Perth, n.d. AA-VIC, MP/742/1, 259/87/197.
79    ibid.
80    E. K. White, Australian–American Co-operation Movement, to Curtin, 5 January 1942; Sydney Secretary of Australian Comforts Fund to National Secretary, 20 January 1942; letters, memorandum from Secretary of Department of Defence Co-ordination, 14, 28 January 1942. AA-VIC: MP508/1, 95/701/93.
81    Thomas W. Meagher to Consul, 17 June 1942. GR 1942, vol. 2.
82    ibid., *passim.*
83    15 May 1942, in ibid.
84    24 June 1942, in ibid.
85    12 August 1942, in ibid.
86    Premier's Department to Consul, 27 July 1942, in ibid.
87    Patricia Boyle, Hon. Sec., Information Bureau for all Overseas Men in Uniform, 20 July 1942, in ibid.

## Chapter Five—A PERVASIVE PRESENCE

1     USNA: '98-BIG-0.1 Base 6 (Perth) History—draft.' 'HT Queen Mary and HT Queen Elizabeth—Transport of first American troops to Australia, April 1942.' AA-VIC: MP1587/1, 278.
2     27 March 1942. GR 1942, vol. 5.
3     USNA: '98-BIG-0.1 Base 6 (Perth) History—draft'.
4     ibid.
5     'A Narrative History of Engineer Headquarters United States Army Forces in Australia, January 1942 to 30 June 1942.' USNA: RG 407 (The Adjutant-General's Office)—98-USF37-0.2 USAIFA.
6     USNA: '98-BIG-0.1 Base 6 (Perth) History—draft'.
7     ibid.
8     'Lists of Deaths of US Citizens in Perth district 1942.' GR 1942, vol. 4.
9     USNA: '98-BIG-0.1 Base 6 (Perth) History—draft'.
10    USNA: 'Narrative History of Engineer Headquarters United States Army Forces in Australia'.
11    Interview: Ian Edgar.
12    ibid.
13    ibid.
14    ibid.
15    ibid.
16    ibid.

17 ibid.

18 Interview: Mrs Nicholls.

19 USNA: '98-BIG-0.1 Base 6 (Perth) History—draft'.

20 Courtland Christiani, 'Basic Information for American Ex-Servicemen Contemplating Residence in Western Australia', 30 October 1945. CF, 1945.

21 'Notes on Exmouth Gulf Advanced Base—World War II Operation "Potshot".' AA-VIC: MP1587/1, 186W.

22 'Base Facilities Report: U.S. Naval Activities Southwest Pacific Area.' Battye: PR 6186, p. 7.

23 Interview: Mrs J. Balcombe.

24 Interview: Jacquie Bunney.

25 *Daily News,* 19 February 1942.

26 'General information about Perth', 26 May 1942. GR 1942, vol. 2.

27 'Works carried out on behalf of United States Navy in Western Australia, 1942–43'. AA-VIC: MP1049/5, 2017/2/130.

28 Interview: Pat Catt.

29 UWA: Currie to US Commanding Officer, 18, 27, 29 April 1942. Koenig, *Catalinas on the Swan River,* pp. 4–5. Christine Shervington, *University Voices: Traces from the Past* (Nedlands, Western Australia, 1987), p. 43.

30 'Works carried out on behalf of United States Navy in Western Australia, 1942–43.' AA-VIC: MP1049/5, 2017/2/130.

31 Interview: E. V. Taylor.

32 Interview: Marjorie Ward; name of one interviewee withheld by request.

33 Interview: Gwen George (née Anderson).

34 'Anti-Aircraft Defence U.S.N. Anchorage, Albany', 6 September 1942. AA-VIC: MP729/6, 26/404/262. Interview: David Bird.

35 Interviews: David Bird, Phyllis Gurley.

36 Interviews: Johnson Head, Bill Barker.

37 Interview: Johnson Head.

38 Interviews: Johnson Head, George May.

39 Interview: George May.

40 ibid.

41 ibid.

42 Interview: Bill Barker.

43 'American Convoys', 9 January 1942. GR 1942, vol. 1.

44 Ely Thompson to Turner, 9 March 1942, in ibid.

45 Causey to Canty, 12 March 1942; Turner to Palmer, 24 March 1942, in ibid.

46 'Request of British Ministry of War Transport for Tonnage for Supply of American Troops, 1942.' AA-ACT, A5954, 292/13.

47 Petersen to Brown, 18 February 1943. CF 1943.

48 Turner to Palmer, 21 July 1943. CF 1943.

*Chapter Six*—THE QUEST FOR COMFORT

1   'Works carried out on behalf of the United States Navy in Western Australia.' AA-VIC, MP1049/5, 2017/2/130.
2   ibid.
3   ibid.
4   ibid.
5   UWA.
6   Interview: Mrs Lee.
7   Koenig, *Catalinas on the Swan River*, p. 6.
8   Fremantle Defence Committee—Reports and Minutes, 2, 21 April 1942. AA-VIC: MP1185/8, 1855/10/1.
9   ibid., 28 April, 5 May 1942.
10  ibid.
11  AA-VIC, MP1049/5, 2017/2/130.
12  ibid.
13  ibid.
14  Correspondence from the Fremantle Town Clerk to Officer in Charge, Arthur's Battery, 15 April 1942. City of Fremantle Council—General Correspondence. Battye: AN 217/6.
15  *Current Notes on International Events*, vol. 14, 3 February 1943, p. 29. 'Co-ordination—Rationing of US Forces'. AA-ACT: A816/131/301/3735/3.
16  Interview: Michael Papadoulis.
17  Interview: Marjorie Ward.
18  Shervington, *University Voices*, p. 42.
19  Interview: Bill Barker.
20  Interview: Larry Pfoff.
21  Interview: Phyllis Gurley.
22  Interview: Pat Tully.
23  Interview: David Bird.
24  Interview: George May.
25  ibid.
26  ibid.
27  Interview: Johnson Head.
28  Interview: Pat Catt.
29  *West Australian,* 19 August 1943.
30  Interviews: Mrs Sundstrom, Mrs Smith.
31  Interview: Michael Papadoulis.
32  Interview: Joy Anderson.
33  Interview: Dalveen Timms (née Lawson).
34  Interview: David Bird.
35  Interview: Homer White.

36  State Secretary, Women's Service Guild, to Perth Town Clerk, 1 April 1942. WSG, correspondence with the Municipality of Perth. Battye: 1949 MN 393, vol. 65.

37  Interview: Michael Papadoulis.

38  Interviewee's name withheld by request.

39  Interview: Andy Andersen.

40  'Hostels and Hospitality Centres for Use of Servicemen on Leave in Perth and Fremantle (WA).' AA-VIC: MP/742/1, 259/87/197.

41  26 May 1942. GR 1942, vol. 2.

42  Interview: Carl Uphoff.

43  Interview: Pat Catt.

44  Interviews: Pat Tully, Bill Barker.

45  Interview: Bill Barker.

46  Interview: George May.

47  Interview: Johnson Head.

48  *Geraldton Guardian,* 2 December 1942.

49  Interview: Bill Barker.

50  Interview: Johnson Head.

51  ibid.

52  Interview: Phyllis Gurley.

53  Interview: David Bird.

54  ibid.

55  *Albany Advertiser,* 29 June 1942.

56  Pat Elphinstone, 'Breakfast at Bernie's', *Panorama* (June 1994), pp. 36–39.

57  ibid. Interviews: Bill Barker, Syd Harvey, Joy Anderson.

58  Interview: Syd Harvey.

59  ibid.

60  ibid.

61  ibid.

62  ibid.

63  ibid.

64  ibid.

65  ibid.

66  ibid.

67  Colonel L. S. Ostrander to all Commanding Officers, all Base Sections, USAFIA, 24 June 1942. AA-ACT: A817/1, 12.

68  J. S. Gibson to C. McKerihan, 2 December 1942, in ibid.

69  AA-WA: PP102/1, USN1943/44/30; PP102/1, USN/1943/44/68.

70  Interview: Jack Glotzbach.

71  Diane Collins, *Hollywood Down Under: Australians at the Movies: 1896 to the Present Day* (North Ryde, NSW, 1987), p. 210.

72  *Fremantle and Districts Sentinel,* 23 April 1942.

73    Fremantle City Council Minutes, vol. 41, 25 May 1944, vol. 42, 19 June 1944. Battye: AN 217/2. Correspondence from Fremantle Town Clerk to Commanding Officer, US Navy, 19 May 1942. Battye: AN 217/6.

74    'Hostels and Hospitality Centres for Use of Servicemen on Leave in Perth and Fremantle (WA).' AA-VIC: MP/742/1, 259/87/197.

75    Interview: Jim Purcell.

76    ibid.

77    ibid.

78    ibid.

79    J. V. Peterson to Currie, 29 April 1942. UWA.

80    Currie to Commanding Officer, RAAF, 18 April 1942. UWA.

81    Dean of Engineering to Currie, 6 January 1943. UWA.

82    Currie to Rear-Admiral Lockwood, 28 January 1943. UWA.

83    Dean of Engineering to Currie, 27 September 1945. UWA.

84    'Works carried out on behalf of the United States Navy in Western Australia.' AA-VIC, MP1049/5, 2017/2/130.

85    Currie to Lt Commander Donaho, 15 September 1942. UWA.

86    Donaho to Currie, 12 October 1942. UWA.

87    J. M. Thomson to Currie, 16 October 1943. UWA.

88    Currie to US Commanding Officer, 6 November 1943. UWA.

89    O. F. Blakey to Currie, 22 March 1943. UWA.

90    Currie to Commander T. A. Christopher, 30 September 1943; Lt Commander W. S. Reid to Currie, 27 October1943. UWA.

91    Currie to US Commanding Officer, 6 November 1943. UWA.

92    Rear Admiral R. W. Christie to Currie, 12 November 1943. UWA.

93    Currie to Administrative Officer, US Forces, 27 March 1944. UWA.

94    Currie to Personnel Officer, US Navy, 17 April 1944. UWA.

95    Currie to Donaho, 18 December 1942. UWA.

96    Interview: Bill Barker.

Chapter Seven—GIRL QUESTIONS

1    Eli Daniel and Annette Potts, 'American Newsmen and Australian Wartime Propaganda and Censorship 1940–1942.' Historical Studies, vol. 21, no. 85, October 1985, p. 570.

2    Daily News, 26 March 1942.

3    Prime Minister J. Curtin, Commonwealth of Australia Parliamentary Debates, vol. 117, p. 825.

4    Interview: Cecil Anderson.

5    'Submarine Operations ex Australian bases. USN, RN and RNN. WW II.' AA-ACT: MP 1587/1, 173F.

6 Dixon Wecter, 'The Aussie and the Yank,' *Atlantic Monthly*, May 1946, p. 54.
7 Interview: Pat Catt.
8 Interview: Bill Barker.
9 31 July 1945. GR 1945, vol. 1.
10 *Albany Advertiser,* 20, 30 April 1942.
11 Interview: Bill Barker.
12 31 July 1945. GR 1945, vol. 1.
13 Interview: Bill Barker.
14 Major-General F. H. Berryman, circular to military units, 8 December 1942. AA-VIC: MP1587/1, 282M.
15 Squibb, 'Fremantle Solidarity', p. 56.
16 Interviews: Pat Catt, Pat Tully.
17 Interviews: Larry Pfoff, Mrs Smith.
18 *Geraldton Guardian*, 28 July 1942.
19 Interview: Syd Harvey.
20 ibid.
21 ibid.
22 ibid. *Porthole: Official Journal of the American Red Cross Club*, 4, 18 October, 11 November 1944.
23 Interview: Jim Purcell, *Porthole*, 18 October 1944.
24 Interview: Pat Tully.
25 AA-ACT: A373/1, 7431.
26 Interview: Pat Catt. Dorothy Hewett, *Wild Card: An Autobiography 1923–1958* (Ringwood, Victoria, 1990), p. 85.
27 Interview: Syd Harvey.
28 Interview: Pat Catt.
29 ibid.
30 Interview: Bill Barker.
31 Interview: Jack Glotzbach, *Daily News,* 9 March 1942.
32 *Albany Advertiser*, 23, 30 March 1942.
33 Interview: Phyllis Gurley.
34 ibid.
35 Interview: David Bird.
36 ibid. Interview: Phyllis Gurley.
37 Interview: Marjorie Ward.
38 ibid.
39 Interview: Bill Barker.
40 Interviews: Syd Harvey, George May, Mrs Nicholls.
41 Interviews: Pat Tully, Pat Catt.
42 ibid.
43 Interview: Pat Catt.
44 Interview: Pat Tully.

45   ibid.
46   Interview: Syd Harvey.
47   Interviewee's name withheld by request.
48   [Name of correspondent withheld to protect family's identity] to Consul, 11 May 1942. GR 1942, vol. 3.
49   Turner to Sydney consulate, 29 September 1944. CF 1944.
50   Minutes of the State Executive of the Women's Service Guild 1938–1953, 20 March 1942. Battye: A2530 MN 585 vol. 44.
51   *Daily News,* 26 March 1942.
52   State Secretary, WSG to Town Clerk (and reply), 1 April 1942. Women's Service Guild, correspondence with the Municipality of Perth. Battye: 1949 MN 393, vol. 65.
53   Minutes of the State Executive of the Women's Service Guild 1938–1953, 17 April 1942.
54   See for example 'Evidence Submitted by the WSG of WA Before the Royal Commission to Inquire into the Administration of Health and Building Bylaws of the City of Perth', June 1938, in ibid.
55   Women Justices Association Of WA Minute Books, 8 April 1942. Battye: 1929A MN375, vol. 7.
56   Minutes of Labor Women Central Executive, 2 June 1942. Battye: 2011A/3MN 407. Modern Women's Club to WSG, 28 May 1942; Mother's Union to WSG, 23 May 1942; WA Women's Progressive League to WSG, 20 May 1942, Women's Service Guild State Executive Minute Book. Battye: 1949A, MN 393, vol. 74.
57   *The Dawn: Journal of the Women's Service Guild,* 15 September 1942.
58   Women Justices Association Of WA Minute Books, 12 August 1942.
59   *The Dawn,* 17 June 1942.
60   ibid., 15 September 1942.
61   Mason to Solicitor-General, 9 September 1942; Solicitor-General to Mason, 15 September 1942. GR 1942, vol. 3.
62   Turner to Sydney consulate, 15 September 1942, in ibid.
63   Police Department Annual Report 1942. Battye: Acc. No. 430, An 5/3, Item 3246, 1942.
64   ibid.
65   ibid.
66   ibid.
67   Women's Service Guild State Executive Minute Book, 6 October 1942. Battye: 1949A, MN 393, vol. 74.
68   Women Justices Association Of WA Annual Reports. 11 November 1942. Battye: 1929A, MN 375, vol. 7.
69   Perth City Council: Correspondence Files. Battye: AN 20/5.
70   Women Justices Association Of WA Annual Reports. 11 November 1942.

71   'Annual Report of the Chief Surgeon, South West Pacific Area, for the Year 1942.' USNA: RG 407, 98-SS3-26.
72   Perth City Council: Correspondence Files. Battye: AN 20/5.
73   Interview: Jack Glotzbach. Correspondence with F. Wood, New Hampshire.
74   Dr F. H. Baker to Sydney Consulate-General, 6 July 1943. GR 1943, vol. 1.
75   Interview: G. Handcock (WA Police Force).
76   Interview: Carl Uphoff.
77   Interview: David Bird.
78   ibid.
79   Interview: Pat Catt.
80   Interview: Carl Uphoff.
81   Interview: Mrs Lee.
82   Correspondence from the S. H. Lamb Printing House to Fremantle Town Clerk, 12 March 1942. Battye: AN 217/6.
83   Fremantle City Council Minutes, vol. 42, 17 June 1944. Battye: AN 217/2.
84   ibid., 25 May 1944.
85   ibid., vol. 43, 19 February 1945.
86   WA National Council of Women—Minutes of the General Council and Executive, 26 June 1944. Battye: 1389A MN 187, vol. 13.
87   Gavin B. Casey, State Publicity Censor to Bonney, 1 April 1943. AA-VIC: SP109/3/1, 337/24A.
88   *Fremantle and Districts Sentinel,* 16 April 1942.
89   ibid., 5 May 1942.
90   ibid., 14 May 1942.
91   ibid., 25 June 1942
92   ibid., 2, 16 July 1942.
93   ibid., 10 September 1942.
94   Norman McRae (Casey's successor) to Bonney, 9 February 1944.
95   'Marriage of Australian Girls to American Soldiers.' AA-VIC: MP508/1, 115/701/352.
96   Palmer to Turner, 19 October 1942. GR 1942, vol. 4.
97   Summary of Business forms 1941–42 for Perth Consulate. GR 1942, vol. 2.
98   'Remarks' section on December 1942 form in ibid.
99   [Name withheld to protect identity] to Consul, 18 June 1942. CF 1942.
100  Turner to J. L. Walker, WA Solicitor-General, 9 September 1942; Walker to Turner, 15 September 1942. GR 1942, vol. 3.
101  [Name withheld to protect identity] to Turner, 13 August 1945, and Turner's reply. GR 1945, vol. 5.
102  Memorandum 14 October 1942. GR 1942, vol. 5.
103  Circular from Director General of Man Power (NSW), 6 September 1944, referring to a letter to Deputy Director of Man Power in Perth (dated 5 August 1943). AA-NSW: SP60/2, LA 452.

104 'Marriage of Australian Girls to American Soldiers [Conference with Mr Dickover, American Consul-General], 26 March 1942. AA-VIC: MP508/1, 115/701/352. Correspondence re Status of Australian Women Married to US servicemen. GR 1942, vol. 4.

105 Correspondence re Status of Australian Women Married to US servicemen. GR 1942, vol. 4.

106 'Australian Women, Wives and Fiancees of US Servicemen', 1942–46. AA-ACT, A659, 1946/1/1527.

107 Charles O. Thompson to J. L. Walker, 19 August 1942. GR 1942, vol. 3.

108 *The Dawn*, 16 February 1944.

109 ibid., 19 January 1944.

## Chapter Eight—THE RACIAL NEGATIVE

1 Secret cable (deciphered) from Australian Minister in Washington to Department of External Affairs, 9 January 1942; reply 14 January 1942. AA-ACT: A1608/1, B45/1/10.

2 Secret cable (deciphered) from Australian Minister in Washington to Department of External Affairs, 9 January 1942; 'Memo for the Minister', 13 January 1942; 'Most Secret' Secretary, Department of Defence Co-Ordination, to Secretary, Department of External Affairs, 13 January 1942. AA-ACT: A981, WAR 35A.

3 Wilson to Secretary, Department of Interior, 13 January 1942. A433, 42/2/258.

4 Memorandum to Secretary, Department of External Affairs, 20 January 1942, in ibid.

5 Cablegram from Casey, External Affairs, to Australian Minister in Washington, 16 January 1942. AA-ACT: A981, WAR 35A.

6 W. R. Hodgson, Secretary, Department of External Affairs, to Secretary, Department of Interior, 19 January 1942. AA-ACT: A433, 45/2/6281.

7 Advisory War Council Minute (Secret), 20 January 1942. AA-ACT: A2684/3, 1330. Department of External Affairs to Australian Minister in Washington, 21 January 1942. AA-ACT: A1608/1, B45/1/10.

8 J. J. Barry, Queensland A/Collector of Customs, to Secretary, Department of Interior, 27 March 1942. AA-ACT: A433, 45/2/6281.

9 E. G. Bonney, Chief Publicity Censor, to Lieutenant Colonel Lloyd Lehrbas, Press Relations Officer, Headquarters, USA Army Forces in Australia, Melbourne, 9 April 1942. AA-ACT: SP109/3, 308/17.

10 H. H. Mansell, State Publicity Censor, NSW, to Bonney, 11 April 1942, in ibid.

11 'War Section—American Coloured Troops', 1942–43. AA-ACT: A1608/1, B45/1/10.

12 Report signed Sgt D. J. Foster, 16 April 1942. AWM 60: 59/1/730.

13 A. E. Lavis, State Publicity Censor, Queensland, to Bonney, 17 April 1942. AA: SP109/3, 308/17.

14 Col. L. A. Diller, Press Relations Officer, US Army, to Bonney, 20 April 1942, in ibid.

15 Censorship files, 28 June 1942. AA-NSW: PC17, part 1.

16 Major General J. A. Ulio, Adjutant General, War Department, Washington, Order re Publicity on Negro Troops sent to Commanding Generals of all US forces, 23 June 1942. Diller to Bonney, 15 July 1942. AA-ACT: SP109/3, 308/17.

17 'Instructions re Negro Troops', 15 July 1942, in ibid.

18 Richard Dalfiume, 'The Forgotten Years of the Negro Revolution', *Journal of American History*, vol. 55, 1968–69, pp. 90–106. Lee Finkle, 'The Conservative Aims of Militant Rhetoric: Black Protest During World War II', ibid., vol. 60, 1973–74, pp. 692–713.

19 'Instructions re Negro Troops', 15 July 1942. AA-ACT: SP109/3, 308/17.

20 For example: 'It is desired that action be taken to discourage Australian troops from fraternising or drinking with American coloured troops. Such fraternisation is not permitted or thought of on the part of American white troops and it is undesirable that it should continue on the part of Australian troops.' Confidential circular to Australian officers in Queensland from HQ, Queensland L. of C. area, 18 May 1942. AWM 60: 59/1/730. Similar comments in HQ Queensland, L. of C. area, 1 August 1942. AWM 60: 75/1/74.

21 Forde to G. W. Martens, MP, 22 August 1942. AA-VIC: MP508/1, 50/703/35.

22 Secretary, Department of Defence, to Secretary, Prime Minister's Department, 15 August 1942 (Secret). AA-ACT: A2684/3, 1330.

23 C. W. Neilson, Asst. Manager for Queensland, Qantas Empire Airways Ltd, to Assistant Director of Civil Aviation, Melbourne, 14 September 1942. E. C. Johnston, Director-General of Civil Aviation, to Secretary, Qantas, Sydney, 24 September 1942. AA-VIC: MP131/1, 192/136/87.

24 H. Harman, Secretary, Qantas, to Director-General of Civil Aviation, 30 September 1942, in ibid.

25 ibid.

26 Major T. F. Ryan, Chief of Air Section, United States Army Services of Supply, South West Pacific Area, to E. C. Johnston, Director-General of Civil Aviation, 19 October 1942, in ibid.

27 For example: Extract from Letter Addressed to Prime Minister from Trades and Labour Council, Ipswich, n.d. 'We desire to protest to the Federal Government against an Army Order directing Australian armed forces not to fraternise with the black skinned soldiers from America, as such displeases the white skinned soldier from America. As the black skinned soldiers are members of the working class, are here to defend Australia and defeat Fascism, we urge that our Army Authorities not be allowed to succumb to such racial superiority theories which are Fascist in character.' AWM 60: 59/1/730.

28  D. A. Alexander, Acting Inspector, Investigation Branch, Sydney, to the Director, Commonwealth Investigation Branch, Canberra, 12 May 1942. AA-ACT: A373/1, 2837.

29  'Re Negro Soldiers and White Chauvinism', in ibid.

30  Circular from Deputy Director of Security to all states, 14 October 1942; reply from Deputy Directors of Security, all states, 17–26 October. AA-ACT: A373/1, 2837.

31  ibid.

32  'West Australia L. of C. Weekly Security Summary No. 1, 10 May 1943.' AWM 54: 883/2/16.

33  *The Mirror*, 17 March 1945.

34  ibid., 10 March 1945.

35  Interview: Syd Harvey.

36  Interviews: Jim Purcell, Pat Tully, Pat Catt.

37  Interviews: Pat Tully, Pat Catt.

38  Interview: Mrs J. Balcombe.

39  Interview: Informant's name withheld by request.

40  Interview: E. V. Taylor.

41  Interview: George May.

42  Interviews: Jack Hanks, George May, Michael Papadoulis.

43  Interviews: Carl Uphoff, George May.

44  Interviews: Informants' names withheld by request.

45  *West Australian*, 14 August 1944.

46  ibid., 24 August 1944.

47  *Daily News*, 22 March 1943.

48  ibid., 5 April 1944.

49  ibid., 21 April 1944.

## Chapter Nine—PETTY VIOLENCE

1  'Strikes, Riots and Brawls—References to', 1939–42. AA-NSW: SP106, PC17 PART 1.

2  Major-General F. H. Berryman, circular to numerous military units, 8 December 1942, 'Disturbances Between Australian and American Troops.' AA-VIC: MP1587/1, 282M.

3  Potts and Potts, *Yanks Down Under*, pp. 302–15.

4  Berryman, circular: 'Disturbances Between Australian and American Troops.'

5  Interview: Pat Catt.

6  *West Australian*, 'Big Weekend' Section, 5 February 1994.

7  Interview: Marjorie Ward.

8  Suzanne Welborn, *Swan: The History of a Brewery* (Nedlands, 1987), p. 172.

9    *Daily News*, 19 March 1942.

10   Report from Sergeant Sholl in 'Report re: Brawl in Fremantle on April 11, 1944 between Allied and other Servicemen', Police Department. Battye: AN 5, Acc. No. 430, File 1609, 1944.

11   *West Australian*, 14 January 1943.

12   Correspondence with R. Moffitt, Washington, USA.

13   Welborn, *Swan,* p. 174.

14   Interview: Cec Anderson.

15   Interview: T. Richards.

16   'Visiting Servicemen—American. Customs Duty on Liquor Imported by Officers Clubs, 1945.' AA-ACT: Department of External Affairs, Correspondence File No. I.C. 45/54/3/1.

17   Correspondence from Premier of Western Australia to the Fremantle Town Clerk, 18 March 1942.

18   Interview: Dewey Balcombe.

19   Correspondence with E. Dwyer, New Hampshire, USA.

20   Correspondence with R. Moffitt, Washington, USA.

21   Interview: Bill Barker.

22   *Commonwealth of Australia Parliamentary Debates,* vol. 171, p. 1793.

23   Interview: Irving Sizik.

24   Berryman, Circular: 'Disturbances Between Australian and American Troops.'

25   *Albany Advertiser,* 11 June 1942, p. 4.

26   Interview: George May.

27   Interview: Bill Barker.

28   Interviews: Marjorie Ward, George May.

29   Interviews: George May, Jack Sue, Syd Harvey.

30   Interview: Michael Papadoulis.

31   Mrs Ashton to Turner, 4 September 1945. GR 1945, vol. 5.

32   Turner to Mrs Ashton, 19 September 1945, in ibid.

33   Interview: Mrs Lee.

34   Interview: Bill Barker.

35   ibid.

36   ibid.

37   ibid.

38   ibid.

39   ibid.


## Chapter Ten—VIOLENT FREMANTLE

1    Interview: Jim Purcell.

2    For example, interviews: Pat Tully, Pat Catt.

3    Beryl Hackner, *Rosa: A Biography of Rosa Townsend* (Nedlands, 1994), p. 59.

4    Philip Ward, 'Reflections: Comrades in Arms', *Fremantle Herald*, 19 October 1992.

5    Hackner, *Rosa*, p. 59.

6    Correspondence from Fremantle Town Clerk to the Commissioner of Police, 8 January 1942. City of Fremantle, General Correspondence. Battye: AN 217/6.

7    *Sunday Times*, 22 March 1942.

8    Fremantle City Council Minutes, 17 April 1944. Battye: AN 217/6.

9    Correspondence from S. H. Lamb Printing House to Town Clerk, 12 March 1942. City of Fremantle, General Correspondence.

10   AA-VIC: MP508/1, 85/750/134.

11   AA-VIC: MP1049/5, 2026/8/714.

12   ibid.

13   AA-NSW: SP106, PC17 PART 1.

14   AA-ACT, A981, CHIN 8.

15   Report on Organisation and Activities of Security Service—Perth Branch. 1943, 'Annexure G'. AA-ACT: A373/1, 7431.

16   ibid.

17   Finding of Facts—signed by Victor Sadd, Lieut. Cdr USNR; see also EN3-8 (Perth) A9/P13, Serial No. 03, January 22 1943. CF 1943.

18   Turner to Luckenbach Steamship Coy Inc., 30 April 1943, in ibid.

19   Ely E. Palmer, US Consul, Sydney, but dated American Consulate Perth, 6 February 1943, in ibid.

20   Report on Organisation and Activities of Security Service—Perth Branch, 1943, 'Annexure G'.

21   Harold P. Petersen to Charles E. Brown, Regional Director, Anzac Area, US War Shipping Administration, 23 January, 11 February 1943. CF 1943.

22   Lynn to Richter, 7 September 1943. GR 1943, vol. 4.

23   Report on Organisation and Activities of Security Service—Perth Branch, 1943, 'Annexure G'.

24   ibid. The Security Service claimed that news of these methods had 'spread throughout the whole of the Merchant Service with the result that desertions are decreasing daily'. From March to the beginning of September 1943 some 62 American seamen had been interned, 'the majority of whom were held only for a few days before being placed back on other liberty ships'.

25   Fremantle Defence Committee—Reports of Meetings. AA-VIC: MP1185/8, 1855/10/1.

26   Report on Organisation and Activities of Security Service—Perth Branch. 1943, 'Annexure H'.

27   ibid.

28   'Shooting of Motorist by Peace Officer at Fremantle Wharves, 1942.' AA-ACT, A432/85, 1942/947.

29   ibid.

30  ibid.

31  ibid.

32  ibid.

33  ibid.

34  Copy of urgent telegram received from Deputy Superintending Peace Officer, Perth, 6 November 1942, by H. E. Jones, Superintending Peace Officer, Canberra, in ibid.

35  West Australia L. of C. Area, 'Weekly Security Summary', No. 3 to 22 May 1943, p. 2. AWM 54: 883/2/16.

36  ibid.

37  ibid. p. 4.

38  West Australia L. of C. Area, 'Weekly Security Summary', No. 2 to 15 May 1943, p. 3.

39  West Australia L. of C. Area, 'Weekly Security Summary', No. 3 to 22 May 1943, p. 4.

40  ibid.

41  Casey to Bonney, 1 April 1943. AA-VIC: SP109/3/1, 337/24A.

42  Case No. Ph-628-242, United States Coast Guard, Merchant Marine Detail, Fremantle, 20 September 1944. CF 1944.

43  Interviews: Andy Andersen, Homer White, Mrs Mona Nicholls, Larry Pfoff.

44  Interviews: Larry Pfoff, Homer White.

45  Interview: Pat Tully.

46  Report from Sergeant Sholl in 'Report re: Brawl in Fremantle on April 11, 1944 between Allied and other Servicemen'.

47  Interviews: Bill Barker, Homer White, Irving Sizik, Carl Uphoff, Mrs Mona Nicholls, Michael Papadoulis.

48  Report from Sergeant Sholl in 'Report re: Brawl in Fremantle on April 11, 1944 between Allied and other Servicemen'.

49  Report from Inspector Read in ibid.

50  ibid.

51  ibid.

52  H. Baker in ibid.

53  ibid.

54  Darcy Agarnia Nepia, in ibid.

55  Report from Inspector Read in ibid.

56  E. Armfield in ibid.

57  Interview: Bill Barker.

58  *The Mirror*, 7 July 1944.

59  Fremantle City Council Minutes, 17 April 1944.

60  ibid.

61  Report from Sergeant Sholl in 'Report re: Brawl in Fremantle on April 11, 1944 between Allied and other Servicemen'.

*Chapter Eleven*—RETURN TO NORMALCY

1     *The Broadcaster,* 7 July 1943, pp. 20–21.

2     'Works Carried out on behalf of the United States Navy in Western Australia.' AA-VIC: MP1049/5, 2017/2/130. Blakey (Engineering) to Currie, 19, 27 September 1945. C. L. Thorpe, Assistant Director of Hirings, Western Command, to Currie, 29 November, 10 December 1945. UWA.

3     Interview: George May.

4     Interviews: Bill Barker, Pat Tully.

5     Fremantle City Council Minutes, vol. 42, March 20, 1944. Battye, AN 217/2.

6     *West Australian,* 23 December 1944.

7     ibid.

8     ibid. Correspondence with Heather Anderson, Western Australia.

9     *West Australian,* 4 May 1945.

10    ibid., 1, 3, 4, 5 May 1945.

11    ibid., 8 May 1945.

12    ibid.

13    ibid.

14    ibid., 15 August 1945.

15    ibid., 17 August 1945.

16    ibid., 16, 17 August 1945.

17    Interview: Pat Catt.

18    ibid.

19    ibid.

20    *West Australian,* 17 August 1945.

21    Phyllis Dean to Frank Forde, 1 March 1945. AA-VIC: MP/742/1, 259/87/197.

22    Dean to Senator Fraser, Acting Minister for Army, 14 May 1945; Dorothy Tangney to Fraser, 22 May 1945, in ibid.

23    Department of the Army, Minute Paper, 23 May 1945, in ibid.

24    Mary S. McKinlay to Fraser, 31 May 1945, in ibid.

25    Tom Burke to Forde, [?], 20 December 1945, in ibid.

26    J. J. Simons to Forde, 15 December 1945, in ibid.

27    Interview: Syd Harvey.

28    *West Australian,* 10 April 1945, p.3.

29    T. W. Meagher to Fraser, 30 May 1945. AA-VIC: MP/742/1, 259/87/197.

30    McKinlay to Fraser, 31 May 1945, in ibid.

31    Dean to Forde, 23 July 1945, in ibid.

32    Burke to Forde, [?] December 1945, in ibid.

33    Simons to Forde, 15 December 1945, in ibid.

34    Senator George McLeay to A. A. Calwell, 5 October 1945; Calwell to McLeay, 19 October 1945. AA-ACT: A436, 45/5/971.

35    John R. Minter, US Legation, Canberra, to Lieutenant-Colonel W. R. Hodgson,

Secretary, Department of External Affairs, 10 March 1944. AA-ACT: A989, 1944/950/5/4/15. Department of Interior Circular, 1945. AA-ACT: A1066, G45/1/21.

36   'Basic Information for American Ex-Servicemen Contemplating Residence in Western Australia' prepared by Courtland Christiani, 30 October 1945. GR 1945, vol. 1.

37   Miss M. O'Neill to Turner, 9 December 1945; Turner to Miss O'Neill, 13 December 1945, in ibid.

38   E. V. Tate to US Ambassador, Canberra, 21 October 1945; Turner to Tate, 28 November 1945, in ibid.

39   Carl W. Mims to Turner, 19 February 1945; Turner to Mims, 23 February 1945, in ibid.

40   'Basic Information for American Ex-Servicemen Contemplating Residence in Western Australia.'

41   ibid.

42   *West Australian,* 16 August 1943.

43   ibid.

44   Michael Sturma, 'Loving the Alien: The Underside of Relations Between American Servicemen and Australian Women in Queensland 1942–1945.' *Journal of Australian Studies,* vol. 24, 1989, p. 12; Turner to Sydney consulate, 5 April 1944. GR 1944, vol. 4.

45   GR 1944, vol. 4, *passim.*

46   Interviews: Johnson and Triss (Beatrice) Head.

47   ibid.

48   Turner to Sydney Consulate, 5 April 1944. GR 1944, vol. 4.

49   Cuttings from Sydney *Daily Telegraph,* 6 December 1944, *Argus,* 21 March 1945, in 'Australian Women, Wives and Fiancees of U.S. Servicemen.' AA-ACT: A659, 1946/1/1527.

50   Annette Potts and Lucinda Strauss, *For the Love of a Soldier: Australian War Brides and their GIs* (Crow's Nest, NSW, 1987 ), pp. 68–69.

51   Interviews: Mrs Lee, Mrs Willshire.

52   Cuttings from *News* and *Mail,* 1 September 1945, and from *Adelaide Advertiser,* 4 September 1945. GR 1945, vol. 5.

53   Cuttings in 'Australian Women, Wives and Fiancees of U.S. Servicemen', AA-ACT: A659, 1946/1/1527.

54   ibid.

55   ibid.

56   Handwritten letter in 'Australian Women, Wives and Fiancees of U.S. Servicemen', AA-ACT: A659, 1946/1/1527.

57   Interview: Pat Catt.

58   ibid. Lois Battle, *War Brides* (London, 1982).

59   Interview: Pat Catt.

60   ibid.

61   Information supplied by Victor Fisher, Swanbourne, Western Australia.

62   Interview: Avis Koenig.

63   ibid.

64   ibid.

65   ibid.; interview: Triss Head.

66   Interviews: Avis Koenig, Johnson and Triss Head.

67   Mrs Roy Murnane, Killora Stud, Elgin PO, to Turner, 3 September 1945. GR 1945, vol. 5.

68   Mrs O'Neill, Carlisle, to Turner, 2 December 1945, in ibid.

69   Miss J. O'Neill to Consul, 10 December 1945, in ibid.

70   Turner to Mrs Murnane, 8 September 1945, in ibid.

71   Mrs Mary Teague to Turner, 5 September 1945, in ibid.

## CONCLUSION

1   'Bodies of American Servicemen Buried in US Army Cemeteries in Australia— Transfer to USA', 1947–48. AA-ACT: 1431, 1947/2351.

2   ibid.

3   Security measures make precise figures hard to determine. Interviews with veterans such as Bill Barker and Johnson Head suggest that, at the most, half a dozen Catalina men died—and these mostly in accidents—whereas some eleven submarines operating out of Fremantle, with a total of many hundreds of men aboard, were lost: Squibb, 'Fremantle Solidarity', p. 50.

# BIBLIOGRAPHY

## ARCHIVAL SOURCES

AUSTRALIAN ARCHIVES, Australian Capital Territory, New South Wales, Victoria and
    Western Australia
Records of the following departments, agencies and individuals have been consulted:
Advisory War Council
Attorney-General
Censorship
Civil Aviation
Defence
Defence, Navy Office
External Affairs
Health
Information
Interior
Navy
Prime Minister
Security Service
Sir Frederick Shedden
War Cabinet


AUSTRALIAN WAR MEMORIAL, Canberra
From the Memorial's extensive records most use has been made of material dealing
    with the wartime atmosphere in Western Australia, especially before the arrival
    of the Americans, for example:
'Breaches of Censorship—Correspondence', 1941. 54, 175/7/1.
'Extracts from War Historians' Diaries', 1 March 1942 [Owen Stanley's Reports]. 54,
    577/7/32.
'Final Voyage Report. H.T. "QX" ("Queen Mary")', 1940–41. 54, 963/13/23.
'Geraldton District: Possibility of Enemy Action: Plans for Protection of Civilians.'
    1942. 54, 183/5/13.
'Reconnaisssance Report Gingin Area,' 1941–42. 54, 831/3/60.
'Voyage Report HMAT "S1", Fremantle to Suez, 1940.' 54, 963/13/18.
'Voyage Report HMT "QX 1" Queen Mary, O/C Troops Brigadier J. J. Murray,
    Fremantle to Bombay, 1940.' 54, 963/13/22.
'Western Australia L. of C. Area: Weekly Security Summary,' 1943. 54, 883/2/16.

BATTYE LIBRARY, Perth

Army and Navy Canteen Documents, High Street, Fremantle, 1940–1945. PR7455.

Base Facilities Report. United States Naval Activities, Southwest Pacific Area. Compiled by the Commander of the Seventh Fleet. 1944. PR6185.

'Bickley Battery, Rottnest Island.' PR 11032.

Casey, Major General Hugh J., 'Airfield and Base Development. Report of Operations. U.S. Army Forces in the Far East, South West Pacific Area Army Forces, Pacific.' 1951. PR11614

Fremantle City Council Departments—General Correspondence. AN 217/6.

Fremantle City Council—Records and Minute Books, 1941–1945. AN 217/2.

Fremantle Municipal Tramways and Electric Lighting Board Minutes 1939–1943. Acc. 1331, AN 306, Item 13, 1939–43.

Hicks, B., 'Personal Reminiscences of World War Two in Albany.' PR 8817/2.

Hospitality and Information Bureau. (Pamphlet material.) PR 8482.

Labor Women Central Executive: Minutes. 2011A/3MN 407.

Perth City Council Records: Minutes. AN 20/1.

Perth City Council Records: Correspondence Files. AN 20/5.

Police Department Records. AN 5, Acc. No. 430.

Ryan, Jan, 'Geraldton 1942: A Year to Remember.' Q994.12 Ger.

WA National Council of Women—Minutes of the General Council and Executive. 1389A MN 187, vol. 13.

Women's Service Guild of WA: Minutes of the State Executive 1938–1953. A2530 MN 585, vol. 44.

Women Justices Association Of WA: Minute Books and Annual Reports. 1929A, MN 375, vol. 7.


NATIONAL LIBRARY OF AUSTRALIA, Canberra

Sir Richard Boyer Papers. MS 3181, Box 8.


UNITED STATES NATIONAL ARCHIVES AND RECORDS SERVICE, Washington, DC (and Annexe, Suitland, Maryland)

| | |
|---|---|
| RG 38 | Records of the Office of the Chief of Naval Operations 1937–46. [These records were examined but yielded little useful information.] |
| RG 84 | Records of the Foreign Service Posts of the Department of State. General Records and Confidential Files of the Perth Consular District, 1937–1949. |
| RG 407 | Records of the Adjutant-General's Office, 1917– . |

| 98-B1G-0.1 | Base 6 (Perth) History—draft 3 March 1942–45. January 1943. |
| 98-USF37-0.2 USAIFA | Report of Organization and Activities—United States Army Forces in Australia, 7 December 1941–30 June 1942, with Inclosures 1 to 30 and Appendices 1 to 23. |
| 98-USF37-2.18 USAFIA | G-2 Memoranda and Miscellaneous Papers. |
| 98-SS3-0.1 USASOS,SWPA | 'History Incomplete 1941–1944.' |
| 98-SS3-0.2 USASOS,SWPA | 'History of the Efforts Made by the Original United States Army Agencies in Australia Early in 1942 to Relieve as Much as was Possible the Beleaguered Troops in the Philippines During the Closing Phases of the Campaign Against the Japanese in that Area', 4 August 1944. |
| 98-SS3-26 USASOS | Medical Diary—Office of the Chief Surgeon, 10 December 1941–30 June 1942. |

THE UNIVERSITY OF WESTERN AUSTRALIA ARCHIVES
Crawley Grounds and Buildings. Use by Armed Forces, 29 January 1945–10 October 1947. UWA: Acc. No. 3696, File 7/8.


MISCELLANEOUS UNPUBLISHED MATERIAL

American Red Cross, 'Brides Program—Australia.' 24 July 1946.

Anderson, Heather, Western Australia. Correspondence with Lisa Jackson.

Booth, C., 'Americans in Fremantle 1942 Onward.' Notes compiled 21 March 1989. Held in the Fremantle Local History Collection.

Dyer, Edwin, New Hampshire, USA. Correspondence with Lisa Jackson.

Fisher, Victor, Swanbourne, Western Australia. Information supplied to Tony Barker, January 1995.

Itoh, William H., former US Consul-General in Perth. Information supplied to Tony Barker, August 1993.

Moffitt, Roy, Washington, USA. Correspondence with Lisa Jackson.

Peet, Lindsay, 'American Military Activities—Western Australia.' Notes compiled 1991.

Squibb, John P., 'Fremantle Solidarity: The Response of a Port City to World War Two.' Unpublished honours dissertation, Department of History, The University of Western Australia, 1984.

Surridge, Robin, United States Information Service, Perth. Information supplied to
Tony Barker, December 1994.
Wood, Col. Frederick, New Hampshire, USA. Correspondence with Lisa Jackson.


## ORAL HISTORY

MATERIAL HELD IN BATTYE LIBRARY, Perth
(collected principally by Jacquie Bunney)

| | |
|---|---|
| Andersen, Andy | American submariner |
| Anderson, Cecil | Australian submariner |
| Balcombe, Dewey | American Army |
| Balcombe, Mrs Jean | Young woman in Perth and war bride |
| Glotzbach, Jack | American Navy |
| Handcock, G. | WA plainclothes policeman during the war |
| Hanks, Jack | American submariner |
| Papadoulis, Michael | Child living in North Perth during the war |
| Richards, T. | Australian Army |
| Sizak, Irving | American submariner |
| Sue, Jack | Australian submariner |
| Uphoff, Carl | American Navy |


INTERVIEWS CONDUCTED BY AUTHORS

| | |
|---|---|
| Anderson, Mrs Joy (née Gawned) | Child in Wembley during the war |
| Barker, Bill | American Catalina serviceman |
| Bird, David | Child and teenager in Albany and Perth during the war |
| Bunney, Jacquie | Oral historian |
| Catt, Mrs Pat (née White) | Subiaco resident during the war, sister of war bride, aunt of Lois Battle |
| Edgar, Ian | Gingin farmer during the war |
| George, Gwen (née Anderson) | Northam telephonist during the war |
| Greenhalgh, Robert | Cottesloe resident during the war |
| Gurley, Phyllis (née Vaughan) | Young woman in Albany and war bride |
| Harvey, Syd | Secretary, ANA Club, Perth, during the war |
| Head, Johnson | Executive Officer, US Catalina base, Geraldton, during the war |

Head, Triss (Beatrice)          Nurse in Geraldton and war bride of Johnson Head
Hudson, Mrs Lyn                 Fremantle resident during the war
Koenig, Mrs Avis                Radar operator and war bride
     (née Grounds-Weston)
Lee, Mrs Edna                   Dance instructor at the Embassy Ballroom
Matthews, Mrs Pat               Wartime girlfriend of Bill Barker; Swan Dive hostess
     (née Tully)
May, George                     Geraldton resident during the war
Melancon, Mrs K.                War bride
Nicholls, Mrs Mona              Kalamunda resident during the war
Peet, Lindsay                   Perth resident during the war, historian
Pfoff, Larry and Flo            American submariner and his Australian wife
Pouleris, Kath                  War bride of American submariner
Purcell, James                  Field Director, American Red Cross, Perth, 1943–44
Smith, Mrs Maidee               Applecross resident during the war
Sundstrum, Mrs Marty            Applecross resident during the war
Timms, Mrs Dalveen              Child in Perth during the war
     (née Lawson)
Taylor, E. V.                   Nedlands resident during the war
Ward, Mrs Marjorie              Proprietor of Derward Hotel, Murray Street, Perth,
                                during the war
White, Homer                    American submariner
Willshire, Mrs Mona             War bride

## PRINTED PRIMARY SOURCES

NEWSPAPERS AND MAGAZINES
*Albany Advertiser* (Albany)
*Australian Women's Weekly* (Sydney)
*Broadcaster* (Perth)
*Christian Science Monitor* (Boston)
*Daily News* (Perth)
*Dawn: Journal of the Women's Service Guilds of Western Australia* (Perth)
*Fremantle and Districts Sentinel* (Fremantle)
*Geraldton Guardian* (Geraldton)
*Mirror* (Perth)
*Porthole: Official Journal of the American Red Cross Club* (Perth)
*Sunday Times* (Perth)
*West Australian* (Perth)

## BOOKS AND PAMPHLETS

*City and Suburban Plans and Street Index*, 1947.

*Commonwealth of Australia Parliamentary Debates.*

*Current Notes on International Events*, vols 13–17.

*The Secession Referendum Act, 1932, and the Secession Referendum Act, 1934... The Case of the People of Western Australia in Support of Their Desire to Withdraw from the Commonwealth of the Australian Constitutional Act (Imperial).* Perth, 1934.

*Souvenir of the Land of the Southern Cross.* From the US Army Forces in Australia.

*Western Australia Parliamentary Debates.*

*The Western Cricketer: Western Australian Cricket Association Inc., 1993–94 Year Book.*


## SECONDARY SOURCES


### BOOKS — HISTORY AND BIOGRAPHY

Adam Smith, Patsy. *Australian Women at War.* Melbourne, 1984.

Alexander, Fred. *Campus at Crawley: A Narrative and Critical Appreciation of the First Fifty Years of The University of Western Australia.* Melbourne, 1963.

Aitchison, R., *Thanks to the Yanks? The Americans and Australia.* Melbourne, 1972.

Bain, Mary. *Full Fathom Five.* Perth, 1982.

Bell, Philip and Bell, Roger. *Implicated: The United States in Australia.* Melbourne, 1993.

Bell, Roger. *Unequal Allies: Australian–American Relations and the Pacific War.* Carlton, Victoria, 1977.

Blair, C. *Silent Victory.* Philadelphia, 1975.

Cairns, Lynne. *Submarines in the Harbour: The World War Two Allied Submarine Base at Fremantle.* Fremantle, 1994.

Campbell, Rosemary. *Heroes and Lovers: A Question of National Identity.* Sydney, 1989.

Churchward, L. G. *Australia and America 1788–1972.* Sydney, 1979.

Collins, D. *Hollywood Down Under: Australians at the Movies 1896 to the Present Day.* North Ryde, New South Wales, 1987.

Cooksey, R., ed. *The Great Depression in Australia.* Canberra, 1970.

Costello, J. *Love, Sex and War: Changing Values, 1939–45.* London, 1985.

Craven, W. F. and Cate, J. L., eds. *The Army Air Forces, Volume One: Plans and Early Operations, January 1939–August 1942.* Chicago, 1948.

Creed, D. *Operations of the Fremantle Submarine Base 1942–45.* Sydney, 1979.

Crowley, F. K. *A New History of Western Australia.* Melbourne, 1974.

Crowley, F. K. *Australia's Western Third.* London, 1960.

Crowley, F. K. *Westralian Suburb: A History of South Perth, Western Australia.* Perth, 1962.

Darian-Smith, K. *On the Home Front: Melbourne In Wartime, 1939–1945.* South Melbourne, 1990.

Ewers, J. K. *The Western Gateway: A History of Fremantle*, Second Revised Edition. Perth, 1971.

Gregory, J. (ed.). *Western Australia Between the Wars 1919–1939*. Perth, 1990.

Hackner, Beryl. *Rosa: A Biography of Rosa Townsend*. Nedlands, Western Australia, 1994, p. 59.

Harper, N. *Australia and the United States: Documents and Readings in Australian History.* Melbourne, 1971.

Harper, N., ed. *Pacific Orbit: Australian–American Relations Since 1942.* Melbourne, 1968.

Hasluck, P. *The Government and the People 1939–1941*. Canberra, 1952.

Hasluck, P. *The Government and the People 1942–1945*. Canberra, 1970.

Hewett, D. *Wild Card: An Autobiography 1923–1958*. Ringwood, Victoria, 1990.

Hilvert, J. *Blue Pencil Warriors: Censorship and Propaganda in World War Two*. St Lucia, Queensland, 1984.

Horner, D. M. *High Command: Australia and Allied Strategy 1939–1945*. Sydney, 1982.

Jamieson, Brigadier Commander W. D. *The History of the Army in Western Australia in World War Two*. Perth, 1978.

Koenig, Avis M. *Catalinas on the Swan River — Perth*. Perth, 1994.

Knightley, P. *The First Casualty: The War Correspondent as Hero, Propagandist and Myth Maker*. London, 1975.

Little, R. *Statistical Register of Western Australia for 1941–42*. Perth, 1944.
*Statistical Register of Western Australia for 1942–43*. Perth, 1946.
*Statistical Register of Western Australia for 1943–44*. Perth, 1947.
*Statistical Register of Western Australia for 1944–45*. Perth, 1948.
*Statistical Register of Western Australia for 1945–46*. Perth, 1949.

McKernan, M. *All In! Australia During the Second World War.* Melbourne, 1983.

McKernan, M. and Browne, M., eds. *Australia, Two Centuries of War and Peace*. Canberra, 1988.

Meaney, N. *Australia and the World: A Documentary History from the 1870's to the 1970's*. Melbourne, 1985.

Moore, J. Hammond, ed. *The American Alliance: Australia, New Zealand and the United States: 1940–1970*. Melbourne, 1970.

Moore, J. Hammond. *Over-Sexed, Over-Paid and Over Here: Americans In Australia 1941–1945*. St Lucia, Queensland, 1981.

Phillips, D. H. *Ambivalent Allies: Myth and Reality in the Australian–American Relationship*. Ringwood, Victoria, 1988.

Potts, Annette and Strauss, Lucinda. *For the Love of a Soldier: Australian War Brides and their GIs*. Crow's Nest, NSW, 1987.

Potts, E. Daniel and Potts, Annette. *Yanks Down Under 1941–45: The American Impact on Australia*. Melbourne, 1985.

Prime, M. *WA's Pearl Harbour: The Japanese Raid on Broome*. Bullcreek, Western Australia, n.d.

Reese, Trevor R. *Australia, New Zealand and the United States: A Survey Of International Relations 1941–1968*. London, 1969.

Robertson, J. *Australia At War 1939–45*. Melbourne, 1981.

Shervington, Christine. *University Voices: Traces from the Past*. Nedlands, Western Australia, 1987.

Spillman, K. *Identity Prized: A History of Subiaco*. Nedlands, Western Australia, 1985.

Stannage, C. T. *The People of Perth: A Social History of Western Australia's Capital City*. Perth, 1979.

Stevenson, J. and Darling, H., eds. *The WAAAF Book*. Sydney, 1984.

Thomson, J. *The WAAAF in Wartime Australia*. Melbourne, 1991.

Welborn, Suzanne. *Swan: The History of a Brewery*. Nedlands, Western Australia, 1987.

Williams, A. E. *Nedlands: From Campsite to City*. Nedlands, Western Australia, 1984.


BOOKS — FICTION

Battle, Lois. *War Brides*. London, 1982.

Cusack, Dymphna and James, Florence. *Come In Spinner*. London, 1951.

Drake-Brockman, Henrietta. *The Fatal Days*. Sydney, 1947.

Herbert, Xavier. *Soldiers' Women*. London, 1962.

Sheiner, Robin. *Smile, the War is Over*. South Melbourne, 1983.

Stow, Randolph. *The Merry-Go-Round in the Sea*. London, 1965.


ARTICLES

'Australia—The American Impact.' *The Round Table, A Quarterly Review of the Politics of the British Commonwealth,* September 1942, pp. 51–58.

Barrett, J., 'Living in Australia, 1939–1945.' *Journal of Australian Studies,* no. 2, November 1977, pp. 107–118.

Bartlett, N. 'Perth in the Turbulent Thirties.' *Westerly,* no. 4, December 1977, pp. 61–70.

Bell, R. 'Australian–American Discord: Negotiations for Post-War Bases and Security Arrangements in the Pacific 1944–46.' *Australian Outlook,* vol. 27, no. 1, April 1973, pp. 12–33.

Bell, R. 'Censorship and War: Australia's Curious Experience 1939–45.' *Media Information Australia,* no. 6, 1977, pp. 1–3.

Bolton, G. 'A Local Identity. Paul Hasluck and the Western Australian Self Concept.' *Westerly,* no. 4, December 1977, pp. 71–78.

Bosworth, Michal. 'Fremantle Interned: the Italian Experience', in Richard Bosworth and Romano Ugolini, eds. *War, Internment and Mass Migration: The Italo-Australian Experience*. Rome, 1992.

Craig, Terry. 'Radical and Conservative Theatre in Perth in the 1930s', in Jenny Gregory, *Western Australia Between the Wars, 1919–1939*. Perth, 1990.

Cramp, K. R. 'Food—The First Munition of War (Australian–American Cooperation).' *Royal Australian Historical Society Journal and Proceedings,* vol. 21, part two, 1945, pp. 65–91.

Dalfiume, Richard. 'The Forgotten Years of the Negro Revolution.' *Journal of American History*, vol. 55, 1968–69, pp. 90–106.

Dedman, J. J. 'The Brisbane Line.' *Australian Outlook*, no. 2, vol. 22, 1968, pp. 141–161.

Eliot, G. F. 'Australia, Keystone of Far Eastern Strategy.' *Foreign Affairs: An American Quarterly Review,* vol. 20, no. 3, April 1942, pp. 402–410.

Elphinstone, Pat. 'Breakfast at Bernie's.' *Panorama*, June 1994, pp. 36–39.

Finkle, Lee. 'The Conservative Aims of Militant Rhetoric: Black Protest During World War II.' *Journal of American History*, vol. 60, 1973–74, pp. 692–713.

Hilvert, J. 'More on Australia's Curious War Censorship.' *Media Information Australia,* no. 7, 1978, pp. 41–44.

Portus, G. V. 'Americans and Australians.' *The Australian Quarterly*, vol. 14, no. 2, June 1942, pp. 30–41.

Potts, E. D. and Potts, A., 'American Newsmen and Australian Wartime Propaganda and Censorship 1940–1942.' *Historical Studies*, vol. 21, no. 85, October 1985, pp. 565–572.

Reekie, G. 'War, Sexuality and Feminism; Perth's Women's Organisations, 1938–1945.' *Historical Studies*, vol. 21, no. 85, October 1985, pp. 576–591.

Reekie, G. 'Women's Responses to War Work in Western Australia 1942–1946.' *Studies in Western Australian History,* vol. 7, December 1987, pp. 46–67.

Robertson, J. 'Australian War Policy.' *Historical Studies*, vol. 17, no. 69, October 1977, pp. 489–504.

Spaull, A. D. 'The American Presence in Australian Schools, 1939–46.' *Journal of the Australian and New Zealand History of Education Society*, vol. 6 and 7, 1977–1978, pp. 16–25.

Sturma, M., 'Loving the Alien: The Underside of Relations Between American Servicemen and Australian Women in Queensland 1942–1945.' *Journal of Australian Studies*, no. 24, May 1989, pp. 3–17.

Ward, Philip. 'Reflections: Comrades in Arms.' *Fremantle Herald*, 19 October 1992.

Wecter, D. 'The Aussie and the Yank.' *Atlantic Monthly*, vol. 117, May 1946, pp. 52–56.

# INDEX